RABBIT TOWN

Kevin Radley

About the author

In 1985, after travelling around Australia as a young man, Kevin worked as an Editorial Officer with the NSW Department of Agriculture, before taking on a role as a story-liner for a new television series, "Neighbours". From his work in this role, Kevin learned to appreciate the value of several concepts in writing a long running storyline. He recognised the role of accuracy and continuity so that each stage of a story would waterfall to the next with cohesion and without contradiction. He also learned the importance of developing depth of characters which viewers and readers would identify with and be intrigued by.

Later, Kevin began a teaching career in the western suburbs of Sydney, whilst maintaining an interest in writing. He has written and published his memoir, "The Teacher's Secrets", which tells of his days as an educator, juxtaposed with the personal twists and turns of his home-life in the Blue Mountains, west of Sydney. He also self-published a novel, "Thundersong", which portrays a retired lawyer who has spent his lifetime defending desperate and downtrodden people who survive on society's margins. Through circumstances, he is drawn back into playing his role in one last struggle for justice.

Kevin presently lives on the mid-north coast of New South Wales with his wife, where he continues to write, and has his next novel in the works already.

First published in 2023 by Contempo Publishing.
652 Hogans Rd North Tumbulgum NSW 2490.
www.contempopublishing.com

Copyright © Kevin Radley 2023.

This book is a work of fiction. Any reference to historical events, real people or real places are used fictitiously. Other names, characters, places, and events are products of the authors imagination, and any resemblance to actual events or places or persons, living or dead, is entirely coincidental.

All right reserved. No part of this book may be reproduced or transmitted by any person or entity, including internet search engines or retailers (including, but not limited to, Google and Amazon), in any form or by any means, electronic or mechanical, including photocopying (except under the statutory exceptions provisions of the Australian Copyright Act 1968), recording, scanning or by any information storage and retrieval system without the prior written permission of Contempo Publishing.

A catalogue entry for this book is available from the National Library of Australia.

ISBN (Paperback):   978-0-6458077-4-5
ISBN (E-book):   978-0-6458077-5-2

Cover design and illustration by Rubi Creations Digital.
Internal design by Contempo Publishing.

Printed and distributed internationally by Ingram Spark.

Dedicated to those who live on society's margins.

Part One: Happy Valley
1st October 1932

1. Rabbitoh!

When Tom was fourteen years old, he helped his father, Charlie, carry a large piece of canvas onto a tram for the journey to La Perouse on the coast. He'd never been that far from home before. The boarded-up shops and closed-down factories of Newtown were behind them and sweating it out under the heavy load was putting Tom in good stead for what lay ahead.

It was late in the afternoon when they got to the limit of the tram's journey, 'La Loop', as it was known, where it stopped for the passengers to get off. Tom gazed towards Botany Bay where the cannons on Bare Island jutted into the sky.

He looked over his shoulder and watched the tram move off again. It circled around a large wood and iron building that served as a station of sorts, before it stopped once more for people to get aboard for the trip back to the city.

They traipsed along a street of weatherboard houses before turning into a track through some scrubby bush that led to the place his father called Happy Valley. It was too late to think about going all the way back to Newtown where the air was thick with grit from the rail yards. Tom's mother Rose and two younger sisters would be there, packing whatever they could carry into hessian bags for the trip east.

Charlie and Tom worked hard to prop up the canvas with solid branches and make a shelter for the night. They would make it stronger in the morning, for this would be their new home, at least until they could build something more substantial.

In Newtown, Charlie hadn't paid any rent for weeks, for with what resources he had, putting food into the bellies of his family took priority. Other desperate men, who like Charlie once had jobs, told him of the shanty town on the outskirts of Sydney. When his landlord gave him five days to make other arrangements, Happy Valley loomed as his only option.

They dumped the heavy load on a gap of ground between several huts made of corrugated iron and wood. Puffs of smoke rose into the sky from dwellings scattered about Happy Valley, people making use of what daylight remained to cook with.

As the skies began to darken on that October day in 1932, Charlie pulled out a hard lump of bread and gave it to his son, steeling himself to deal with the intense pangs of hunger that constantly gnawed at his insides.

They sat under the canvas. Tom sucked on the crust until his saliva softened it enough for him to swallow while his father stared into the darkness that was setting upon the rows of huts. *Christ, I hope they're orright back there.*

Charlie stood and took a few steps away from the shelter, bending to gather some small sticks he could start a fire with. Not that he had anything to cook, but a fire would make it feel more like a proper camp.

He sat down next to Tom and threw the collection of twigs on the ground, when as if from nowhere, two black men appeared. Their grey whiskers made it hard to tell how old they were, probably somewhere between thirty and forty. Charlie responded by jumping to his feet and shaping up in self-defence. The two Gadigal men spoke to each other in words that made no sense to Tom or his father and then walked in the direction of the Aboriginal mission on the other side of Happy Valley.

For the moment, the immediate threat had been averted but they knew that when it got darker, they'd need to be on their guard. Tom moved closer to his father, broke the remainder of his bread in half and passed it to him. Charlie put it in his mouth to soften, grateful for the distraction. Side by side they sat and waited for the rising moon to give them some light.

Campfires scattered about the settlement glowed red. Swallowed up by the night, Tom was grateful for his father's presence and was startled when he sprang to his feet again as the two Gadigal men re-appeared. Charlie raised his fists again to warn them off. The taller of the two black men held out a charred rabbit with a long piece of wood through it.

'Here, take this... good tucka.'

It was with that gesture, that the new arrivals joined in with the respectful arrangement that had grown between the two collectives, desperate unemployed whitefellas who were doing their best to survive in their shanties and the dispossessed blackfellas who were pretty much trying to do the same thing. For now, on their first night in Happy Valley, physical exhaustion and meat in their bellies gave them peace and with that came sleep.

~

They woke early the next morning, using the feeble grey light of dawn to move about, chewing on chunks of stringy rabbit until it could be swallowed. The smell of smoke told them that others nearby were awake.

A sheet of wood serving as a door, was pushed outwards from the closest hut. A wiry and whiskered man with his wife emerged and walked over to them carrying saucepans of sweet, black tea and with that they met their immediate neighbours.

The rest of the morning was hard work finding wood that was strong enough to hold up the part of the tent that was missing a pole. To do this they ventured into the bush that ran down to the bay where they felled a small tree to trim.

When they got back to the tent, they continued fixing it until they were satisfied that the structure was held together well enough to withstand the elements. With some shelter now established, they began the journey back across the outskirts to the city and then back to Newtown. It would be another day before they'd return with Tom's mother and sisters and a load of blankets, clothes, pots and some food.

It was a dour existence with a distinct division of chores. The small girls helped their mother collect sticks and whatever else they could use as fuel. They'd wash clothes in water gathered from one of the public taps or from a nearby creek that flowed to the bay. They turned flour and anything else they could scrounge into meals to cook over the coals.

Tom and his father spent the daylight hours tramping large distances on foot. When the opportunity arose, they would jump onto a tram without paying to cover distances more quickly. They searched for any chore or job that paid even a small amount of money. Most days they returned with empty pockets and empty bellies but occasionally they earned a 'bob', the colloquialism for the currency of a shilling. On a good day, they worked for a few hours, perhaps chopping a pile of wood for a well-to-do widower or digging the ground to make a vegetable patch for someone who owned both a house and enough resources to shield them from the economic depression.

One such property sat on a hill with views over the Chinese market gardens of La Perouse. It was full of stooped Asian men and women covered in farming clothes and topped with coolie hats. Halfway up the hill, Tom paused for breath and watched his father look down at the gardens, rubbing his whiskered chin. *It'd be easy to get in there when it gets dark; we could get some of them carrots and greens.*

At the top, they stood outside the front door of a large, weatherboard house. Charlie used his fingers to brush back his hair. He gave Tom a slap on the back to do the same thing, and he knocked on the door.

A moment later, the door opened and Charlie introduced themselves to the lady of the house, Mrs Anderson. She explained to them that the usual man who ran errands for her, had fallen foul with the constabulary. They were in luck and their job was to take two hessian bags to the markets near Railway Square and purchase a piece of mutton and other groceries.

'Forgive me for asking, Mrs,' said Charlie, 'but what makes you sure that I won't run off with the money... or the groceries?'

'That's an easy question to answer, my man,' she replied, 'if you do, you'll be sure to enjoy yourselves for a day or two... but no more. Return my mutton before nightfall and you'll become my new help. I'll give you money for the tram. What you do with that is up to you. Just be back with what I want before dark and then I'll pay you for your trouble.'

With the money for the goods stashed in one pocket and the coins for the fare tucked safely in another, Charlie gave Tom the nod when the tram slowed near a junction for some horses to cross. They had come to know this to be a reliable spot to get aboard, running alongside and then hopping up near the back exit.

They jumped off when the tram approached the markets near Railway Square where a bustling collection of buyers were trying to beat down prices from hawkers. Most shopfronts were boarded up, though a scattering of some that had so far defied the odds remained open. The ground was littered with cabbage leaves and scraps and Tom noticed a rat scurry along the gutter to flee down a drain.

Wafts of intense foul odours made Tom heave and he stayed close to his father while they searched for what they needed. They happened upon an alcove where a carcass was being butchered, and it all became too much for Tom. He turned his head to the side and lost what little was in his stomach to the ground. Charlie gave him a wry smile. 'Okay, mate?'

'I'll be 'right.'

They continued walking between the different stalls, Charlie focussed on getting the best piece of mutton that he could for Mrs Anderson's money. With persistence he secured a bigger and fattier lump of meat for a few pennies less than the first pieces being offered by the butchers.

The hessian bag became full and as they finished acquiring the groceries, Charlie noticed a hawker across the street prizing open a wooden box and lifting out a pair of dead rabbits by their ears. Along that side of the street were some stalls set up against the back walls of closed-down shops, flogging different stuff.

'Rabbits... two bob a head, three bob for two!' the scrawny hawker yelled in a high pitch over the noise of the street. A group of about ten men were gathered next to his stall, all clambering around a central figure standing on a wooden box relaying information from the wireless he could hear out of the back window of an old shop. 'He's on ninety-eight!' he yelled, to which they responded with a collective gasp of suspense.

'C'mon, Tom,' said his father, attracted to the hawker who was trying to sell rabbits. Tom had the hessian bag slung over his shoulder and followed his father across the road, dodging people who were walking in the opposite direction until they were up close to the rabbit man. Charlie fingered the coins in his pocket, making sure that with the tram money, he had nine bob.

'I'm after six rabbits. How much is that?'

'Three bob for two, so that makes it nine bob,' said the hawker.

'I can give you seven'.

A cheer erupted from the nearby gathering and the men slapped each other on their backs in celebration.

'No mate, but I'll do it for eight... only because I'm in a good mood. Bradman just got his hundred! Reckon we'll beat the Poms in this one!'

'You beauty!' Charlie was buoyed by what was happening in the cricket. 'Could do with some good news after the first test!'

He counted out the coins, handed them over and opened the other hessian bag. 'Put 'em in here, mate.'

That was the first purchase of what was to become a focal point of the family's existence for the next five years. Their work was done, and they walked back to where the tram would be moving slowly. Jumping onto it was more difficult now because of the loaded sacks but after stumbling, they secured their feet, wedging them into brackets on the outside of the tram carriage. They hung on for dear life as they bumped their way towards the Chinese gardens and Mrs Anderson's house on the hill.

Charlie yelled above the rattles and clunks, explaining to Tom how the eight bob he spent that day was going to be worth more than double that in the next few days. He remembered when he was a kid and men would traipse the streets of the inner-city, flogging rabbits. Legend had it that the local football team once rubbed rabbit blood into their jerseys before they played in honour of the dogged people from which they were spawned.

'We'll keep two, that'll feed us and save at least four bob from not buying other food,' he shouted, 'keep the pelts too, dry and salt 'em, good fur in that.'

'That leaves four more,' Tom called out.

'Give one to the blackfellas; remember our first night at Happy Valley?'

'Yeah, that's fair enough but what about the other three?'

'I would have been happy to pay two bob each, even three,' he said, 'so reckon we can flog 'em for four bob a head. People got a taste for rabbit these days.'

'When will we do that?'

'Tomorrow, we'll get up early.'

'Do you mean we have to come back all this way again tomorrow?'

'Yeah, then if we sell what we've got, we're close enough to get some more.'

~

Mrs Anderson was impressed. The meat was better than she had expected, and they brought back everything that was on the list. All of this was done before the sun had begun to set. 'Well,' she said, rummaging through the goods, 'every Wednesday morning, the earlier the better. I'll have errands for you. Interested?'

Charlie's eyed widened and he took a moment to find his voice. 'Every Wednesday!' His eyes nearly popped out of his head when she passed over a note, not coins but a note! They clambered down the hill and with nightfall almost upon them, hid behind some tall bull rushes at the edge of a swamp. From there they could gaze across the rows of raised earth full of green and yellow produce. Across the way on the other side of the field, the last of the workers in coolie hats left through a gate, turning to lock a chain before walking off.

With that, Charlie and Tom crept closer to the fields and pulled aside some loose palings to step through. It was getting dark, and they were startled when they heard several other men behind them.

'Oi,' one of them said, 'Don't take too much! We don't want the chinks getting too angry. They have shotguns.'

~

The mood back at the tent was sullen. Another day of dreary and arduous chores was not yet over. The males hadn't been there for any of it, and it was much later than expected when they eventually got back. The fire was going and Tom's mother, Rose, was kneading some flour for another doughy and tasteless meal. Charlie, oblivious to her mood, could hardly wait to tell her about their good fortunes.

Across from their squat, some men had gathered around a neighbour's fire to talk about politics and the downturn. A short man who had been talking loudly about the government gave Charlie a wave.

He returned the gesture and then began relaying the events of the day to Rose who managed a smile, her first for hours. Gradually, the mood spread throughout the family, and for a fleeting moment, Charlie was once again a worthy breadwinner.

Getting to work, the man of the house skinned a rabbit, cut it up and tossed it into the water bubbling away in the big iron pot. He tipped the vegetables out of the bag and roughly chopped a couple of onions, carrots and some other green leaves that he had no clue about. He threw them on top of the rabbit pieces with a small handful of salt. 'Tonight, we have a feast!'

'I'll add some flour in a while, when those juices get cooked up,' said Rose, joining in with the good news of the day, 'we can mop up the gravy with the dough boys.'

'We'll sleep with full bellies,' said Charlie. 'Tomorrow, me and Tom will flog off the other rabbits. Hopefully in a while, not too long I hope, we'll be able to buy some more canvas and thick blankets... saw some at the markets... make us some decent beds.'

~

From that glorious day onwards, after scratching together whatever they could to make ends meet, the luxury of routine was once more a part of their lives. Life was tough, but each of the Davis family was more content with their lot, knowing that there would be a bit more money around and they could put more than just flour and water together to sustain them each day.

Wednesdays were set aside for the males to do errands and chores for Mrs Anderson and to get fresh vegetables on their way home. The days either side were for tramping the suburbs, selling some rabbits and, on a good day, going back to the markets for more.

One evening after lugging rabbits all day, Tom was holding onto the rails at the back of the tram when he had an idea. 'Reckon we could split up, Da.'

'Wotcha mean?' yelled his father over the wind and noise of the tracks.

'I know all the good places now. There's too many to get to when we're together.'

'Reckon you could do it?'

'Yeah, been watching for ages now... I know what to do, what to say, how much to get for a rabbit... Reckon I could. Besides, I'm fifteen now.'

'Orright. Give it a go tomorrow. After the markets, you do the Redfern streets and I'll do Newtown.'

After a couple of weeks of working separately there was distinctly more money in their pockets and the thought of sleeping on more comfortable bedding was closer to becoming a reality.

~

Evidence of the hard times was everywhere on the streets of Redfern. It was a tough suburb and the struggle for survival was etched in lines on the faces of people Tom encountered along the way. Hawking rabbits was difficult work, mile after mile lugging the heavy load to where the regular customers were.

Along the way he would pass dishevelled men, some squatting on wads of old newspapers in doorways and others in camps they had made in small public spaces. Some existed quietly in their squalor and others were mad from the drink, abusing Tom if he got too close.

There was one small house, towards the end of his run that he looked forward to getting to. It was crowded with Catholics, as his father had previously said, seven or eight kids greeting them excitedly each time they had passed them by. One of them was the prettiest girl Tom had ever seen and thinking about her kept a spring in his step all the way up Cleveland Street to where they lived. As he got closer to the house, he anticipated her smile and the way she would look at him.

'Rabbitoh,' he called, just like his father had told him, but louder than he had been in the other streets for he wanted to make sure she would hear. 'Rabbitoh!' he called again as he stood outside her front gate.

There was no sign of her. He sighed, his shoulders dropping as he began walking away, kicking a rock as he went. When he heard the gate squeak open, he stopped dead in his tracks and turned around. There she stood, the only one of the brood, with an empty house behind her.

'Gotcha rabbits, miss,' said Tom. 'Where's everyone else?'

'Pa's gone bush, the little twins got sick, and Ma's gone looking for someone to help. The others went with her.'

'How come you didn't go?'

'I'm supposed to make sure we get the rabbits.' She spoke with a soft Irish brogue that intrigued him. 'How come you're on your own again? Did your father die or something?'

'We split up… He's doing Newtown and I'm here. It's better that way.'

'Well, can we get two?'

'Sure.' Tom lifted out two sets of ears and passed the dead animals over the fence. 'It's eight bob for these.'

'Oh no,' she gasped, 'Ma forgot to give me the money.'

'Well… er…'

'We can pay double next week…to be sure…'

'I don't think…'

Her eyes upon him made him look away.

'Aw, come on… You know we'll pay. Why don't you come inside, and I can make you some tea. You can have a rest and think about it.'

The thought of being alone in a house with her made his heart thump. He looked at her strawberry blond hair tied back in a ribbon made from old yellow cloth, the same colour as the patches sown into her dress. 'Well, a cup o'tea does sound good.'

He opened the gate wider and put the bag of rabbits next to the front door.

'Better not leave them there. They may not hop away, but someone will take 'em to be sure. Come in, shut the door behind you.'

Tom laughed, picked up the sack, and followed her down a narrow hallway. The girl nodded towards the floor. 'Just leave 'em there.' She held out her hand for him to take. 'My name is Hazel.'

'I'm Tom.'

He wondered if he should really be alone in the house with her. She kept hold of his hand and took a step closer. 'I look forward to you coming around every Friday.'

He knew that something was happening but had no idea what it was. He tried to speak. 'Er… um…'

Hazel put her other hand on his shoulder as they stood facing each other.

'How about that tea, miss… I mean, Hazel?'

'Maybe in a little while… Have you ever kissed a girl before?'

'Um... before what?'

She leant into him and pushed her lips upon his. He stood, not knowing what to do, the urges that had been so strong recently overwhelming him.

'Before this.' The trace of her soft Irish accent made him dizzy. She rubbed the front of his trousers. 'The tea can wait.'

Tom didn't notice the fatigue in his legs that afternoon as he hawked the rest of the rabbits. When the last one was sold, he bounded along the path towards Railway Square and the ride back to Happy Valley.

He couldn't tell anyone what had happened, for he didn't really understand it himself. The last hour was a blur, and now he was eight bob short, not sure how he'd explain that to his father. The only thing he knew for certain, was that the time until next Friday couldn't pass quickly enough. If he was lucky, Hazel's younger twin sisters might be sick again.

2. Conception

'Stay away from that house,' Charlie said.

They had ventured further afield, trying to flog rabbits as they tramped along the street, taunted by glimpses of the ocean through the gaps between the stately homes along Maroubra Road. It was autumn, though the heat persisted in the late morning sun as they made a quest for territory closer to home.

'This was a mistake, I reckon.'

'Yeah, haven't sold one rabbit. What's wrong with that house, Da?'

'The word about the place is that she lives there... Tilly Devine... Don't reckon she'd take too kindly to a couple of rabbitohs.'

'Is that because she's rich?'

They trudged further along the street. 'Nah, Tom, it's because of what she does and who she does it with. Just stay away.'

'Orright.'

They walked on in silence, disappointed from the day so far.

'Not doing any good, are we?' said Tom.

His father grimaced. 'Waste of time around these parts. They're not hungry enough around here for our rabbits... Reckon we split up again tomorrow, go back to what we were doing. I was just hoping we'd find a quicker way to sell... have more time back at Happy Valley if we could.'

'To fix the place up a bit?'

13

'Yeah, we need to get going on it quick... they've gone you know... the Browns next to us... He's gone off, fighting out in the bush.'

'But they were there yesterday.'

'But not today; he told me to my face. They know someone at St Marys who'll take 'em in, and he'll go off boxing... already got one fight lined up in Penrith, and if he wins, well who knows what it could lead to. He might be able to travel around, Tent Boxing, get a name for himself. His missus will be looked after at St Marys while he's gone.'

'What if he comes back to Happy Valley, Da?'

'Like I said, he told me to my face; collapse the old place so his no-hoper brother doesn't try and take it over. We can use the wood and iron to make a new place for us.'

The load of rabbits wasn't getting any lighter and their legs were heavy.

'Not selling any of these here,' said Tom. 'Still plenty of daylight; why don't we go back and get started.'

'Yeah, sell this lot tomorrow, I'll do Newtown and you go back to Redfern.'

'But tomorrow's Wednesday... Mrs Anderson's errands.'

'Ah yeah. Reckon you can do 'em both, Newtown and Redfern? And I do Mrs Anderson's errands.'

'What, all of these?'

'Reckon you can?'

'Orright.'

It had been more than a week since Tom had walked the streets around Hazel's place and four months since he lay with her on the cool stone floor of the kitchen. Her mother didn't usually buy rabbits on a Wednesday, but he might get to see her anyway. The thought of getting close enough to touch her, sent a buzz through his body. With more purpose in his step, he paced it out.

'C'mon, Da,' he said, 'we've got a house to build.'

~

It was unusual to be back at the camp with so much light ahead of them and Charlie was determined to have the Browns' shack taken apart by night fall. He had planned how the re-build could be made in a space behind their tent amongst the scrubby bushes to double the size of their squat.

The mood of the whole family had lifted since the men had found some reliable income. Life remained hard though, and Rose considered it one of her duties to do what she could to keep their spirits up. Sometimes when she noticed the family's mood dipping, she would give them a jolt rather than try to placate them, reminding them that their lot in life could be a lot worse and that they were lucky to usually have a full belly so they could sleep at night.

Life was harsh and physically demanding for even the youngest children, however those who lived in the shanty town were free of one demon, that being the anxiety of trying to find rent money when there simply wasn't any.

Those in the valley were free to mix it up with the Aboriginal people from the nearby mission. There was an acceptance of mixed-race relationships at La Perouse and babies that resulted were affectionately cradled by women of all skin colours. Judgement of moral inferiority was left behind with the bills, rent payments and perceived respectability of life as it was before the crash.

On that Wednesday, when his father did the errands for Mrs Anderson before pinching some vegetables from the Chinese gardens just on sunset, Tom spent the entire day tramping the streets from Railway Square to Newtown and then back to Redfern.

It was a dawn to dusk effort, culminating in legs of exhaustion by late afternoon. Thankfully, the load over his shoulder had lightened over the day, with just one pair of rabbits remaining when it was time to walk up Cleveland Street, noisy with the clip-clop of horses and a small number of automobiles trying to get past them.

He saved that part of the route until last, the stretch of closely packed house frontages that almost came right up to the front fences. Many of them had newspaper covering the inside of their windows. Most of the shops leading to the main intersection with

Crown Street were closed and boarded up with sheets of wood. He walked with haste, thinking of an imminent encounter with Hazel and maybe being alone with her again.

He made no call along the street, for there was nothing to sell but the two he'd saved for Hazel... if she wanted them.

When he got to her front gate he stopped and put the bag on the ground. 'Rabbitoh! Rabbitoh!'

Nothing. *Maybe I've made a mistake leaving it to the last part of the day... They've all gone out, maybe even gone bush to catch up with the father... She probably doesn't like me anymore.*

He picked up the sack and turned around to start the long trek back to Railway Square without so much as a glimpse of her. He began to walk away, jolting to a stop when from behind he heard a door open to a barrage of shrill shouts.

'Come back right now, Hazel!' yelled the mother. 'You stay away from that boy; wait until your Pa is back! Come back right now!'

Tom turned to see Hazel struggle free from her mother's grip and run to the gate. 'Tom! Tom, I must see you!' She ran through the broken gate and into the street. 'Tom, wait!'

'If you go with him,' screamed her mother from the doorway, 'don't ever come back!'

Tom dropped his hessian sack. He stood wide-eyed and stunned as Hazel wrapped her arms around him. 'Tom, I need to talk to you.'

'What's going on, Hazel? Why is your Ma so angry?'

The front door slammed behind them. 'Oh Tom, I'm in trouble... we're in trouble... you got me in trouble.'

'What kind of trouble?'

'Oh, you daft bugger.' Her face was wet with tears as she reached down and grabbed his hand, placing it on her belly. 'I'm going to have a baby... your baby.'

'But... but...'

'It's true, Tom Davis, a baby.'

'But...'

There were no words forming from the commotion in his head. He was just fifteen and babies were what older people had. Would he have to marry her? Where would they live? Would he have to build another shack at Happy Valley?

'Ma says... I can't... see you anymore.' Her words broke up as she pushed through. 'She says that now... now she'll have another sprog to feed, and she can't even afford to feed the ones she's got.'

'I'll... I can... I...'

'You're just talking dribble.' Hazel tried to take control of the moment. 'I just wanted you to know. Ma says I can't see you for what you done to me... but I wanted you to know. My Pa will be back in a while... He don't know a thing about it yet. Ma is right, I can't be seeing you no more and I don't know what will happen when Pa gets back.'

'Here,' said Tom, bending down to pull out the last pair of rabbits. 'You better take these.'

'Thank you, Tom, but it will take more than some rabbits to fix the fine old mess I'm in.'

She grabbed the animals by the ears and turned, taking slow wretched steps back to her house.

'But I want to keep seeing you,' he called.

She looked over her shoulder and shook her head.

'I gotta go now,' he called out, 'but I want to keep seeing you.'

At that moment, Happy Valley seemed like it was at the ends of the Earth.

~

With the changing seasons, days were getting shorter, and nights were nippy, meaning that the Davis family had to fit as much as they could into the dwindling amount of daylight. Ironically, in a period of massive unemployment, Tom and his father were busier than they had been in a long while, selling rabbits, running errands for Mrs Anderson on Wednesdays and constructing the cabin behind their tent.

After scrounging a bunch of nails, they put in a succession of late afternoons and evenings when they worked through the twilight until it was pitch black. Being busy suited Tom fine, distracting him from his problems.

Finally, they saw the completion of the new structure. It was a rectangle of timber and iron cladding under a tin roof with the walls softened with hessian bags and rabbit pelts. When the final nail was hammered into place, Charlie took a step back, smiled, and put his arm around Tom. They would keep the tent erected as well, glad of the extra space.

Life went on. Rose and the girls completing their chores each day, washing their few clothes and struggling to dry them in cooler weather. After that, they would look for enough wood from the dwindling supply to keep the fire smouldering to cook on. Time spent at the local school was a break for the girls and a chance to play with other kids, though it was not unusual for them to miss several days in a row to help their mother out.

It was obvious to his parents that something was troubling Tom, and when they sat around the fire to eat and drink tea, they probed for details. Tom, however, was keeping things to himself, and his detachment was tangible.

It was more than a month since he'd walked back from Cleveland Street after Hazel told him about the baby, and since then he hadn't been back. His father was concerned that Tom was in some sort of trouble. Twice his son had come home eight bob short after a day on the streets. Maybe that had something to do with it, for when Tom had tried to explain why, it hadn't rung true.

For the past month, Tom continued to hawk rabbits around the streets but turned back at the Crown Street intersection, a couple of hundred yards short of Hazel's house. Although he longed to see her when he was so close to where he knew she'd be, going any closer would be terrible for Hazel.

Upon returning to Happy Valley after one day of hawking, he walked straight past the rest of the family who had settled around the camp-stove while a stew was simmering away. Charlie had splashed out, buying a piece of mutton and some potatoes at the market. The mood was bright, though completely lost on Tom when he slipped through the gap between the tent wall and the timber cladding behind it and collapsed on the stack of cloth that was his bed.

Rose had had enough of wondering what was so wrong in her son's life. She passed a ladle to one of the younger girls and told her to move the stew around every few minutes. Then she looked at the boy's father. 'Come on, Da. It's time we found out what is going on.'

They sat either side of him and what followed was a needling for information that only a mother could get away with. Charlie sat and listened to Rose recall some of the happy moments in the boy's life that would evoke feelings of warmth and security. She intertwined the conversation with simple questions followed by more complicated ones, drawing on Tom's emotions until his defences began to fracture.

'There's a girl,' he began. 'I sell her family rabbits sometimes.'

With that, both parents felt some relief with the age-old explanation for the boy's blues. His mother probed for more information and over the next few moments they learned of Hazel, one of a tribe of Catholic kids in Redfern. It wasn't until Tom told them that he wasn't allowed to see her anymore that the seeds of more serious concern were planted.

'And why would that be, Tom?' Rose spoke with fire in her eyes. 'Is it because you're not a Catholic?'

'Well, I don't reckon, Ma.'

'Come on boy, out with it.'

'Some some something happened,' he stammered, 'last year, I think it was.'

His father sat more upright, anticipating news he'd rather not know.

'What did you do, boy?'

'She's... she's...'

'She's what?'

'She's going to have... a... baby.'

19

Charlie looked down and dropped his forehead into his hand. 'Ah, Jesus Christ.'

'What am I going to do, Ma?'

Rose was quiet, drawing in a deep breath and sighing. She processed what was happening and recalled the time when she herself, just fifteen years old, was telling her mother a similar thing.

'Sit up properly, Tom,' she said. 'You're going to have some stew for supper. Your Da got us a nice piece of mutton. Then we'll drink some tea. Then, when we're ready, we'll have a long talk, the three of us. You might have been barred from seeing young Hazel, but we're not. The whole lot of us are going to have to get together at some stage.'

'But Ma...'

'But nothing. It's time for us all to have something to eat.'

'Not very hungry, Ma.'

'We'll all eat and then we'll sleep. Tomorrow we'll talk.'

3. Desperation

There was no fanfare when Hazel's Pa returned from the bush in winter. He brought back two main things from his wanderings about the central west of New South Wales. He scooped the first from his pocket and slapped it on the table in front of his wife: a handful of coins and a few pound notes. She counted the offerings, gave him a spiteful glare and squirreled them into a tin that sat on the bench in the kitchen. 'That's it?'

The second thing he came back with was a craving for rum. The small, noisy house was suffocating after the months he had spent on the track. The road had been hard, and many was a night he'd gone to bed with an empty belly, save a swig of rum to dull the pain. Though wherever he lay, be it in a shed on some property where he'd worked for a day or two, or under a tree on a plain somewhere, there was quiet space around him, and he was content with his solitude.

Each of his kids took their turn in greeting their father, a man they didn't really know. One by one they would spiel a rehearsed pleasantry before getting back to whatever they had been doing; chores for the older ones or the younger ones playing with clothes pegs and whatever else they could turn into some type of toy.

When it was Hazel's turn to welcome her father home, her mother intervened, telling him that there was news he needed to prepare himself for. 'And this one,' she continued after the warning, 'as you can plainly see, this one is with child.'

It was all too familiar for the returned traveller, a man who found it difficult to remember any time in their life together during which there was not a pregnancy. 'I see,' he said, 'and do we have a father that we know of?'

'The boy who did this,' said the mother, 'the boy...'

'His name is Tom,' interjected Hazel, 'and he's a sweet boy.'

'He's the Protestant boy who knocked you up!' said her mother, 'and I've warned him off! He's not to see her.'

The man was quiet, slipping into his thoughts and how just a week earlier he was lodged in a farm shed near Penrith. It was where he slept after cutting hay for a dairy farmer. He worked there for lodgings and rum and although there was no monetary payment for his labour, it was the most peaceful week of his time away.

He wished that he was there again, physically spent after a day's work and about to eat his fill of beef from a recently slaughtered beast and boiled vegetables that he'd have picked from their gardens. The drink to follow would soften his shoulders and massage his head, delivering him into a sublime tranquillity and sleep. What he'd do, to smell the pastures and cattle once more and have a long, sweet swill of the dark spirit.

'We need to meet the boy,' he said. 'There'll be certain arrangements that need to be made.'

'What?' Hazel's mother was angry. 'I think not; he's not even Catholic!'

~

Miles away, on the coast near La Perouse, the Davis family got on with life, though not without an air of expectancy. The news of Tom's imminent fatherhood was taken on board as another challenge, but rather than cast a problematic shadow over them, Rose made sure that it added a further sense of purpose to their existence.

She spoke of their good fortune in having added the wooden dwelling, for they would surely need the extra space. What they wanted now, was some certainty about the future, commitment from Hazel's family and themselves, over the role they would be playing to care for the infant.

Rose's motivation added lively conversation around their meal one evening. 'No Davis has ever denied their own blood... You'll be sure to get your name on that baby's birth certificate, Tom.'

'Orright, Ma.'

'The child will be a Davis... and always have a home with us.'

Tom and his father glanced at each other, both aware that when Rose had her heart set on something, she would remain determined.

'And Tom, it will be up to you to make the first move.'

~

The following day near lunchtime, Tom stood at the front door of Hazel's family house, sodden from the cold, persistent drizzle that fell on him all the way from Railway Square. He was doing as his mother said, making contact with Hazel's family and showing that he was being a man facing his responsibilities.

Hazel's elder sister opened the door. 'Ma!' she yelled over her shoulder. 'It's the mongrel scoundrel dog!'

Tom stood, his hands trembling not from the cold and wet, but from the trepidation that had built since leaving Happy Valley hours earlier. There was the sound of clanging metal pots coming from inside and then the thud of heavy stomps getting louder. The door opened with the mother standing there wearing a scowl on her face. Hazel ran up behind her.

'Well,' snapped the mother, 'you've got some gall!'

'Beg pardon, Mrs O'Brien,' he began, 'Beg pardon, but if I could please...'

'Please what!'

'If I could...'

'Ma,' said Hazel trying to push past, 'Ma, can't you see he's soaked to the skin?'

Perhaps it was Tom's pathetic appearance, dressed in his father's best shirt and trousers that swam all over his cold shivering pink skin, or perhaps it was the desperation in Hazel's voice, or maybe both, but the surprise visit managed to precipitate a kernel of sympathy as the matriarch's face began to soften. 'Come inside, you wretched boy,' she managed. 'Go through and stand by the copper heater in the back room.'

He followed the mother, leaving wet boot prints on the hard floor as he went, passing Hazel, her belly now obviously protruding. 'Hello, Hazel.'

'Oh Tom,' she said, 'why did you come?'

He was led through the narrow hall, past two rooms on the right full of boisterous kids who were frustrated in having to stay inside out of the rain. He stood with his back to the burner, his eyes darting around for a glimpse of Hazel's father. Older kids cradled younger ones or were busy patching clothes while the mother stood at the kitchen table, holding her silent stare.

'Excuse me,' he said, 'is Hazel's father here? I expect he will want to see me.'

'Hmph,' said the mother. 'Whatever you want to say to him, you can say to me.'

'It's just that...'

Hazel resisted the urge to wrap her arms around him. 'Oh Tom, Pa's gone on the track again, couldn't get a day's work on the wharves.'

'Gone bush again,' said the mother, 'so it's just us.'

'Orright.'

'So out with it, you despicable boy,' she pushed. 'What do you have to say?'

~

Later that day, Tom shivered from the wind that blew right through him as he hung off the back of the tram. He felt a strange calm after surviving the meeting with the O'Briens, relieved that her father hadn't been there. It would be easier now when his folks returned with him the following week to further the arrangements.

He arrived back at the shanty town just before dusk, eager to change out of his father's wet clothes and put on dry patched shirt and trousers that he could fill. Outside, a few men gathered as they often did at this time of day to talk. Smoke drifted up from the fires scattered around the settlement, glowing in the darkening sky. Charlie and the men were talking about the government and who was to blame for what. Tom looked on, eager for them to finish and head back to their own tin sheds for there was much he needed to say to his mother and father.

'Hello, young Tom,' called one of the men. 'Come and join us.'

Tom walked to the gathering, happy at least that the rain had ceased, and a few early stars had begun to twinkle in the eastern night sky.

'We're talking about the Premier,' said another of the men. 'Jack Lang's done alright by us, I'd say.'

'And now he's been done in with!' said the first man.

'Since the Sydney Harbour Bridge was finished, no one I know has had a day's work... Well maybe that big bloke down at the bottom part of the valley; he's got himself a day or two on the waterfront, but that's it. No one else has had anything!'

'Not Lang's doing, you know; he's done all he can. It's the other mob, The New Guard... too much power. They've got too much influence. Jack Lang was elected by the people.'

'My word!'

'They've no right to sack him!'

Charlie nodded, rubbing his chin in thought. 'There's a meeting tomorrow,' he said. 'Waterside workers and Miner workers, the big unions. They'll be having something to say about it!'

'You going?' said the first man, 'New South Wales needs a strong communist party. Bring the boy!'

'Wotcha say, Tom?' said Charlie. 'We could do with a day off.'

'Huh? What? Not sure. I think we need to sell rabbits.'

'We'll have a think about it,' said Charlie, 'but for now it looks like Ma has got our supper ready.'

'Ha,' echoed the other men, 'it's time for us all to get back and rustle up something to eat.'

Back to their own company, the family made the most of the stew, mopping up any trace of the juices with dough boys that had been made earlier in the day. When the younger girls were put to bed, and while a saucepan of black tea bubbled on the coals, they sat on the wooden boxes that constituted their furniture, drank the hot, sweet liquid and began to talk about the issue of the day. That night, under a clearing sky that began to sparkle with stars, they each said what they needed to and prepared themselves for the imminent meeting with the O'Brien's.

'We've managed to make ourselves comfortable here, wouldn't you say?' said Rose. 'And more often than not, our bellies are full.'

'Could be worse,' said Charlie.

Tom nodded.

~

In September of 1933, as per the arrangements made between the Davis and O'Brien families, sixteen-year-old Tom accompanied fifteen-year-old Hazel and a baby boy who had been hidden from the world, now wrapped in blankets, all the way from Cleveland Street in Redfern to Happy Valley at La Perouse. Despite her reluctance to Hazel leaving home, her mother felt some relief; the constant effort in keeping the girl out of sight from the prying eyes of Cleveland Street had taken its toll.

Tom wore his father's best clothes for the second time in his life, carrying a case of Hazel's clothes and treasured possessions while she carried baby William. Befitting the occasion, he purchased legitimate fares for the tram ride.

It had been a teary farewell; though while Mrs O'Brien was torn to see her second eldest daughter and her first grandchild walk away with their shame, she was convinced that the Davis family would provide well for them. She had never been to Happy Valley, but a picture had been painted for her of a caring community with enough food and shelter to protect them from the desperation of the times.

The fact that she now had fewer mouths to feed also contributed to the consensus that Hazel's departure was in the best interests for all.

There was one sticking point; the Davis's were not Catholic. Much of the discussion between the two families had been around that. Throughout the talking, Rose insisted that the infant's move to Happy Valley would be the best course of action for all concerned and this came with an assurance, albeit a hollow one at best, that Tom would be converting soon. With that, the arrangements secured the necessary approval from the O'Brien side.

~

Tom's parents had partitioned half of the cabin so there would be a place for the new mother and child, and being Wednesday, errand day for Mrs Anderson, Charlie had spent more money than he should have on a piece of mutton from the markets near Railway Square. He even bought some vegetables and a real loaf of bread to go with what he could pinch from the Chinese gardens on the way home.

The Davis family had grown accustomed to the hard life, and they were proud of what they had been able to put together. Rose was sure that they could not have welcomed the newcomers any more warmly.

At first, the trek eastward was an adventure for Hazel, the wobbly tram taking her somewhere mysterious. However, by the time they passed the Chinese gardens and continued through the scrub, she became more hesitant. When they stopped at La Perouse, she clung protectively to the baby and nestled in closely to Tom when two Gadigal men approached to look at the baby. 'Is this your missus, Tom?' said one. 'Gotta little one too, eh?'

'Yeah, Eric,' said Tom, 'this is Hazel, and the baby is William.'

'Hello, missus,' said Eric. 'You'll like it here, Tom good fella.'

Hazel tensed when a cockatoo screeched as it flew above them. Holding the baby more tightly, she stepped along the path, hesitating when they veered onto a rough track, and continued towards the tent and cabin.

'Here we are,' said Tom. 'Your new home.'

Looking at the dwelling, her stomach was twisted and nauseous as she pondered her future. She slept poorly that first night. It was still spring and although the days were warming up nicely, the cabin chilled off at night. She shared the sectioned-off part of the hut with Tom and baby William cradled between them.

Strange sounds of the night unnerved her and when the baby cried at intervals, she did well not to burst into tears while she rummaged around in the cold dark for what she needed to feed him or to clean him up.

After a tormented night, grey light and crow calls just outside roused the young man lying next to her. Hazel began her first morning at Happy Valley holding William as if she was scared to let him go, and listening to Rose outside, babbling excitedly about having a new infant to care for.

Tom and Charlie heated up a big pot of water on the smouldering fire, pouring some of the steaming liquid into a can for tea and leaving the rest as instructed, for the women to use. Rose, recognising the exhaustion in Hazel's face, insisted that she take the baby off her hands to give him a wash with a warm flannel. Reluctantly, Hazel handed William to his grandmother.

'You're a beautiful boy, young Bill,' said Rose while she gently moved the cloth over his delicate parts.

'Pass him over when you're done,' said Hazel, 'and I'll wrap him up again.'

'Now you just have a rest, my girl. You'll be needing all your energy. There's lots of work in raising one of these. In good hands, is young Bill.'

Hazel's torment spilled into helplessness watching someone she barely knew take over care of William and not even call him by his proper name. Hazel watched Tom's mother wash the baby differently to the way she had done so many times before when she had looked after her baby siblings.

The men ate some of the leftover bread from the last night's meal and washed it down with hot tea knowing that soon they'd be gone and on the tram to Railway Square. It was spring and the days were getting longer. It was the first day Tom was off to provide for his new family. Hazel watched him walk away with his Charlie, left behind with people she really didn't know.

By mid-morning, sleep-deprived and feeling the early heat of the changing season, Hazel sat in the hut and nursed her baby, grimacing in pain as he suckled on her cracked nipples. She felt relief when the feed was over and the intense throbbing started to fade just a little. Though the respite was short lived as William threw up much of the milk over her shoulder. She sobbed, feeling trapped in a world she felt had no place for her, wishing that Tom was there. Drying her eyes and patting the baby on his back, she steeled herself to go outside and join the other females.

'Ah, Hazel,' said Rose. 'Pass young Bill over and go and clean yourself with the hot water on the fire. That'll make you feel better.'

She did as she was told.

'I'll take him for now and when you feel up to it, could you help the girls wash some clothes... might get them dry in this sunshine.'

The young mother persevered for the remainder of the day, helping with chores, stopping only in response to the infant's crying to suffer the pain of feeding William and cleaning him. While the others had grown accustomed to life at Happy Valley and were excited that it now included a baby, for Hazel, her first day with them was drudgery at best.

By the time evening shadows stretched across the settlement and she could smell the first hint of smoke for the evening, Hazel was overwhelmed with misery. She had survived a day, one of many more just the same to follow.

In sharp contrast, Tom had returned with his father before sundown, their spirits high after selling all but one of the rabbits they had bought that morning at the markets. The females enjoyed this part of the day when the men returned home. They would have a story or two about the characters they'd encountered and if it was a particularly good day, they might also bring home something special such as a loaf of bread or even a length of fabric to make something with.

For Hazel, though, the mood of the camp was something she could only watch. It made her bitter towards the others who had no idea how sad she was, nor was anyone there she could talk to about it.

~

As one day rolled into another and weeks became months, the relationship between Hazel and the Davis family failed to become any warmer. Rose had taken firm control of raising William, or Bill as she called him, handing the infant over to his mother when he needed a feed. With the passage of time Hazel began to withdraw even further, her eyes masking the hollowness she felt inside. To Rose, Hazel's behaviour was rude and ungrateful.

Sometimes, rather than bursting into tears, she would go for a walk around Happy Valley, occasionally coming across another woman who would be keen to spend time chatting with her. During these times she would hear about all sorts of things in their lives, dramas and tragedies that at least made her feel that she wasn't totally alone in her misery.

Tom was at a loss as to how he could extract an expression of happiness from her during the daylight hours, and he was totally baffled when sometimes through the night while William was sleeping, she'd come to him. For Hazel, the touch of him and those few moments of intense desire reminded her that she was alive.

Tom would take the passionate union as a sign that she was better again, happy to be there and that the next day would be a better one. Invariably, by morning she would have regressed once more, delving deep inside herself, leaving Tom confused and at his wits end.

It was late one summer morning when something jolted Hazel even further into her darkness. The young girls were away collecting pieces of fuel for the fire, and both men were running errands for Mrs Anderson, leaving Hazel and the baby alone with Rose. Hazel was having a difficult time during which the baby sucked spasmodically, screaming, crying and barely settling to take in any decent amount of milk.

Rose held her arms out to take the baby from her. 'Do pass him over, girl.'

Sleep deprived and worn out, Hazel did as she was told.

'Shh, shh, little Bill,' said Rose, 'that's better. What a good boy you are.'

The baby ceased his crying and a broad smile spread across his face as his eyes locked in with those of his grandmother who rocked him in her arms. The moment hit Hazel hard, and she interpreted it the only way she knew how. William was Bill and he was better off with Rose.

Into the afternoon the thoughts played over and over in her mind and by the time Tom and Charlie returned from running Mrs Anderson's errands, she'd made a decision. With that, she felt a weight of burden lift from her shoulders and for the first time in a long time, she owned a glimmer of happiness.

The conversation offered by Hazel as they put together a watery stew of mutton bones and vegetables, was at first met with suspicion by Rose, for it had been months since she'd volunteered any contribution to discussion. As the cool of night fell over them, they began to warm to her Irish brogue, giving the young mother the benefit of doubt; perhaps after having a hard time of it she was beginning to grow accustomed to their way of life.

Banter was lively as conversation spilled from mouths full of food.

'Would you like a little more, Hazel?' said Rose. 'Need to keep your strength up, feeding young Bill.'

'Well thank you. If there's enough to go round, I would.'

Tom was so taken with the apparent change in Hazel's demeanour that he saddled up close to her and asked quietly how the baby had been that day.

'I'd be thinking your Ma would be better able to answer that. She has a special way with him, and it's grand, what they have.'

Lying on top of the blanket that night, comforted by the drop in temperature after the daytime heat, Hazel began to pack some detail around the bones of her plan. Rose had spoken of another baby, just a couple of months older than Bill, who belonged to a family at the other end of Happy Valley, fed on watered down condensed milk. That little child was apparently doing well, sometimes having his milk topped up with a little softened arrowroot biscuit.

Hazel decided that over the next month or so, while she would feed William what she could, she would also try him on the watered-down condensed milk with some mushy biscuit and get Rose to feed it to him. Gradually, she would put some distance between herself and the baby.

She was sure that Tom's mother would be happy to take on the role of feeding the baby from time to time. Day by day, William would become Bill and would be more and more attached to the older woman. Then, when the time was right, she would leave them a note explaining how Bill was better off with them and that she couldn't raise him as good as they could, and that Tom wasn't to try and find her. With that, she'd be gone.

~

Up to that point, her plan was quite straight forward and without complication; however, in recent weeks she began to feel physically different, a condition that was strangely familiar. She had pushed aside any thought of what was growing inside her. Now she knew that if her plans had any chance of coming to fruition, she must get away as soon as she could and deal with her latest revelation.

She had also heard from some of the women in Happy Valley that for girls who were carrying a baby, there were places they could go where things could be done to have it gone. *I'll get back to Redfern. Ma won't notice for a while. There'll be time to get everything sorted. I'll find the place where they can take it out of me, and Ma will never know.*

~

Six weeks later, after a day of traipsing the streets, Tom and Charlie got back to Happy Valley, tired but in good spirits. They brought home three yards of a woollen blanket from one old fellow who had given it to them to pay off a debt for a month supply of rabbits.

They trod their way up the track to the camp, greeting Eric and his friend along the way. They looked forward to a rest as they walked up and over the rise to the shack and the tent.

Straight away, Charlie could tell from Rose's face, that something was wrong. Tom's young sisters were sitting on the up-turned fruit boxes, either side of their mother who was standing and swaying back and forth, rocking the crying baby. The girls looked on with much more concern than usual until they noticed the men approaching. 'Da!' one of them called, 'Come, Ma's been crying.'

The men hurried their steps to find out what was going on.

'We were only away for a bit,' said Rose. 'We only went down to the creek while she had a little rest... She said she wasn't feeling well.'

'Who?'

'Hazel, of course,' she sobbed. 'I thought she had been so much happier lately too... We all did.'

'What's happened?' said Tom. 'Where is she?'

'Oh, Tom,' said his mother. She walked to the opening of the tent and reached in to pick something up from a wooden bench. She took a few steps towards him and held out a piece of paper with a long pencil-written message on it. 'She's gone, my boy. Read this.'

4. Concealment

It had been a long and sleepless night. Baby Bill had spent his first night sleeping alongside his grandmother in the canvas part of their camp. Tom had tossed and turned in the emptiness of what had been their bed, her murmurs, scent and the disturbances through the night as she tended the baby, all gone. At first light he was splashing water on his face and getting himself ready to find Hazel. 'She'll come back,' he persisted. 'She must!'

'Oh Tom,' said Rose rocking Bill in her arms. 'Not yet. Give her some time. If you go and look for her now, it will make things worse. In a few weeks she'll be missing her baby; then she might want to see you.'

'Oh, but Ma...'

'Come here, Tom. Come and hold your baby boy. There's nothing for us to be too worried about. Da and me will take care of us all, including this little fellow. Whatever happens with Hazel, well... everything will be alright.'

Tom took the baby, wondering how he was ever going to be able to look after him properly. 'How can everything be alright, Ma?'

~

Hazel woke in her Redfern house well before anyone else had stirred. It had been so soft, lying on a real bed in a room with the younger kids who had been excited to have their big sister home again, albeit without the baby she had left with. She had been full of anticipation on her trip back; the comfort of solid walls, a proper floor and the joy of being surrounded by people she grew up with. The other side to that was her mother, who was sure to be difficult. She had prepared a solid spiel about her failed attempt to make a life with the Davis family.

Hazel's mother was shocked the previous evening when she opened the front door to see her daughter standing there with no baby. Emotions spilled over from both, and it took until well into the night, when most of the children were fed, cleaned and put to bed, before they spoke about what had happened over the past five months.

'I thought it was for the best, Ma,' whispered Hazel, aware that while the other kids were in bed, they'd be doing their best to be listening. 'Ma Davis takes such good care of him, so much that I think, that he thinks, that she's his Ma!'

'Ah, you poor mite,' her mother said. 'Maybe you're right. It's all for the best. Baby William will be well cared for.'

Hazel's eyes glistened over as she tried to stifle the flow of tears. 'Oh Ma, will I ever see him again? How will I ever be able to tell my poor baby that I gave him up... just left him with another family?'

'That's it, girl,' said her mother, 'have a good cry and then you'll start to be right again.'

'I don't think so, Ma.'

'You've got to put it all behind you now.' Herr mother pushed on; there was more to be said. 'Who knows? One day you might see him again, maybe when he's grown up a tad, but you can never tell him who you are... or what you did.'

Her mother's message burnt into her mind and Hazel dropped her face into her hands. She pushed the sadness down deep inside where it would never spill out again.

~

Hazel was back in the home of her childhood, but her mother's scrutiny was never far away. Over the past few days, it had become clear that her place in the family had shifted. Each morning, she opened her eyes to the peeling paint on the ceiling, reminding her of where she was. Slowly, reality would creep up upon her and send her mood plummeting.

She had been back for nearly a week when one morning, a physical nausea had her throwing off the bed sheet and dashing out through the back door to the toilet, which was embedded as a small brick room into the back wall of the house.

She heaved and spluttered, holding her hair back and kneeling over the bowl, waiting for another surge from her insides. She heaved again and again, gasping after each episode until finally it was over. She slowly got to her feet, wiped around her mouth and pulled a rope that flushed it all away. She stepped slowly, breathing deeply as she got to the back door where her mother was standing cross-armed, glaring at her.

'And how long has this been happening?' she asked, thinking that for the past five months that Protestant boy would have been doing his best to have his way with her again.

'Ah Ma, just today.' She couldn't look at her mother and stared past her towards the kitchen. 'I feel a lot better now.'

Hazel felt her mother's eyes follow her wherever she went from that moment onwards. As she woke each morning with her stomach feeling the need to purge itself of its contents, she would go as quietly as she could to the outhouse and stifle the moans and groans as best as she could while she tipped her load.

She would creep back into the house softly, slip under her bed sheet and drift off to sleep again, hoping that the curse of her morning sickness wouldn't burden her again later in the day.

When the kitchen became noisy each morning, she would try to join in with her siblings as though everything was normal. She helped with the younger children, getting them some bread and if they were lucky, a small cup of milk, all the while knowing that her mother's eyes remained fixated on her every move.

'Was that you again this morning in the outhouse, Hazel?'

'No, Ma. I was asleep.'

She knew that it was just a matter of time before her Ma would know what was inside her; she needed to act.

At Happy Valley, Tom had given her a few bob each week, money that he trusted her to keep safe for when they might need it. She thought about the place she could go to make her problem go away. What was it like? Would they hurt her? She had no choice; it was time.

The next day Hazel followed her usual charade of disguising her morning sickness before doing her chores. Then she told her mother that she had heard of a woman who lived in the city that might give her some laundry work. The women at Happy Valley had told her about it, but she had forgotten until now.

'It will be grand if I can get us a few more shillings, Ma.'

Her mother interrogated her for details, but Hazel held her nerve and managed to convince her that the story was true. Satisfied that she had placated her mother, she set off for a laneway in Surrey Hills where in exchange for her money, someone would take her problem away.

She walked as quickly as she could, her hands trembling as she got to the other end of Cleveland Street. Today she would find out what having a baby taken out really meant, how it was done and when they could do it. The women at Happy Valley hadn't said much about that. Maybe it would all happen that day and then everything would be back to normal, and she wouldn't have to pretend anymore.

By the time she passed the junction of Railway Square, she wore a heavy film of sweat on her brow. Her head was light and dizzy, and her legs threatened to buckle under her unless she slowed down. She continued down Elizabeth Street and then up a steep hill on Albion Street towards the laneway she'd been told about.

She turned into the dingy lane and felt her heart thump heavily. A narrow strip of cracked road cut between narrow and squashed houses. Her hands shook and, for a moment, she thought about turning around and walking away. Then in the distance she saw it, a red gate in a wooden fence with a shiny brass handle. She baulked, stepping closer until the gate opened inwards. She froze when a young woman in a blue frock, sobbing and hunched over, stepped out and stumbled into the lane.

'Mrs... Hey Mrs...'

Hazel went to her, wanting to help the distressed woman, but not knowing how. 'I'll help you walk, Mrs...'

The woman looked into Hazel's eyes and then to her own ankles, where a thin stream of blood trickled from beneath her frock to the ground. 'No...'

'But you need help.'

'No one can know I'm here,' she managed as she did her best to clean up her inner leg with a handkerchief she pulled from her bag. She held onto her belly and began to walk away, stumbling every few steps.

Hazel's eyes flitted from the poor woman to the red gate with the brass handle that had snapped shut. She wondered what horrors were on the other side of the gate and began to shake. A cold sweat formed on her brow, and she felt sick inside. She turned around and walked away as quickly as she could. *I can't go back to Ma like this. I can't go back to Tom. There's nowhere else... I must think of something... Maybe she knows about me already. If she does, I'm done for.*

The walk back to where the day had begun was long and tortuous. Her legs ached and her head was fuzzy from hunger and thirst. When she made her way up Cleveland Street for the final stint, she was at her lowest ebb. If her mother chose that moment to continue chastising her, she knew she wouldn't be able to contain herself. She would be sure to crumble and betray her facade.

The gate squeaked loudly, and the front door groaned as she crept along the hallway towards the shared bedroom. She was almost there when the third youngest of her siblings raced in from the tiny concrete square of a backyard. 'Hazel, where you been?'

'Shh, Mary,' she snapped. 'Where's Ma?'

'Out back, pegging clothes.'

'Orright,' she said, pushing past the little girl to get to her bed. 'I'm going to lay down for a bit.'

She lay her head back on her lumpy pillow and looked up at the ceiling to the familiar patches where the paint had come away. She closed her eyes and gave in to exhaustion, in her mind picturing Tom and Ma Davis cradling baby William while the younger kids stoked up the fire at Happy Valley.

It may have been minutes or hours, such was the depth of her sleep, when she opened her eyes to her mother standing over her and shaking her shoulder. 'Hazel,' she said. 'No time for that. Now tell me, are you going to do the laundry work?'

'What, Ma?' she said. 'What...'

'I've let you sleep long enough. Now tell me, the laundry work?'

'Ah, that's right... I'm sorry Ma, I was too late...'

Suddenly Hazel felt the sickness in her belly begin to well up again. She sat up and did her best to look as though she was okay, until the urgency of the situation forced her to take a hurried retreat past her mother to the outhouse.

Try as she may, the sounds of her gagging and spluttering were too obvious and after she pulled the rope to flush away the little bit that had been in her stomach, she went back towards the bedroom. 'I'm not feeling too well, Ma. I need to lay down again.'

Her mother's eyes watched her closely for just one more clue that would remove any doubt about her daughter's condition. 'Go on then, rest your head.'

Hazel sat on the bed, laid back and rolled onto her side. Without thought she rubbed her hand over the contours of her belly, oblivious to the close attention of her mother. It was enough to confirm what the older woman had been mulling over for some time. 'So where were you today?' she snapped. 'Were you seeing that boy again?'

'No, Ma,' she answered, 'I told you... I just missed out... like I said.'

'Look at me when I'm talking to you, girl! I want the truth now!'

'Ma, I didn't see Tom. I haven't since I left there.'

'The truth, I said. Did he put a baby inside you again? I'll find out, so you may as well tell me now, girl!'

The silence was a confession, and with that, the blanket of shame once more descended upon the household.

'There's only one thing for it,' said her mother. 'It's St Monica's for you... for you and the likes of you!'

Hazel was too exhausted to take on any of her mother's words. There was nothing left to hide, and the repercussions were sure to be severe. For now though, the urge to sleep was overwhelming and for a brief moment, it gave her respite from the awfulness of reality.

~

Of all the days since Hazel had absconded from Happy Valley, Tom chose that same one to make the trip to try and find her. If Rose was right, Hazel would be aching to see her baby by now. While Hazel had walked for miles through the streets of Surry Hills that morning, he had been making the trek from La Perouse on the coast to the streets of Redfern. For the third time in his life, he was dressed in his father's best shirt and trousers, noticing that this time, his arms and shoulders and thighs almost filled them.

His desire to see her was intense, so much that he had none of the jitters that overwhelmed him on his previous two trips to Cleveland Street. He took long and fast steps, breaking into a jog over the final hundred yards to her front door.

He knocked loudly and breathed in as deeply as he could. Soon he heard the smack of tiny bare feet on the hard surface inside, running to the door. It opened slowly for him to see Hazel's sister, reaching up to grip the doorknob. 'Ma,' she called loudly. 'It's the mongrel scoundrel dog!'

With that he heard dishes being dropped into a sink followed by quick and heavy steps of the mother stomping towards him. 'Get inside Patricia!' she scolded, as the little girl scampered. 'You! How dare you!'

'Please... please, Mrs O'Brien...'

'If my husband was here, he'd beat the day lights out of you!'

'But I only want to see Hazel,' he spluttered. 'She must want to see Bill by now...'

Inside the bedroom, Hazel woke to the commotion and lay still as if paralysed from what she was hearing. Tom was right; she did ache to see baby William and if the truth be known, to see him as well. She knew too, however, that her mother was right, and her union with him was nothing but shameful. Only more grief would come from it.

'I will tell you once, and once only,' she barked, 'and then you will go and not ever return!'

'Please, Mrs O'Brien...'

'Hazel has gone,' she said, emphasising every syllable. 'She's gone to do the only respectable thing. She's at the home for girls like her... in disgrace.'

'Where?' he pleaded, 'What home?'

Hazel hurt with every part of the lie she heard being told, fighting her instincts to rush outside and tell him that she was there, and she wanted to hold William. *Girls like me, shameful and disgraceful... Go away, Tom... Take good care of baby William.*

She rolled onto her side and buried her head into the pillow, folding it over her ears to block out the world.

'That's not for you to know. Away with you and don't come back!' were her final words as she pushed the heavy door shut in his face. She should never have trusted the Protestant Davis family with her daughter in the first place and she vowed never to do it again. *Let them deal with the consequences and keep the shameful William as their own. And let St Monica's take the Protestant's next evil spawn to teach Hazel a lesson once and for all.*

Tom walked slowly along Cleveland Street towards Railway Square. He paid no attention to what was on the road, for he was still trying to take in what Mrs O'Brien had told him and ambled across the street right in front of a horse and buggy. The huge animal baulked suddenly, jolting the man in the buggy forward. 'Have a look where you're going, you drongo!' he yelled.

Tom looked up and waved an apology, as the whiff of fresh horse droppings shot through his nostrils. He walked on, mulling over each thing Hazel's mother had said, helpless to do anything about it. *This hurts so much. She doesn't have a clue that I'm trying to find her. Where is she? What is this 'home for girls like her'?*

Part Two: War

21ˢᵗ May 1940

5. Worthy

Tom Davis, a man of twenty-two years, stood with his family on the platform at Railway Square. He was one of dozens in khaki uniforms under a slouch hat bidding farewell to loved ones. The train to take the soldiers west to an army training camp approached from the direction of the city and rattled its way along the platform, slowly coming to a jerky stop.

There were tears and excitement amongst the crowd, for in their minds, these heroic soldiers would soon be on their way to take on the soulless aggressors in Europe. Women and children stood with the husbands, sons and fathers, proud of the handsome men in uniforms but also frightened of what might happen to them.

'Look after him,' Rose pleaded to Charlie. 'And look after yourself; come back safe.' They were Rose's last words to her husband that day. Her hands trembled, thinking that she may never see either of them again. She wrapped her arms around Tom and hugged him tightly before grabbing her husband and squeezing him with all the love she had.

Tom hugged his sisters one at a time and then bent down to grab Bill's hand and look him in the eye. It was hard to speak. 'Be a good boy... for your grandma.' he managed. 'No more fights... even if the other boys tease you because you're new.'

'If they say mean things about you and Grandma and Grandpa, I'll punch them on the nose.'

Tom wrapped up the seven-year-old boy in his arms and held him longer than he ever had before. 'I'll write you lots of letters and your aunties can read them to you.'

He had said goodbye to Bill many times before but that had been different because he always knew he'd be back. He was the parent that had always been there. This moment tore at his heart strings, worried that one day soon, Bill would think that both of his parents left him behind.

Tom took one step towards the carriage and then another, looking over his shoulder to see his sisters bending down and comforting his crying son. How he wished he could have just one more moment to hold the boy and tell him that everything would be okay. More soldiers followed him into the train, pushing him away from his family.

Outside, the crowds on the platform waved with smiles hiding their tears. Tom and Charlie scrambled inside as the train moved off with a jolt, its wheels turning slowly as the faces outside became smaller until they were gone.

~

Charlie and Tom had plenty of time to think during their trip to the camp at Blacktown on the outskirts of Sydney. Smalltalk mostly, for any conversation about the people they were thinking about was too difficult. Gradually, their talk petered out and they each retreated into their own headspace.

Best case scenario was that this whole mess far away across the seas could be sorted out quickly; maybe within a year or so and then they could all get back to putting their families back together after the years of upheaval from the Great Depression.

Tom's thoughts flitted over what had become of his life during the time at Happy Valley. Paramount in his mind was the ambiguous sighting he had of Hazel just a couple of months earlier when he was returning from his army medical examination at Paddington. He remembered how he walked down a busy Oxford Street where pedestrians' reflections off the glass shopfronts appeared to double the size of the crowd.

Yet amongst the throng, on the opposite side of the street, the woman's face and the strawberry blonde hair made his heart thud. He was stunned by the sight of the beautiful woman, and although, through the crowd he could only see her head and shoulders, he was sure that it was Hazel. The last time he felt like that was seven years earlier on Cleveland Street, when she first paid him for rabbits.

When he called her name in Oxford Street, she looked over her shoulder. 'Hazel!' he yelled again. Amongst the street traffic and struggling through the pedestrians walking in the opposite direction, he yelled it out again, pushing between the obstacles, and apologising to those he bumped into, all while watching her slip away.

Now he was about to go into training and be shipped off to somewhere on the other side of the world, sure that she was somewhere in Paddington. What he would give to get a message to her and tell her about Bill and what a dependable little chap, albeit a feisty one, he'd become.

He wanted to tell her about the narrow terrace house in Newtown that they had moved back to and that she still had a home with them if she wanted it. He was proud of the bits and pieces they had managed to put together from running errands for Mrs Anderson and flogging rabbits and doing any other 'one-off' jobs they could muster, so they could get some of the rent money together.

He wanted to tell her how Charlie managed to convince the landlord that even part-rent was better than no rent, sweetening his argument by agreeing to keep a tab of arrears which he would pay when eventually the whole sorry downturn was over. Now with the first pay from being a soldier coming in, the Davis's were honouring their promise.

The sways and rocking of the train relaxed Tom, freeing his mind to rehearse what he would say to Hazel, when the day came that he found her. He'd tell her how Bill was being raised in a real house with people who cared for him, even sending him to school most days for an education.

He wanted her to see him in uniform, a brave soldier who could now be her breadwinner. In his mind's eye, he saw her, the beautiful girl he knew who had become his child's mother, and he wondered if she ever thought of him... and Bill.

While Tom was deep in thought, Charlie's mind was on what he was leaving behind. He knew how lucky they had been in getting out of Happy Valley just before the New South Wales Golf Club next to the shanty town had influenced the new conservative Government to knock down the eye-sore and clear it out.

The years there had been tough going, sweating it out in summer swelters and shivering through cold, wet winters when the company of hunger pangs were all too familiar. Yet beneath the hardship Charlie had taken to a freedom that he'd never had before. The shillings he earned from the streets were for his family and not a landlord, and he was at home rubbing shoulders with the blackfellas and everyone else at the valley on equal terms.

He recalled the solidarity he felt with the other men there, and how angry they all were when the State Premier, Jack Lang was sacked. He had been the only politician, in their minds, whose actions, no matter how radical, had been in the interests of the common people.

He missed their gatherings at the end of a day at Happy Valley, lamenting the political shifts to the right of both State and Federal Governments. He and the others at Happy Valley had steeled their resolve to join with the growing number of 'red raggers' at gatherings in public places such as the Domain. He felt a shame that since moving back to Newtown, he had lost touch with that part of his life.

Now he was going away, and as the train trundled along to Blacktown, his thoughts moved to the job ahead and making his family proud. The Nazis' aggression in Europe made him eager to do his bit for the allied cause.

When he enlisted, there was the buzz of excitement in his home while he and his son went through the military processes of medicals, and getting fitted out for a uniform. He loved the feeling of the fabric on his skin, and how the look of it told the world that he was part of a greater cause.

Now though, it was all very real, and as he sat in the bumpy carriage, the realisation that he was leaving behind his cherished wife and daughters, hit him with a thud. He was off to places unknown with his oldest child, to confront a foe he didn't understand. It was both frightening and thrilling.

They trundled through the farms and bushlands of Sydney's outskirts and as they were about to come to a stop at Blacktown Station, he was already missing the woman who had always made sense of the world.

The train slowed and jerked to a stop. Men in uniforms grabbed their kits from the overhead racks, humping them over their shoulders and taking turns moving through the carriage to hop down to the platform.

'It all starts here, Tom. You ready for this?'

'Of course, Da,' he answered, forcing a smile, 'It's what we signed up for, isn't it?'

~

While Tom was preparing to embark upon a great ship in a voyage across the ocean to another continent, Hazel lived another day with Arthur and Ester Byrne. Months earlier, in crowded Oxford Street, Paddington, she heard her name being called from across the street. It was a familiar voice; perhaps it was Tom. For a long while she ceased to think about him, yet the unexpected sound of his voice reminded her of her first love.

Into the sea of faces she had searched, holding her little girl's hand tightly as she pushed her way through the crowd to try and locate the source of the voice. For a moment, it was as though time had stood still, the little girl hugging her soft toy lion closely with her spare arm, as her mother looked around to find where the voice had come from. Seconds became minutes and finally she knew that if Tom had been there, he was now gone.

She knew that after her brief time out and about in the streets of Paddington, she would have to return to the ornate Moore Park terrace where she would continue to struggle as a housekeeper for a man she was trying not to love and his family.

~

The journey to that place in time began six years earlier when Hazel was just sixteen years old, while Tom was still at Happy Valley, flogging rabbits and helping his Ma look after baby Bill.

Under the influence of her mother, Hazel was placed at St Monica's in Darlinghurst, a home for unwed pregnant women, just a couple of miles from their house on Cleveland Street. 'Darlo' as the suburb was known, was an eclectic arrangement of houses, shops and businesses as varied as the characters that ran them. Certain streets were off-limits to people who wished to keep out of trouble, especially at night.

Homeless men and a few women, occupied park benches beneath tall fig trees in the few green spaces of the streets set back from the main road, Oxford Street. At night they would shelter where they could, either sleeping under the blanket of night in a tiny park or squirreling themselves away in the alcove of a nearby back-alley. Juxtaposed with this, were pockets of dwellings that attracted musicians, artists and others who gravitated to the avant-garde set.

St Monica's was on a street that was an exception to the crowded conditions of the adjacent streets. The large building occupied more space than surrounding structures and it exuded a clinical harshness, a hint of what it was like inside its walls. From the moment of arrival at the sanctimonious institution, Hazel was made to feel shame for what she was carrying inside and how she should be grateful to the Sisters of St John for taking her unworthy soul into their care.

Her only penance, she was told, would arrive when she handed over her newborn child to respectable and God-fearing people who deserved the joy of raising an infant. Without being able to voice her objections, she galvanised her inner resolve that this would never happen. She had already given up her first born and the dark hole from that was not going to be deepened by doing it again.

Life was hard at St Monica's, so much so, that memories of her days in the family home at Cleveland Street or the time after at Happy Valley didn't seem so bad after all. Having barely settled into her shared room with three other pregnant girls, she was soon put to hot and arduous work in the kitchen. The stoves and ovens were relentless in pumping out heat and odours of overcooked meat and vegetables that made Hazel feel sickly.

One of her jobs each day was to get down on her knees and scrub the floors, a chore that tormented her aching back and made her knees throb in pain, especially as she grew more heavily pregnant. One morning, a nun known as Sister Julianne, who was sensitive to her predicament, told her to use a mop so she wouldn't have to bend down and get on her 'all fours'.

Sister Julianne was the exception to the harshness and coldness that was entrenched in the home. For Hazel, the mop did indeed make the task more manageable and lifted her spirits from hopelessness to at least survival mode.

She continued with this less taxing way of cleaning for two mornings, even managing a small amount of conversation with one or two of the others in the kitchen. On the third morning however, one of the other Sisters came into the kitchen, sensing a small amount of camaraderie amongst the young women. Intent on keeping the girls' spirits broken she barked into action. 'Put down that mop, girl,' she hissed. 'Get down where you belong. A girl like you should be kneeling before our precious Lord.'

There was no payment to any of the girls for their labour. Their work was a humble contribution for their keep while they were confined and waiting for the birth of their bastard children.

The living quarters were overcrowded and despite being kindred spirits in so much that their lives were dour and joyless, their situation meant that the girls had little energy or enthusiasm for talk. It took more than a month before Hazel built up any trust with any of the others. It was a sixteen-year-old girl named Moira, a fellow sufferer at about the same stage of her pregnancy, who she made some connection with.

Despite this tiny amount of company, it remained a desperate and lonely existence. Even when the other girls would break into conversation, she was further crushed in her spirits when talk would centre about the day when their babies would be born and the Sisters would take them away.

The one glimmer of hope arose when Moira spoke of another place, St Steven's, where she wanted to go. It was somewhere, she'd been told by Sister Julianne, where she might be able to stay with her baby. Moira had broken down in tears as she told Hazel how she'd been tricked into signing the papers, surrendering her baby upon its birth and now there was no point in going to St Steven's.

Each day Hazel fought the thoughts of losing another baby, mentally preparing for the battle she knew she would face to keep her child. *I mustn't write my name to anything. Where is this place, St Steven's?*

A part of their orientation at St Monica's was a tour of the labour ward, a clinical and colourless room contained by painted, rendered concrete walls. It was intended to frighten the girls and to remind them of their sins. During the tour, they were told that they were chosen by God to provide babies for worthy, though childless, couples. 'If you really loved your babies,' they were told, 'you would be grateful to the Lord, to be able to give them to a proper and deserving family.'

~

51

Baby O'Brien came into the world, after a long and painful labour in the early hours of the 10th of November 1934. Exhausted, Hazel fought the attempts by the Sisters to take the baby from her, determined to latch the infant onto her nipple as soon as she could. As she had done for the past months, she continued to refuse to sign any pieces of paper that had been shoved in front of her, knowing that just one signature on a cleverly disguised document could mean that baby Nancy would be gone from her forever.

Her reputation amongst the Sisters was that she was trouble, a wilful girl with no appreciation for what had been done for her. With the birth, her mother made a rare visit to St Monica's. When they encountered Hazel's mother, the Sisters were pleased that she sided with them to prize the baby from Hazel and send it in the direction of the awaiting adoptive parents.

Using Hazel's mother as a portal of influence, they put on a facade of care and concern for both the young mother and the infant, portraying the envious life ahead for the baby, should she be placed with good and honourable parents. At first, the ploy was working, and for a while, Hazel's mother accommodated the dialogue. She agreed to take some time alone with her daughter and talk some sense into her.

'It would be for the best, Hazel.'

'No, Ma,' she protested, holding Nancy close to her bosom, 'You don't know what it's like here.'

'I can't be raising another child for you, Hazel. The people at our own church, especially the Nuns, are already gossiping about the whereabouts of your Pa... It doesn't look good... and there are the rumours too, that this isn't the first baby you've had... Oh, how it must look! It takes all o' me strength to keep the talk down. Imagine, my girl, what those tongues would be gossiping about if you were to come home with this one. Try to see reason, girl. There are good people out there who would take better care of her than we can.'

'Ma,' she pleaded, 'I'll find a way. Don't worry about people finding out; I'll find a way.'

Alone with her daughter and new grandchild, the older woman looked into her daughter's eyes, the once bright windows into her soul, now empty hollows in a gaunt face. For the first time in a long while, she felt sympathy instead of shame. 'Ah, Hazel,' she whispered. 'What will become of you?'

'Ma,' she pleaded, 'find out about St Steven's. My only friend, Moira, said that if I could get there, I could keep Nancy. Ma, no-one will ever know of the shame. I'll stay away after that, live somewhere where you can come visit. No one from home will know.'

'I know about St Steven's, Hazel,' said her mother, pausing for thought and leaning in to look at baby Nancy, an infant that carried her blood, nestled into the bosom of her own daughter.

'Ma...'

'She looks like you did,' her mother murmured and stroked the baby's temple.

'Don't you see, Ma?' Hazel pleaded. 'There might be a way and you won't have to live with the shame.'

Hazel's mother turned and walked away.

'Ma, please,' she sobbed.

Outside the ward, Hazel's mother was once again approached by two of the Sisters of St Monica's. 'So, it's all arranged then?' one of the Sisters asked, holding up a clipboard with a pen, 'You might be able to take this in for her to put her name to.'

She looked at the zealous women in front of her, seeing a small part of herself. The image of her frightened and distraught daughter flickered through her mind. 'Excuse me, Sisters,' she said, shuffling past them, 'I have some errands to run.'

~

As it turned out, it was no easy task arranging a transfer from St Monica's to St Steven's. The Sisters had considered Hazel to be trouble, and now her mother, apparently, was made of the same stuff. The Sisters had already earmarked Hazel's baby for a particular couple and were intent on securing any scrawl they could argue was her signature of consent.

After just five days, while Hazel was nursing baby Nancy, she received another visit from her mother along with the most senior Sister. They were in heated, though controlled discussion. 'I thank you for housing Hazel through this time, Sister. I'm sure those at St Steven's will be in touch.'

'Ma,' said Hazel, quite confused. 'What's happening?'

'Finish up what you'd be doing there. The little mite can have some more soon.'

'Are we really going?'

'Pack your bag.'

In a moment that seemed to have come from nowhere, Hazel's mother changed everything. With that, Hazel felt a glimmer of hope. With no opportunity to say goodbye to her friend, Moira, she was gone from St Monica's.

In the time Hazel's mother had made the necessary arrangements for the transfer, she had also decided to not place the move in the trust of the Sisters. She would accompany Hazel with the child to the home, an offshoot of the wider St Vincent's de Paul Society.

'There's a bus in thirty minutes; we'll have to get a hurry-on.'

~

St Steven's was situated in a tree-lined street in a suburb known as Concord. It was to become Hazel's new home, and although the sight of Sisters in black and white tunics beneath a habit of the same colours stirred unpleasant feelings in her gut, she noticed a softer demeanour from the people there. Even the men who came and went, including doctors and figures from the church, offered the young women and babies who lived there benevolence and sympathy.

It was several weeks, however, before Hazel began to accept their trust, having remained guarded after the awful time at St Monica's. Her mother had told her that she was to be grateful to the

Saints for this chance, an opportunity for her to be with the baby while the good name and reputation of their family was safeguarded and hidden from the eyes of society.

Hazel also knew that she was not to allow herself to feel absolutely settled in this new place for it was made very clear that her stay was for twelve months at the most, after which she would face some difficult decisions. Her options would be to either adopt baby Nancy out, leave her at the home or take her when she left.

For Hazel, though, there was only one option. The ensuing twelve months would serve as a period of respite while she determined just how she was to make her way in the world along with her daughter. She knew that her mother's help in getting her to St Steven's, although cherished, would not extend to welcoming her back to the family home where the eyes of the neighbourhood and especially their church, St Agatha's, would be fixed upon them.

~

Each morning the heat, typical of the time of year, would build along with the drone of cicadas that populated the line of gum trees in the properties near St Steven's. The area around the main building was largely grass with several rose gardens and leafy trees spaced across it. Hazel took great pleasure in strolling about this part of the property with Nancy after she had completed her share of the house duties each day.

On the hotter days, she would wait until late afternoon, when the shadows from the trees stretched across the grass, before venturing outside. If it was a particularly humid and oppressive day, she would stay indoors until the predictable thunderstorm from the south had blown the air cool and fresh.

Arthur, a man in his late thirties, held the responsibility of maintaining the grounds so that all who visited were met with a visual splendour that made them feel confident the young women and their babies were being well cared for. Despite the physical nature of his work, he took pride in being well presented, wearing trousers and a stiff collared shirt.

The first time they encountered each other was a Wednesday afternoon, when he greeted Hazel with a smile and a nod as she strolled past. Unbeknown to her, his gaze followed her well after she passed him by.

Over the next week or so, he made sure that he was close when he expected her to be walking past, and soon the routine became a spoken greeting with a small amount of conversation and exchanging of names.

As the weeks passed, Hazel became more relaxed and comfortable in the surroundings of St Steven's. During one of her daily strolls, Arthur paused from the work he was doing in the rose garden when he saw her.

'I was hoping I'd see you today,' he said, dropping the pair of cutters onto the grass. 'I have something for you; actually, it's for the little one, when she gets a bit older.'

Hazel was taken aback by the gesture, not being able to remember the last time she had received a gift. 'That's very kind of you Mr Byrne.'

'Please call me Arthur,' he said as he bent over next to his shovel and rake to retrieve the package wrapped in brown paper. 'I hope you both like it.'

'Thank you, Arthur,' she said, struggling with being on a first name basis with an older man. 'I really wasn't expecting such a thing.'

'Go on,' he said, 'unwrap it.'

Hazel felt like she was a girl having a birthday as she tried her best not to tear the paper. Inside the package was a toy lion, and she could not resist rubbing her face in it, rejoicing in the soft fluffy texture. 'I love it,' she giggled. 'I mean, she will love it. Thank you, Mr, I mean Arthur.'

~

Over the ensuing weeks, their conversations became part of Hazel's afternoons, and over time she learned a little more about his wife and two children. She looked forward to their encounters, to the point that she was disappointed if he wasn't there on a particular day.

One afternoon as the two exchanged polite conversation, it became obvious to Hazel that Arthur was alluding to a topic of conversation that he wasn't prepared to fully broach. As he raked leaves and trimmed some hedges, he told her that his family would be passing by soon, and that he would like to introduce her to them. She was thrilled with the offer, though perplexed as to why it was so hard for Arthur to suggest it.

That day, as the shadows crept across the grass, Arthur dropped his tools on the ground and walked towards the gates where a pretty lady in a green frock held the hands either side of her of a boy who looked to be about nine years old and a slightly younger girl. The children called out to their father, and Hazel noticed the pronounced limp of the mother. As they came together, Arthur kissed his wife on her cheek and bent down to give each child a brief but affectionate hug. 'Come and meet Hazel.'

What followed was a meeting between people who seemed destined to be a part of each other's lives. Baby Nancy was passed around as a treasure to behold, while Hazel watched with joy as the children ran and played.

Two days later, it was as though the Saints had answered her prayers when, upon her afternoon walk in the garden, Arthur put a proposal to her that she needed no time to think through. 'You've probably noticed my wife's problem,' he said, pausing to lean on a garden shovel.

'I've noticed she has a limp, if that's what you mean.'

'It's getting worse lately and the children seem to be needing more and more attention,' he explained. 'At times, Ester finds it quite difficult. So do I if the truth be known. Perhaps I shouldn't be saying this to you, but Ester and I are finding things quite a struggle.'

Hazel felt awkward in that Arthur had confided in her about his family's lives and he picked up on her reaction. 'I'm sorry, Hazel,' he said. 'I've said too much. It's just that I have no one I can talk to about it really.'

'It must be hard,' she said.

'It is, but we do get by. It's just that if there was a way of making things easier.'

There was an uncomfortable silence.

'I was thinking,' he continued. 'Well to be honest, both Ester and I have been thinking... you seem to get on well with our children, and we adore baby Nancy...'

Hazel's heart began to pound heavily in anticipation. Could this be her salvation?

'I think your wife is lovely too.'

'You could come and live with us, Hazel,' he said. 'Of course, we'd need you to help out with things, especially as Ester isn't able to do much anymore, but that could be in return for board and keep for you and the little one.'

She wanted to throw her arms around him and say yes, she'd love to, but for the moment, words evaded her.

'You don't have to tell me today,' he continued. 'Have a think about it.'

~

And so it was that over the six years up to the day she heard Tom's voice across a noisy and crowded Oxford Street in Paddington, Hazel and baby Nancy came to live with Arthur's family. She enjoyed cooking and cleaning in the two-story house that sat in a tree lined avenue of well-to-do Moore Park. Ester, an only child, had inherited the house from her wealthy parents, a godsend to the couple, especially considering the impoverished world her husband was from.

Hazel was now in her twenties and despite the ravages of her life, including the birth of her two children into poverty, she had grown to be a voluptuous woman who looked as though she belonged in every way, to the salubrious place she was now a part of.

In sad contrast, Arthur's wife had become more and more physically depleted. At first, she was very lucky in that she appeared to have made a recovery from the polio she suffered as a teenager.

All these years later however, doctors were not surprised when debilitating symptoms of the disease began to re-emerge.

Her spirit remained as joyous as she could make it, counting blessings rather than misfortunes and ever grateful that Hazel had been a part of their lives for the past six years. On the days when the pain of walking became too much for her to spend time on her feet, she asked more of Hazel who was always happy to do whatever was needed. The two women cared about each other, Hazel for the first time in her life sharing certain intimate details of her past life with someone she felt would understand.

Hazel looked upon Ester's children with loving affection, and as they grew into their restless teenage years, she was thankful that they remained quite sheltered from what the world could do to them, from what it had done to her. Through them, she saw how very young she had been when she first met Tom and lay with him on the cold concrete of her Cleveland Street home.

She loved how they treated Nancy like a younger sister, including her in trips to the park and spending time reading stories to her while Hazel was busy in the house.

Hazel had become as much a part of the family as she could have hoped for, but along the way, something else had grown inside her that she was not equipped to deal with. It was during the nights, late when the world was asleep, that she gave herself permission to think about Arthur.

Sometimes, her desire for him was so powerful that she lay in the dark, tending to herself and thinking about when they first met. In her fantasies, she rolled amongst the fallen leaves with him in the gardens of St Steven's, while Ester would play with Nancy and her own children out of sight, behind the tall hedges of the property.

It was a precarious situation, for Arthur had been drawn towards her since he first saw her. The much younger woman had continued to occupy his thoughts each day. There had been several times when temptation had gotten the better of him, that he almost made advances towards her. On one occasion, it was only the sound of Ester's footsteps approaching that stopped him. During moments of intimacy with his wife, he had almost said Hazel's name, catching himself just in time to avoid an error with catastrophic consequences.

One night, not long after the day Hazel heard Tom's voice in Oxford Street, she lay in the quiet of the large upstairs room she shared with Nancy. Her daughter, worn out from a busy day at school and then playing after dinner with her older house siblings, was in deep contented sleep. The light of a full moon filtered through the lace curtains so that from where she lay, the polished chest of drawers and wardrobe reflected the starry night sky at her. The moonlight flickered over her white nightdress and when she lifted it up it, shone on the milky white flesh of her breasts.

It was easy for her thoughts to wander, and she wondered if it really was Tom calling her name just a few days earlier. The thought made her think of baby William and what had become of him. Her thoughts turned to Arthur, and she wondered if perhaps hearing Tom call her name was some sort of divine message, a warning for her to be careful. The very thought of hurting Ester in any way, especially in such an ultimate betrayal, terrified her.

There had been two men in her life that had stirred her emotions so, one from Happy Valley, who she had run from years ago, and the other, the man who gave her somewhere to run to. It was the latter who was now occupying her mind.

She had accepted that the hunger she felt for Arthur was wrong, hearing her mother's words in her mind admonishing her for the lustful sins that had already landed her in so much disgrace. Yet despite that, she couldn't stop thinking about him and what it would be like to kiss his lips.

That night, with her resistance at its lowest ebb, she was aware that should the opportunity arise, she would be powerless to avoid betraying Ester. At first, she thought she was imagining the sound of someone walking on the wooden floor, surely it was a part of her fantasy. The reality became more obvious as the footsteps ascended the stairs, stopping for a few moments then continuing.

He's coming. He keeps stopping, hesitating... Oh, please no... We can't let Ester know... Please stay asleep, Nancy.

The footsteps stopped just outside her room. Hazel's heart thumped and her breathing was quick and shallow. There were three soft knocks on her door. 'Yes, who is it?' she said, excited and terrified.

'Sorry, Hazel,' came the reply from Ester. 'I didn't think you'd be asleep yet. May I come in?'

The euphoria that had built up inside, crashed as if she had been doused in cold water. She struggled to reply, pulling down her nightdress and finally managing the words to invite her in.

'Sorry to disturb you, Hazel,' said Ester, 'I was going to check with you at dinner, but I forgot... you know how it can be when the kids are noisy and having fun.'

'Yes,' she managed. 'Of course, what is it, Ester?'

'Will you be able to come with me tomorrow, to see Doctor Giles? After the children go to school?'

The question resonated in her head. She would do anything she could to help this lovely woman who had become a dear friend. The realisation of what she had just been prepared to do, and how it would have destroyed her, hit with a thud. *It's too much now, too close. How long can I keep going like this?*

'Of course, Ester. Of course, I'll go with you.'

6. Loss

It took more than a week for Tom to gain his sea legs on the voyage from Sydney to Egypt. His father, Charlie, took to the military routines far more easily upon the grand ship Queen Mary. After coming out of the loose and desperate years of the depression, having to follow orders and knowing his place in the military hierarchy made Charlie feel secure, especially when it meant that he could line up for a plate of stodgy food three times each day. Despite being one of the oldest men on board, his physical strength and tenacious demeanour backed up the age of thirty-eight years he lied about on the attestation forms for enlistment.

The massive troop carrier was pretty much a moving city on the water, thousands of soldiers on route to the Middle East where their training was to be put into good use to thwart the advancing Germans and Italians. It was well into the third week of the voyage before Tom's body began to tolerate the strange feeling of movement across the Indian Ocean and the thick tropical air that he breathed.

The two men were able to enjoy each other's company on only the rare occasion, having been designated places in different sections of this division of the infantry force. This bothered neither of them as they each made their own mates and grew accustomed to the roles they had in the grander scheme of organisation. It was clear to them that their fates during this war were likely to proceed in very different directions.

On the 20th of April 1941, Tom silently wished himself a happy twenty-third birthday. That night, while all those around him bunkered down to sleep, he made certain that no one saw him make his way to the deck. He would be in serious trouble should a superior officer find him anywhere near the bow of the great vessel.

He imagined his mother and siblings back home, making a birthday wish with young Bill on his behalf. He wondered if Hazel might have spared a thought for him too. He brought himself back to the present and stared into the sky, a glorious moonlit night on the high seas. In majestic solitude, he marked the occasion by breaking all the rules and climbing over the rails near the front of the bow. There he was exposed to the rush of air as the great ship cut her way through the vast expanse of water, splashing cooling sea spray over his hot face.

He fastened his feet into the grooves above gigantic bolts and gripped the top of another rail, hanging on for dear life as he looked over his right shoulder to the sea in front. From what he was looking at through his watering eyes, he could see no horizon to tell him where the shimmering of the reflected moonlight on the black ocean stopped and where the sparkling of stars in the sky began. He felt the wind from every one of the twenty knots that the ship was moving and in that exhilarating moment when he knew that just one slip would have him fall into deadly oblivion, he was free from all his worries, content to trust that the people he loved at home were safe and well in each other's care.

~

Weeks later, with the voyage to the Middle East well behind them and following a blistering day of infantry training that had given way to the freezing sands of an Egyptian night, Tom remembered the vista from the bow of the Queen Mary and how he felt at that sublime moment. Now, physically spent from the demands of preparing to do battle, he lay on his bunk and allowed his thoughts to flow.

He thought of home once more, and in his mind's eye he could see his mother holding Bill's hand with his sisters nearby, and he tried to imagine what they'd be doing. The girls were almost of an age when they could leave school and hopefully earn a pound or two in one of the factories or workshops in Newtown.

That, along with the money that he and his father could send, made him confident they'd have all they needed to be warm, sheltered and well fed. With that, young Bill, he decided, was in the best place he could be.

In the blurry state of mind that precedes sleep, his mind flickered once more to the images of the woman he was certain was Hazel, in that crowded Paddington Street months earlier. He allowed his imagination to run, changing the sequence of what happened that day so that he weaved through the people on the footpath and caught up with her.

The fantasy played out in his head as he drifted into sleep.

~

Training in Egypt was hard and brief before both Tom and Charlie were cast into action, albeit both totally unaware of each other's movements. As soon as the troops had learnt barely as much as they needed to know and had become somewhat acclimatised to that harsh part of the world, they were sent north through Palestine, where they readied themselves to do battle in Syria and Lebanon.

Different brigades of Australian troops combined with other allies to be sent to fight the Vichy French, a military force under the control of a French administration which had sympathised with the Nazis after the fall of France to Germany a year earlier. Facing this enemy was the first action of the war that both Charlie and Tom were to face.

Charlie had learned from his fellow troops, of the De-facto French administration set up in the resort city of Vichy, whose job it was to defend the territories in Syria and Lebanon. While Charlie did his best to understand the complex political arrangements that were generated under the stresses of war, those details meant little to Tom.

What he did understand was that the Vichy French were the enemy, and he was eager to fight them.

What made sense to both Tom and Charlie was that if they could defeat the Vichy forces, they would have played a vital role in stopping the Nazi's progress towards Palestine, Egypt and ultimately the Mediterranean.

As his brigade moved further north, Tom was one of the many Australian troops moved further north to engage in fierce and dogged battle on the outskirts of the Lebanese capital, Beirut. Unbeknown to Tom, at the same time his father was one of a separate brigade progressing eastward towards a large airfield near the city of Rayak.

For weeks, the Vichy resistance was every bit as brutal as the allied assaults upon them, and the progression of the predominantly Australian forces on both fronts was slow and bloody.

It was during this campaign that Tom learnt much about his own character. The men around him were strangers just months earlier, but now they were the people in the world who he placed his utmost trust in. He knew that these men would put their lives on the line for him at the most perilous of times, and he hoped, that if tested, he would do the same for them.

Several weeks into the conflict, towards nightfall after a particularly heavy day's fighting, Tom was working hard with Snowy Jones and Bluey Reid, two soldiers with whom he'd become as close as brothers, when a screeching missile shook the ground.

The impact was catastrophic, and Tom was thrown flat on his back, numb and stunned as a piercing shrill rang through his head. It could have been seconds or minutes before he was able to move, firstly to his knees and then struggling to stand, when he saw Snowy stumbling towards what was left of Bluey. Together, they did what they could, blood oozing through their fingers and hands as they attempted to plug the gaping wounds.

For Tom, the events of that dark day were to eat away at his very soul and change him forever. In the desperate circumstances there was no time afforded for him or his mates to process what had happened before they were once again thrust back into the heat of battle. Living on instinct, he continued to do what he'd been trained for, all the while fighting another battle within. A surge of guilt swam through his head because it was Bluey who was gone and not him, for they had swapped places in their roles only minutes earlier.

Later, as the gravity of the day fell upon him, he felt shame when feelings of gratitude flicked through his head that he was still alive to fight another day. These were the first tragic scars of war that he pushed deep down into the furthest reaches of his being, where they would lay, never to be disturbed.

The Syrian and Lebanese campaigns were ruthless in the personal toll it inflicted upon Tom. Weeks later, when the dust finally settled and the allies had secured the strategic locations they had been fighting for, he found out the fate of his father. Charlie's fighting brigade had attacked the Vichy French further east near Rayak, close to the Syrian border. The fighting was intense and protracted and the toll of casualties on both sides was high.

Charlie was just one of the soldiers who had expected the enemy to offer only token resistance. After all, how could their hearts really be in winning this battle, especially since France itself has already been taken over and occupied by the Germans?

Charlie's assumption could not have been further from the truth, and the exchanges of fire were brutal. Before the allies succeeded in securing the region, continuing their progression towards Damascus, hundreds of soldiers from both sides had been killed, with hundreds more including Charlie, injured, many critically and disfigured for life.

Following that conflict, Charlie had been returned to Egypt where he spent his final days in a delirium. Mercifully, his madding fever took his mind back to the days of his youth, back to a familiar place, flitting in and out of his life at Happy Valley. On the 28th of July 1941, Charlie Davis, one of the many men who had lowered their age on the enlistment papers to join up, drew his last breath.

Tom's fractured life was further ripped apart. In a time when he needed to be comforted by his family, and to grieve, there was no such thing. It tore at him to know that on the other side of the world, his mother and sisters would be grieving the loss of the man who had always got them through their struggles. He couldn't imagine how his mother would be able to mask her own grief when she had to tell young Bill that he'd never see his grandfather again. He knew, firsthand, how quickly death could come, and he wondered how long it would be before his mother was telling Bill that his dad too would not be coming home.

~

In early 1942, as the situation in the Middle East became slightly more stable, a diplomatic row was being waged between the Australian Prime Minister, John Curtin, and the British Prime Minister, Winston Churchill. Both leaders had commitments in mind for the 7th Division, the Australian force of which the grieving Tom was a soldier. With the Japanese threat growing more perilous by the day in Southeast Asia, Curtin stepped up from his lower rung of the political hierarchy and called the division home, against instructions from Churchill.

To that point in time, the British were confident in the strength of their military in Singapore, sure that the Japanese would not be able to make any impact on their bastion there. Churchill's opinion was that he had better use for the thousands of soldiers like Tom, who had already proven themselves in battle, than to lose them back to Australia.

Unbeknown to those in Tom's brigade, while they were doing battle in Syria, the war had erupted closer to their homeland in the Pacific. Japan, buoyed by its successful advances into China, was objecting to American insistence that they withdraw from its geographical neighbour. Their anger with America had reached an explosive point, and they bombed the United States Hawaiian base at Pearl Harbour, bringing another giant global power into the world conflict.

Curtin, attuned to the ferocity of Japanese advances and being aware that Australia's geography placed it in a perilous situation, had ideas totally contrary to Churchill. He turned to President Roosevelt and the Americans for allegiance, already sympathetic to them after the damage they had suffered in Pearl Harbour.

Curtin's insistence to bring home the Australian troops, including the 7th Division, created strange and conflicting emotions for Tom. On the one hand, he was joyous that he was on a ship heading in the direction of his homeland, but it ripped him apart knowing that his father remained behind, buried in the sands of Egypt.

Despite being dismissed by Churchill as an act of disloyalty to the British, Curtin's decision proved to be the correct one from an Australian point of view. While Tom's division was upon the seas returning to Australia, conflict was heating up in Asia. During the early days of February 1942, the Japanese advanced their position by engaging in ferocious battles that shocked the western world.

To Churchill's horror, the Japanese destroyed any semblance of British domination in Singapore, and tens of thousands of allied soldiers, including Australians, were killed or taken prisoner in the fall of the once-great British bastion. The infliction of terror went beyond those of the thousands of soldiers suffering terrible deaths in awful labour camps, and many thousands of Chinese civilians living in Singapore were also slaughtered.

The fate of Australia was suddenly at its most precarious, and only days after the fall of Singapore, the Japanese bombed Darwin in the first of many deadly air raids. For Tom, the news of this filtered through in frustrating instalments, making him desperate to get back. For now, the intense grief he had over the loss of his father needed to be put on hold, shoved deep inside, amongst the accumulation of festering sorrow that was already there.

By the time Tom disembarked in Australia, the situation was dire and in desperate need for consolidation of the union between Australian and American forces. In the tropical north of Queensland, Tom was one of thousands of troops given some time for respite from the ordeals of the African campaign before going into intense preparatory jungle training for the next chapter of the war, now against the fanatical Japanese empire.

For Tom, it felt as though he'd left one war and had gone home to fight in an entirely different one, against a mysterious foe intent on taking his country. The rainforests of North Queensland were a world away from the sands of Lebanon and Syria, and although Sydney town was more than fifteen hundred miles to the south, he was on home soil and desperate to protect it. Along with his soldier mates around him, Tom focussed his energy on his immediate future, for the word was that soon they would be off to defend against the Japanese aggression in the jungles of New Guinea.

Many more air raids upon Northern Australia occurred, as Darwin had become strategically important for both the Japanese and the allied forces. The small city at the top end of the country was demolished and many Australian soldiers and civilians were killed or suffered horrible injuries.

While the Australian forces were coming to terms with the imminent threat from the Japanese, things were getting desperate from yet another direction as news gathered of fiery battles involving Australians and Americans fending off the enemy to the east, in the Coral Sea.

Usually, at the end of the day, when the troops had a small amount of time to gather amongst themselves and unwind, their talk would gravitate to the latest news and the rumours that had been heard. One piece of hearsay was about political talk from Australia's south. If the situation became worse, the country would establish a defensive line from Brisbane westwards, thus protecting the lands south of that but conceding anything north to the Japanese.

Tom's gut reaction was one of anger and disappointment. The rumour of the 'Brisbane Line' had not been substantiated, though the mere mention of it made him feel betrayed. How could his own country not have enough faith in the thousands of soldiers, white and indigenous, who were with him, ready and prepared to defend them.

'We're up here ready to take on the yellow bastards and the politicians are down there ready to throw in the towel!' he said amongst a gathering of troops sitting in the mess tent smoking.

Jimmy Donovan was an Aboriginal man from the mid north coast of New South Wales. He called himself a proud Biripi man, but neither Tom nor anyone else in his unit had any idea what that meant. It had not been easy for Jimmy to get into the army, being knocked back twice for manufactured reasons to cover up the real reason for his rejection. On his third attempt, the decision makers changed their mind, not only for Jimmy but for many others like him; the Japanese threat had become more real and the need for more men was desperate.

'My mob knows what invasion feels like,' he said, pulling no punches, 'and be fucked if we gunna let it happen again, Tom!'

'Too right, Jimmy!'

'Blackfellas, whitefellas, we all gotta do our bit now,' said Jimmy, whose displaced family existed on the margins of society with so many others in similar situations. As the demand for more soldiers became intensified, he and other men from indigenous nations across Australia slowly gained acceptance into the military.

They shared with the rest of the army a fierce determination to defend Australia, but for different reasons. Tom, Snowy and the others like them were fighting for the sons and daughters of Britain who now called Australia home. As far as Australia's leaders were concerned, when this dreadful war was over, the nation would once again stand proudly according to the White Australia Policy, a prosperous outpost for its British offspring to call home. Jimmy and those like him were fighting a different war. They were defending the land itself, their mother, from yet another invasion.

~

In the fields of battle, regardless of colour, the soldiers depended on the trust they placed in each other. During the quiet times of the training in North Queensland, Tom came to look forward to exchanging talk with Jimmy; he felt that he could say things to him that he couldn't mention to his other mates. Each day, he began to understand things more from Jimmy's point of view.

Tom told him about his son back home and about the boy's mother, and that hopefully, one day he would find her. In turn, Jimmy spoke about the heartbreak of losing his place on country and not being accepted as a fellow person outside his place on the mission.

One night, after a gruelling day's work, Tom said to Jimmy that maybe the government would be able to make things better for him and his people. He told him of the blackfellas he lived alongside at Happy Valley during the depression, and how they looked out for each other.

'Like we'll be looking out for each other up in New Guinea, eh, Tom?' said Jimmy. 'But after the war things will be just the same for my mob.'

'How can you be so sure?'

'You'll see, Tom. My people cared for country way before whitefellas, and you know what else? We're not citizens, can't even vote for guv'ment.'

Tom went quiet, letting what he had just been told sink in. 'You know, Jimmy,' he said, before getting ready to turn in for the day. 'We're just the same, you and me. Dunno if we'll be together in New Guinea, but after the war, maybe we can stay mates.'

'Funny thing, Tom,' he answered. 'I'm like you here, and when we fight the Japs, we be just the same. But I reckon after, if we get back home, you'll go one way and good luck to you... but me... I'll go back to being just another poor blackfella.'

Towards the end of the training days for their movement north to New Guinea, fragments of news reached them of Japanese midget submarines invading Sydney Harbour and firing upon civilian ferry vessels. The invading submarines were destroyed but details of anything more than that were scant. For the troops about to embark for transport north, the news meant that their mission had become even more critical. Tom's heart was torn between what he knew he had to do - fight the invaders up north, and what he desperately wanted to do - take off in the middle of the night, somehow get to Sydney and embrace what was left of his family.

In January of 1943, at Townsville in North Queensland, Tom embarked upon the MS Taroona and headed for Port Moresby, New Guinea. While he travelled north for several days on that ship, his mind had gone in the opposite direction, thinking of his family, especially young Bill. When he could find some quiet time to himself, he tried to picture his young son's face, but to his own anguish, he couldn't.

He wondered how the little boy was, aware that Bill was facing his own battles. In the treasured letters he'd received from home, he learnt more and more of his son getting into scraps with other kids. He didn't like him getting into trouble, but part of him couldn't stop from being proud of the boy's willingness to stand up to anyone who had a bad word to say about his family.

Tom thought of the others back home and how they would be coping with their sadness and loss. He fantasised that they may have heard from Hazel and that she would be asking for news of him. He had only fractured memories of her now, and he craved to be able to picture her face in his head again. *If I make it through this damn war, I will find her.*

~

The invasion by Japanese midget submarines in the harbour brought the war close to home in the minds of many Sydney residents. In their Moore Park terrace house, Arthur complied with the public address instruction that windows be covered in brown paper and that safety rules be followed when advised. One of these rules was that houses were to be blacked out at night to dim the view of the city during anticipated air raids. Along with Hazel and the children who were now much older, they busied themselves on step ladders and chairs, reaching up to tape paper over every window in the house.

Ester would do what she could for the cause, measuring and cutting the pieces to be used.

It was an anxious time for many as news trickled through from Europe and from what was happening on Australia's doorstep. With the war reaching Australian soil, the population was typically divided in attitude.

Large sections chose to remain distant from the war time conflict and assumed that their protectors, the Australian soldiers and their allies, would keep them safe. Others more connected with global events were doing what they could in preparation for what may come. Each morning before Nancy was taken to school by one of the grown-up children, Hazel would make sure that her identification tag was secure in its place around her neck. This measure was being taken by the school to help reunite kids with their parents should they be evacuated to one of the shelters that had been prepared across the city.

For Hazel and Arthur, the preparations that were made to deal with a Japanese air raid, or other unanticipated form of invasion, filled them with suspense. They each secretly harboured fears about what life would be like under the rule of the Japanese.

Beneath that fear was a further layer of anguish, a tension that had been simmering for years. Each day, they both pushed through what had to be done, tormented by a longing for each other. At times, when alone in each other's company, working on a common task such as moving some furniture, Hazel's arm would brush lightly across Arthur's, sparking the sexual tension between them.

Too often, they would catch each other's eye, the connection deep and amorous. There existed a maddening itch, one Hazel knew she couldn't scratch; if she did, irreparable damage would be done to their families, and it wouldn't be the Japanese who inflicted it.

~

The summer heat of Sydney had been typically oppressive, particularly on those days when the humidity made people sticky with sweat and eager for relief to come. If they were lucky, a weather change would roll its way up the coast from the south. As the weeks rolled by, the stifling weather was compounded by the prospect of Japanese invasion.

By the time the chills of winter arrived, news from the fighting in New Guinea was filtering through on a weekly basis, mainly in the form of news reels at the cinema, the details spreading out from there by word of mouth. One nippy morning as the household gathered around the kitchen for breakfast, Arthur suggested that they have a break from the tension of recent weeks and have a day in town to watch a movie at the cinema.

Hazel and Nancy were excited at the prospect of such an outing, while for Ester, just the thought of travelling into the city made her feel tired and worn. The others, too, were not thrilled about spending a day with their parents, more intent upon enjoying the company of their friends and new workmates. Although Ester quite liked the prospect of a quiet day to herself, she recognised that such an excursion would be a welcomed distraction for her husband.

With her encouragement, Arthur and Hazel left the house mid-morning, Nancy walking between them along the pavement on their way towards Anzac Parade and the bus stop. The little girl was all smiles, happy to hold her mother's hand and then thrilled when Arthur scooped her up and put her on his shoulders for the final part of the walk.

It was exciting to be on the bus, trundling towards the city knowing that in an hour or so they would be sitting in front of a big cinema screen. From where they disembarked in the city, they could see the Tatler Theatre standing proudly on the corner of Liverpool Street, its grand stature, designed by the renowned architect, Walter Burley Griffen, justifying the fuss made about it around many Sydney dinner tables.

Arthur looked in awe at the beautiful building, part of him imagining the worst-case scenario of the impressive theatre housing Japanese members of an occupying military. Pushing those thoughts away, he looked at Hazel, feeling an excitement to be out with just her and Nancy.

The session at the cinema began with a newsreel from New Guinea. Legendary wartime photographer, Damian Parer's footage of what was happening so close to Australia's north, had the cinema audience captivated. A stirring commentary accompanied the visual account of heroic Australian troops mucking it through the mud of the jungles. Footage of native New Guineans, dubbed the 'Fuzzy Wuzzy Angels', lugging supplies and carrying injured Australian soldiers up and down the thick, sticky terrain drew collective gasps from the movie watchers.

Towards the end of the newsreel, Damian Parer himself made a plea to those who were watching, urging them to get behind our brave troops in this battle, expressing his frustration at those Australians who were yet to give a thought for the tremendous hardship faced by Australian troops in battle against a cunning and ruthless foe.

As the footage rolled on, Hazel, sitting in the soft theatre chair, though mesmerised by what she was watching, was oblivious to a passage of film showing Tom in a line of exhausted soldiers struggling up a muddy jungle slope.

Nancy, sitting between them, just a bit too low in her seat to see everything on the screen, was propped up by Arthur's thick coat, rolled up and folded in such a way to give her seat a boost. She didn't understand much of what was being said in the narration but was very happy to see the moving pictures on such a big scale. Again, Parer reminded the audience that the war was on Australia's doorstep and the troops needed the whole country to get behind them.

The effect of the newsreel upon the audience was palpable. Arthur was just one of those in the crowd appreciative of what the troops were up against in New Guinea but also jolted by the very real threat of a Japanese invasion. As the news-reel finished, he looked at Hazel, thinking that if the worst scenario of the war came true, and they became lost to Japanese control, he may never have a moment like this again.

Hazel felt his gaze upon her and caught his eye. She too felt the intense connection and lifted her arm over the back of Nancy's seat to rest her hand on Arthur's shoulder. In a moment of intoxicating euphoria, Arthur tilted his head to embrace the touch, firstly on the side of his face, then turning ever so slightly, to kiss her hand.

The curtains moved across to cover the big screen and quickly opened again, announcing the beginning of the main movie. It was a welcome distraction, one that gave both Hazel and Arthur a chance to recalibrate their emotional states and be immersed in the escapism of watching Errol Flynn portray Custer's involvement during a tumultuous period of American history.

For the next hour or so, they each burned for the chance to take that intimate moment further. As the movie ended, and her emotions became tempered, Hazel realised that the honourable thing to do was to pretend that the moment never happened. Arthur, however, had other ideas.

7. Lust

The mountainous jungles of New Guinea were Tom's home for most of 1942 and 1943. In the many battles defending Port Moresby, he bore witness to bloodshed and atrocities that burnt their images into his mind. The memory of Jimmy Donovan falling like a rock right next to him during one exchange of gunfire would stay with him forever.

On home soil for most of 1944, Tom yearned for the war to finish, so he could be re-united with his son once more. He knew from the correspondence he received that Bill, now eleven years old, was facing his own battles on the home front. School, it seemed, was not a perfect match for the boy and it was not unusual for him to be on the wrong end of the stick, usually as a punishment for fighting. What weren't communicated so clearly were the reasons for Bill's fights; namely, that he couldn't stand by when a schoolyard bully was inflicting torment on someone who couldn't defend themselves.

Throughout the war, the desire to find Hazel one day had become an obsession, at times the driving force that gave Tom the will to deal with what was happening all around him. Several times, since getting back from New Guinea and while based in the Atherton tablelands of North Queensland, he almost did the unthinkable and planned a run south.

On one occasion, it was Snowy Jones, his closest mate and someone he confided in, who physically stopped him from going 'Absent Without Leave'. It began with Tom telling him of his plan over several bottles of beer. A heated argument followed and grew into an exchange of fists. It ended with tears and an embrace between the two men - Tom promising to stay put.

~

In many ways the conflict in the Pacific and Southeast Asia was like a separate war to that in Europe where the allied forces had taken control. The Italian dictator, Mussolini, while attempting to flee from Italy to Switzerland, was captured by Italian partisans and executed.

With the Soviets surrounding Berlin, Adolf Hitler and his lover Eva Braun followed through with a suicide pact. Just one week later, on the 7th of May 1945, Germany surrendered unconditionally to the allied forces in Europe.

As knowledge of these victories filtered through, Tom felt solace that his father's sacrifice had not been made in vain, though he ached with the realisation that Charlie never had the chance to hear the news for himself.

~

Tom survived the years in New Guinea, but the war was not yet finished for him. While he was preparing for yet another tour of duty, this time to Borneo, life for Hazel in Sydney had grown complicated. From the time after the kiss on the hand at the cinema, the atmosphere in the Byrne household became tense. Hazel was nervous and overpolite towards Arthur, an awkward attempt to return the dynamics in the house to normal.

The tension between Arthur and Hazel was not lost on Ester who began to suspect that there was something going on that she was not privy to. With that, in her mind, she conjured up scenario after scenario in which Hazel had become much more than a friend to Arthur.

She was not a bitter woman by nature, but the way she felt when delving into her sordid imaginings made her upset, and she began to question her own character. As weeks became months, she came to be more irritated by Hazel's mere presence, the younger woman's voluptuous body reminding her of her own physical shortcomings.

To Nancy, her mother had become preoccupied. 'Mum,' she said one night in their room as they were preparing for bed, 'why don't you ask me about school anymore?'

'Pardon, Nancy?'

'You didn't ask me about school, and you know I had a mathematics test.'

'You did?' she replied. 'I mean, of course you did. Was it difficult?'

The young girl was miffed. 'Don't worry about it.'

'I'm sorry, Nancy,' she said. 'Please... how was the spelling test?'

Nancy glared at her mother and stormed off.

Life in the house fumbled along, all those in it carrying on with a facade of polite conversation and trying not to needle one another. They maintained an outward appearance that everything was normal. Everything, however, was not normal and Arthur tried to cover up his demeanour, claiming that if his wife thought he was acting strange, it was because of the news each week about the situation in New Guinea. He would parrot his spiel about how precarious the situation was and that if the Australian soldiers didn't hold their place, firstly it would be Port Moresby that would fall and then Australia.

Ester understood these concerns, for they all had them, but she could see through him. It was obvious he was hiding something. She could see it whenever Hazel entered a room and how if he was sitting, he'd become more upright, and his eyes would widen.

Ester became expert at using her peripheral vision, especially in the sitting room after dinner. While she stared blankly into the pages of a book, she would catch Arthur's eyes moving to the younger woman whenever she walked past. She was becoming more and more convinced of her husband's infatuation with Hazel and wondered if it was mutual. All through the summer and well into 1944, Ester became more suspicious; everyone in the house was living on tenterhooks.

As one long year of the war led into another, and as news from battlefields near and far began to become more encouraging from the allied forces point of view, the pressure in the Byrne house was becoming intolerable.

The allies had Germany on the ropes in Europe, though in the Pacific, fighting continued against a fanatical Japanese foe. However, for Arthur, it was his domestic situation that was having a far more telling effect on his life.

Early in 1945, more than a year and a half after the cinema kiss, Arthur arrived home early from his work at St Steven's. He knew that Ester would have been taken to her medical appointment by one of his children and the other one would be at work. He knew too that Nancy would be at school and so Hazel was more than likely at home on her own.

Hazel was in the kitchen preparing food for their dinner, and when he came through the door, she gasped and dropped the large knife she was using.

'Sorry to startle you, Hazel.'

'Oh, I'll be fine,' she managed. 'I didn't expect you home just now.'

'Ah, I finished all the work early... We both know that things have become difficult, and I thought we could talk.'

'About what?' she said, moving to the tap and washing her hands for way too long. Her heart thumped heavily as it was only on the rare occasion that they found themselves alone together.

A cold sweat formed on Arthur's brow. 'Well, I'm not sure how to begin really... It's just that...'

'Just what, Arthur,' she said. 'I'd be telling a lie if I said that you weren't making me feel a wee bit nervous.'

'Oh, I'm sorry. I'm not trying to... I think I should get to the point...'

'Please do.'

'We have never spoken about it, Hazel.'

'Again, I say, about what?'

'Remember the cinema?'

'Well, I try not to think about it,' she said, her breathing becoming rapid.

'That's the trouble... I can't stop thinking about it.'

Hazel wiped her hands on her apron and then used it to wipe the moisture from her eyes. 'I'm sorry,' she said with a sniffle. 'I try not to... but it's so hard...and Ester...'

She began to sob, and he moved forward to wrap his arms around her. 'We can't go on pretending.'

She looked into his eyes as he wiped a tear from her cheek.

I'm so sorry. I'm sorry Ester. I'm sorry Ma. I'm sorry Nancy.

Arthur put his lips to hers, the heavy beating of her heart giving way to a quivering that spread throughout her body as she opened her mouth to his. He burned for her, his hand gliding down her back and over her buttock. In the moment of passion, she saw the hard kitchen floor and thought of her first time so long ago, with Tom at Cleveland Street.

'No,' she said, 'not here.'

He led her up the wooden staircase, through her bedroom door and kissed her again, firstly on the mouth and then on her neck causing her to shudder with ecstasy. She had imagined this moment a hundred times, and as he unbuttoned his shirt to reveal the skin of his chest, she kissed him over and over. There was no turning back, the pressure that had been building and simmering for years, engulfed them as the constraint they had used to keep it in check for all that time, was blown apart.

8. Surrender

By 1945, the allied forces' defences had become galvanised in much of the contested territory. Although the Japanese were buckling under the strain of lost access to their supply lines, their fanaticism remained resolute, and they refused to give in.

In Borneo, Tom's brigade could sense that they were getting on top of things. Without becoming careless or arrogant, there was a more confident air amongst the troops when they were on a patrol or carrying out any other duty.

At the end of a day, if they had any period of free time, Tom, Snowy and a few of their mates would gather at the southern end of their base, just on the edge of the rainforest where they had cleared a patch of ground and rolled in a few logs to sit on. The tropical nights were black as pitch when there was no moon to speak of, and as they sat and smoked, Tom would gaze up through the gaps in the tree canopy and look for familiar stars. He would imagine that his mother, Rose, and his sisters might be on the beach near Happy Valley with Bill, looking at the same stars.

Unbeknown to him, at the same time far away in America, the new President, Harry Truman, was in deep consultation with his decision makers. The debate was about whether to use the results of the top-secret Manhattan Project, namely, nuclear warheads, to finish this costly war that lingered and refused to die.

~

Things had changed in the Byrne house. Since that passionate afternoon during which all inhibitions were cast aside, it was as though a building storm had finally burst and calm had followed. While Arthur tried not to be obviously smitten with Hazel, the shift in his demeanour did not go unnoticed with Ester.

Hazel did what she could to avoid being alone with her. She knew the conversation would be intolerable. At the end of each evening, upon retiring for the night, Ester would be cold and short, and Arthur would try to compensate with fabricated attempts at discussion, only making the situation worse.

Whenever Hazel was to be alone in the afternoon, Arthur would arrive home early from St Steven's. Their fervent lovemaking continued unabated, the passion between them bubbling away with the guilt and shame that simmered just beneath the surface.

The morning household rituals had evolved to accommodate the awkwardness that existed in the household. Hazel would prepare what she had to in the kitchen and then use the excuse of helping Nancy get ready for school to make herself scarce. Arthur and Ester would sit at the table and eat their breakfast in silence, apart from Arthur's feeble attempts at small talk. One morning, towards the end of winter, Arthur forcing himself to eat some breakfast, was encouraged when Ester contributed to the conversation. 'The roses should be pruned soon.'

At hearing those words, he joined in quickly, thinking that perhaps his secret was safe. 'Yes, it's that time of year again,' he chirped. 'At St Steven's too... the rose garden is looking a little shabby.'

'Well, I must come and have a look, when you've tidied it up... perhaps this afternoon, after my appointment. I feel that I have a little more energy today.'

'Today?' he baulked. 'Well, I'm not sure if I'll have it all done by then.'

'It doesn't matter then.'

'Er... What I mean to say is that I can have a good old crack at it this morning... Should be able to have it nice and tidy by day's end.'

'Hmph,' she said. 'Well, I'll see how I'm feeling later; might pay you a visit about three.'

The ambiguity left him in a quandary, knowing that his wife would be out of the house from mid-morning and that Hazel would be alone from then. He immediately began to plot a course of action that would have him soon out of the house so that he could return as his wife left. Time with Hazel, and then back at St Steven's by mid-afternoon. It was possible.

Feeling Ester's eyes upon him, he hurried through his breakfast to get away.

'Best be off then,' he said, 'busy morning coming up.'

He bent down to kiss her, pushing his luck somewhat, not really surprised when she suddenly pulled back and turned her head to the side.

Upstairs, Hazel listened for the departure of firstly Arthur and then, sometime later, Ester with her eldest child. Only then, when she was certain that the house was empty, did she return herself to her household duties, beginning with cleaning up the breakfast dishes and then moving to the laundry. It would be just a few hours, she was sure, when Arthur would get home and they would be together.

Arthur's plans for the day had been shaken up. There was no time to go all the way to St Steven's and then come back, only to return before three o'clock. Perhaps he would forget about seeing Hazel, he pondered, just this one time, and spend the whole day at his work, and hopefully in doing so, begin to quash his wife's suspicions. That line of thought lasted but briefly, for when he sensed that Hazel was alone in the house at that very moment, the pull to see her took over.

From the bus stop, he chose to return to the house by an alternative route to make sure he didn't encounter Ester who may be heading in his direction. The much longer walk around the famous Sydney sporting arena and back home was done in double-quick time, and he was puffing to regain his breath when he came through the front door, catching Hazel by surprise.

'We haven't got long.'

'But why are you not at St Steven's?' said Hazel, dropping the basket of clothes she was carrying.

'Ester might be coming by later to see me at work,' he said. 'I'm not sure why... maybe to check up on me, I don't know.'

Arthur's unexpected appearance shook her as she had been trying to process her feelings of guilt that had continued to fester that morning. There was something else too that didn't feel right, although it would be some time before she would be able to navigate her way through that.

He led her up the stairs and to her room. They undressed more quickly than ever before and fell onto the bed. He moved his hands over her breasts; her mind was elsewhere. She was distracted by the worn, fluffy Lion in the corner of the room that had fallen from a storage box. She remembered how much Nancy once loved the toy.

'Are you alright?' said Arthur.

'Er... yes,' she managed, 'a wee bit surprised that you're here.'

Their lovemaking that morning was rushed, leaving Hazel less than satisfied. When they were finished, she lay there trying to work out what exactly was troubling her about Arthur's unforeseen early return to the house. It was all over so quickly and now Arthur was hurrying away again. She thought of the first words he said to her that morning, 'we haven't got long', as though she was some type of convenience.

Arthur pulled up his trousers and buttoned his shirt. He ran his fingers through his hair, adjusted his attire and leant over to kiss her on the forehead. The cursory gesture irritated her further and for the first time since their initial indiscretion, she felt sick with remorse about how she had hurt Ester.

As he left the house, Arthur figured that he had ample time to get to St Steven's, well before his wife, to establish the facade that he'd been there all day. He ambled towards the bus stop, knowing he'd have time to bask in the winter sunshine while he waited for the bus, confident that he'd got away with the latest incident of infidelity. He hoped so, for he knew that the stakes were high; if he was found out, there would be a huge price to pay.

The bus stop on Anzac Parade was a busy place, acting as an intersection where commuters would change from a bus returning from the city to another that went to the inner suburbs. Many people there also made a swap at the nearby tram station. The gentle sun felt soothing upon his face, and he was able to quell the thoughts that had been swimming in his head.

Now dozy, he heard the distinct rumble of a distant bus getting louder and thought it to be the city bus, for there were still fifteen minutes before his was due. He closed his eyes, content to sit there as several people around him rose from the benches to meet the tall green double-decker as it grumbled and whined to a halt. A conductor in his uniform held onto the silver pole at the open back door, swinging backwards to create a pathway out for the commuters.

Arthur remained sitting on the bench, his eyes closed to the commotion of people getting off and others scrambling on to swap one or two coins with the conductor for a small paper ticket. The bus continued to idle, the smell of burnt fuel wafting across the road. For a moment there was a slight delay in proceedings as the conductor paused in his collection of the fares to focus on someone who seemed to be having difficulty stepping down from the bus to the road.

'Hang on, just a minute, Mrs,' he said. 'I'll give you a hand.'

'Thanks, but we'll be fine,' replied the young woman who was helping the older woman negotiate the exit.

At the sound of those words, Arthur's eyes widened with terror. *Jesus Christ!*

'Dad! What are you doing here?' his daughter asked, holding her mother's arm as they stepped up to the pavement.

He sat, stunned as his wife's spiteful eyes glared at him.

Without referring specifically to nuclear warheads, America's President Truman issued grave warnings to the Japanese. The call was to surrender or face swift and total destruction. The information from American intelligence, however, was that Japanese emperor, Hirohito, would not surrender and fight to the end.

It was obvious to the troops in Tom's brigade in Borneo, that the table had been turned against the Japanese he had come to despise. Nonetheless, by painful experience, they had learned not to get too relaxed or casual with their daily routines. The enemy would remain fanatical until the end, and he knew that dying in defence of the emperor would be an honour.

In the jungles of Borneo, the Australians had no idea of the political decisions being made by their American allies. With no formal reply from Emperor Hirohito to Truman's demand to surrender, the order was given to drop the bomb, reportedly on the understanding that the target would be a military one. On the 6th of August 1945, the American bomber, 'Enola Gray', dropped the five-ton atomic bomb known as 'Little Boy' on the Japanese city of Hiroshima. Eighty thousand people were instantly vaporised with tens of thousands more dying over the following weeks from radiation poisoning.

Three days later, a bomber dropped another one, 'Fat Man', on the city of Nagasaki wiping out more than forty thousand citizens. A few days later, Emperor Hirohito unconditionally surrendered to the allied forces, closing the book on World War Two and opening another on a fresh set of global tensions. As defeated parts of the world were carved up under the jurisdiction of the victors, the seeds of resentment were sewn for the next generation of conflicts, including the Cold War.

In Borneo, Tom and his fellow troops received the news of victory with elation, for it meant that they were one step closer to getting home, hopefully this time for good. Despite this, the men knew that their job was not yet over, and that despite the victory, there were enemy soldiers who had not surrendered or been captured, remaining in the jungles unaware of their emperor's capitulation.

For days after the news of victory, the men walked with an extra spring in their step until their enthusiasm began to wear off amidst the daily grind of regular duties. As the calendar extended into spring, the hot tropical weather was made even more oppressive by the humidity that built up preceding the monsoon. The conditions made Tom and all the troops there with him, uncomfortable and more frustrated with the lack of any newsworthy announcements.

A consequence of being stuck in a foreign land after the formal surrender of the Japanese was that at times when on routine patrols, some of the soldiers were not as vigilant as they had been before. This was brought home to them one morning when the leading scouts of a party proceeded far too casually about their patrol.

Tom was at the rear of the unit when the commotion broke out. There was the familiar sound of gun fire, followed by shouting as the Australians hit the ground and returned fire at a suspected part of the jungle. As far as he could tell, there was no obvious sign that any of his mates had been hit and instinctively, he fell into battle mode, his eyes darting around for any evidence of the enemy.

The men hadn't seen action for more than a month, yet in a flash they were doing what they had been trained to do, each of them like a vital part of the overall machine. The entire episode lasted no more than fifteen minutes as they dragged themselves on their bellies across the forest floor, strategically eliminating the threat from each patch of ground until they were certain that whatever peril had been there was now gone.

That day marked a shift in the mindset of the soldiers in Tom's unit. They now knew that while the war may have been declared over, there was still a long way to go before they would tread on Australian soil. In the weeks following, news did begin to flow in including the details of what remained to be done in Borneo as a part of the mop up from this dreadful war.

Sometimes Snowy and Tom would sit, smoking on the logs in their special clearing, long after the others had retired for the night.

'So, when all this is done,' Snowy said, drawing on his smoke. 'What then, Tom?'

'Hmph,' came the reply, 'all I've been able to think about for years now is getting home... see my Ma and sisters and my boy. Try and tell 'em something at least, not sure what... something about my Da, what happened to him.'

Snowy nodded, understanding.

'Christ, I miss him... All through the depression he kept us safe... He made sure we had something in our bellies, most days anyway... and clothes on our back.'

'Another good man lost, Tom.'

'And back then I was pretty much just a boy m'self, so he was more of a Da to Bill than I was.'

'Sounds like there's a bit of your father in the boy... tough little fella from what you've told me.'

Tom breathed in his smoke long and hard. 'Yeah... and he'll be thirteen by now.'

'So, like I said, after all this... what then?'

'I'm not sure... Been a soldier for years now,' said Tom. It was the first time he was made to think about this. Ever since leaving his father buried in the Middle East, he'd yearned to go home and be with those he loved. He dreamed about finding Hazel and hearing about everything she had been through since Happy Valley. What he hadn't thought of was how he would support himself.

'Y'know what, Snowy?' he went on, 'I'm buggered if I know what I'll do.'

'You could come with me for a while, Tom.'

'To Japan?' he snorted. 'In that occupation thing you've been talking about?'

'It wouldn't be forever, mate. Maybe a year or so, another year's pay. Who knows?'

'I fucken hate Japan, Snowy... Nah mate, I'll be home as soon as I can... You and I, we'll catch up when you eventually get back.'

'So, what will you do?'

'Can't say. Get a job I s'pose...

'Yeah, you and every other bastard getting back from the war.'

'Hmph. Yeah, me and every other bastard.'

As it happened, Tom need not have given much more thought about going home for some time. The army had plenty of mopping up for the Australian soldiers to get through, especially as the thousands of Japanese prisoners had to be supervised and moved. At the same time, they were needed to help restore civilian administration and oversee the start of the reconstruction of Borneo.

It was during these months that Tom and many of his fellow troops helped with the liberation of the allied prisoners that were held in numerous Japanese camps around Borneo. Tom was affected by what he saw in the men who somehow had survived, and it cut him to the core, burning images in his brain that galvanised the hatred he felt.

~

In January of 1946, Tom embarked on a ship and left the war behind. Snowy stayed behind with the many others who still had to wait. Over the days and nights of the voyage, Tom tried to forget the atrocities he had witnessed but failed dismally. At night, he would fall in and out of tortured sleep.

In mid-January, six years after going off to war with his father, Tom, along with a thousand others stood on the ship's deck with packs slung over their shoulders, staring at the first glimpses of Sydney Harbour. He closed his eyes and though he tried, he failed to picture the faces of those he was coming back to.

The images that were in his head belonged to those who were dead now; those he vowed never to forget. He tried again to remember his Ma and Bill, but they remained faceless. He thought of Hazel and when he couldn't see her in his mind's eye, he whacked his own forehead hard to give it a jolt. He felt the ache in his chest from holding back tears, so intense that he couldn't gain a breath. He looked at the heads of Sydney in the distance and once more pushed the anguish down inside, deeper and deeper, locking it away with the accumulation of grief that was already there.

9. Home

Tom was granted leave and it felt strange to open the small metal gate to the semi-detached house in Newtown he left six years earlier. At first, he wasn't sure if he was in the right place, his mother looking so much older that he almost didn't recognise her. Young Bill, a small child when he left, was now almost as tall as he was.

Sanding in the doorway, words were hard to come by and when Tom tried to speak, his words faltered. With that, he wrapped his arms around them both and tried not to cry.

Rose took him through to the room that his sisters had shared before they moved out a few months earlier. He dumped his bag there and then they proceeded to the small living room. Rose sat next to Bill and then Tom joined them. He listened to the news about his sisters, hanging off every word and devouring every bit of domestic information he had been starved of for so long.

Rose leant forward to take a cigarette from the packet on the small table in front of the lounge chair.

'And when did you start smoking?'

'Ah, not long after you left,' she said, striking a match and sucking the smoke in. 'Mrs Jones next door gave me one, oh, must have been five years ago, when we were both waiting for news from the war.'

'Fair enough.'

'Helped to calm us down when we got worried, you know, worked up about what was happening,' she explained, breaking her words with a cough.

Tom listened to how his eldest sister had become pregnant and was quickly married to a very young serviceman who had joined up in the latter stages of the war but was never deployed to see action. They had moved to his father's sheep station, hundreds of miles west. His other sister moved in with them too, as Rose explained, to give the expecting mother some company and to lend another pair of hands to the running of the station.

Tom wanted to hear as much as he could about his son; however, Bill, now a gangly teenager, found it difficult to say much. He was still unsure how to take his father after all this time. He was happy to listen to his grandmother take the lead and answer his father's questions.

There was much to catch up on, and as they talked a tension hung in the room. Finally, it was Bill who cracked open the subject, interrupting the discussion with an abrupt question. 'Why hasn't anyone spoken about Grandpa?'

Tom looked to the floor as Rose covered her mouth and gasped for air.

'It's not fair,' Bill pushed on. 'Grandpa didn't even need to go. He was old enough to stay with us.'

'You're right about that, Bill,' said his father. 'It isn't fair... Thing is though, he wanted to go... He had a fire in his belly about so many things... He figured that the war was his chance to do something, right a few wrongs.'

Rose coughed again and put her arm around the boy who was fast approaching manhood. 'Your father is right about that. I remember that look on his face. For the first time in years, he was proud of himself. He had a job to do.' Her voice began to quiver. 'The night before your father and Grandpa Charlie went off, he hugged me so hard and asked me if I was proud to be his missus.'

'What did you say, Grandma?'

'I told him that I had always been proud to be his missus, even when he'd gone off flogging rabbits. I told him that he was the most handsome man I'd ever seen, and I would remember him standing tall in that uniform every day until he got back home.'

'Oh, Ma,' said Tom holding back his tears while Bill turned to hug his grandmother.

'Thing is,' she said sobbing freely now, 'he's never going to come back home.'

~

The short period of army leave served two purposes. Firstly, it gave Tom the chance to reunite with loved ones, albeit, not with Hazel, the woman whose image he carried in his mind throughout the war. Secondly, it gave him time to mull over what he would do as a provider for his family when he left the army.

When his turn to leave the army came, he sat with a rehabilitation officer who rushed through a dozen questions. Tom provided cursory answers, before he was declared fit to move on to the next stage. There, he was told of what monetary entitlements he could expect, and where he could go to seek employment. Civilian life was a daunting prospect for Tom, the army being the only proper job he'd ever had.

He was told how to apply for a war-service home loan that offered attractive subsidies; however, the prospect of ever owning a home had always been unthinkable to Tom. That type of thing was for other people, those who hadn't spent years in unemployment camps before the war.

As more was explained, he heard of fellow soldiers who were no different to him taking on such a commitment and his interest was pricked. It triggered something, an urge to find work and apply for one of the loans. If he could do that, he would have so much more to offer Hazel when he found her.

~

Following the war, life in the Byrne house was difficult for all. The only thing that saved Arthur from being thrown out of the house by his wife was the fear of public embarrassment if news broke of his infidelity with the house-help. For her part, Hazel, if she was to remain there, was banished to her own quarters with her daughter, save the time she required to complete cooking, cleaning, and washing. Her workload had been increased significantly and no longer was she a part of the family in any way; she was the maid.

Arthur had become cool towards her in the event of their paths crossing, manufacturing an outward bitterness that he displayed for Ester's benefit to preserve his own well-being. He knew where his bread was buttered, Ester having been very careful in the legal arrangements concerning the family assets, when she inherited the house.

Their children, now young adults, had been kept away from any details of what had happened between Arthur and Hazel, and they agreed between themselves that their parents had simply become old, bitter and unbearable. They thought the treatment of Hazel and Nancy was unfair.

When it was possible, without creating a scene with their parents, they would covertly spend time in Hazel and Nancy's large room, stifling laughter and relaying stories about their unreasonable parents. Hazel cherished their company, though she would invariably defend their parents, the guilt from what she had done never far from her thoughts.

If she had the means, she would certainly have left and started again somewhere, but for now and the foreseeable future, that was just a pipe dream. Gradually over time, Hazel adapted to the mood of the house by simply going through the motions of day-to-day existence and finding comfort in routine.

One morning in early November of 1947, Nancy woke to the sunshine streaming in through the window upon her face. It was already warm and humid, one of those Sydney mornings that promised a hot day ahead and if they were lucky, a storm in the evening to cool things down. It was a school day and her mother had deliberately pulled apart the curtains earlier than usual in a bid to wake her.

Hazel sat on the side of her daughter's bed and held out a package wrapped in red paper. 'Happy thirteenth birthday, Nancy!'

'Er, thanks, Mum,' she said, rubbing her eyes and yawning.

'Open it.'

Nancy sat up in bed and a smile spread across her face. She unwrapped the gift carefully so that she might be able to use the red paper again. 'Ooh, Mum... it's lovely.' She ran her hands around the wooden sewing box, opened it up and lifted out a cardboard sheet with needles and buttons embedded upon it.

'Look, Mum... there's a tape measure and three different cotton reels! And what's this?'

'Ah, it's a wee thing to put over your finger, it's called a thimble,' said Hazel, happy that her daughter was so excited. 'And look if you lift this up, there's some pieces of material you can make something with.'

'Thanks Mum, I love it.'

Nancy packed the box up, staring at the letters of her name and the year 1947, expertly carved into its top. She got up and slid her gift under her bed and put on her dressing gown.

'You take your time getting ready, Nancy,' said her mother, looking at her daughter and recognising how she was fast becoming a woman. She saw her daughter's high cheekbones and perfectly symmetrical face, one that men would find alluring. 'I must go down and start cooking breakfast. I'll bring you up something to eat.'

'I'll come down too; I'll help.'

They rattled around in the kitchen, Nancy setting the table in preparation for the Byrne family while Hazel beat some eggs and boiled water. As soon as they heard Arthur and Ester coming down the steps at six thirty, they would place the hot plates of food in the middle of the table with tongs and cutlery for them to help themselves. The rest of the family would come down some time after that.

That morning however, they were caught by surprise. Just after six, Arthur, still in his dressing gown, stepped briskly down the steps holding a small gift. 'Good morning,' he said. 'Ester is in the bath, so I thought I'd take the opportunity to bring this down now. It's for you, Nancy. Happy birthday.'

Each year since Hazel arrived at their house and before things had turned sour, Arthur and Ester had given something to

Nancy on her birthday. On her twelfth birthday, Nancy felt the absence of their gift and had taken it to heart, not understanding why things had become so awful. This year, she expected that the lack of acknowledgement from the Byrnes would continue; when Arthur passed over the gift, she was taken aback.

'Thank you, Mr Byrnes,' she said, accepting the small package, 'I wasn't expecting...'

'That's all very well, Nancy,' he managed. 'Er... just so you know... it's from me... No need to mention it to anyone else.'

'Yes, thank you Arthur,' said Hazel, perplexed by the first hint of kindness in such a long time.

'Well, I'll get back to Mrs Byrnes,' he said, 'before she misses me.'

'Alright then,' said Hazel.

He turned to walk away and then stopped and turned his head. 'Just so you know, nothing has changed between us. Just a small gift for Nancy, that's all.'

Hazel watched until he was gone. 'Do you want to open it now?' she asked.

'I don't think so,' answered Nancy, slipping the little package into the pocket of her gown. 'Maybe later, when we're in our room.'

'Very well,' said Hazel. 'We had best get a hurry-on then; they'll be down for breakfast soon.'

10. Searching

Settling into civilian life was a challenge for Tom. When he knew that his mother or son were nearby, he presented the face of a man who was coping well. Only when he was sure that no one could see him, would he drop his guard, lay back on the bed and wallow in despair until he felt as though he could face other people again.

After demobilisation, he was filled with an urgency to get on with things - land himself a job and get a war-service home loan. The weeks and months that followed, however, had not proven fruitful in finding work. The offers of going away to work in the bush or as part of a distant regional engineering project filled him with dread. The thought of leaving his family again was too much.

There was talk about town of re-joining the military, and for several men the secure employment that came with it was tempting. Already, still within two years of the war's end, tensions were re-emerging across the globe as the carve-up of Germany by America and the Soviets fed the beginning of a new power struggle. Tom recognised the opportunities that a military life could bring, but the more he thought about it, the more he knew he would not be able to stomach it.

In 1947, more than a year since being demobilised, Tom committed to a full-time job at the glass factory in the industrial area across the road from Moore Park golf course. It felt strange to be working so close to the streets of his rabbitoh days, and he thought back to the first time he ever saw Hazel.

The work was hot and hard, especially when he had to turn huge amounts of heavy substances manually to form a mix. The most exhausting part of the work was when they had to load the mix to where it was channelled towards an intense heat source that began to meld the raw materials together.

Tom kept to himself at work, where the physical exertion was an outlet for the torments and frustrations that had built up in his life. After his years in the army, where progress was measured in territory gained or enemy lives taken, it felt good to be part of a system that made things for people to use. He collected a regular wage and as the cold days of winter began to give way to the softer warmth of spring, he came closer to gaining a war service home loan. The shift in Tom's demeanour was not lost on Rose or Bill, and for the time being their lives felt secure because there was a happier breadwinner coming through the front door each night.

For Tom though, alone in the dark, small hours of night, he would stare at the glimmers of light flickering on the ceiling - afraid to close his eyes. It was in sleep that his demons would make their presence felt.

Some mornings he would wake exhausted from the ordeals of the night. Relief would come with sunlight, and once again he would be able to resume his role in the civilian world and work towards his goal. After a few months of regular work, he was rewarded with great news. He was able to get the loan to purchase a narrow frontage house in Surry Hills, a suburb not far from the familiar streets of Redfern.

The street of his new house was near some blocks of housing commission dwellings earmarked for demolition. Plans were already underway to produce a multilevel, high-density public housing estate in their place. The speculation of the associated noise and disruption resulting from the development lowered the asking price of the house, making it an affordable proposition. The house needed significant repairs, but that didn't worry him at all. As they settled in, the fact that there were three small bedrooms made him feel like a king.

What unsettled him, though, was being in the part of Sydney that evoked certain memories. It was only a short distance from Surry Hills to the streets of Redfern where he had traipsed fifteen years earlier with a bag of rabbits over his shoulder and his father by his side. The thought of one street troubled him the most, and he would go well out of his way to steer clear of Hazel's old house. He knew that she wouldn't still be there but perhaps her angry mother was.

He grew accustomed to his new life, working regular hours and coming home at the end of each day, and with that, his confidence grew. Gradually the thought of walking past Hazel's family home was becoming less daunting. He finally felt like he was getting on top of things.

He decided that soon he would face Cleveland Street and begin his search for Hazel. He knew that her mother despised him, but hopefully over the passage of time, she may have softened enough to tell him something at least about Hazel.

Life in the new house meant different things to each of them. The move was no big deal for Rose. Since the loss of Charlie, being with her son and grandson was all she cared about, no matter where that was. In some ways, it was as though she hadn't left their old rental house, especially once her heavy lounge chair was positioned next to the stand with the wireless and her cigarettes on top.

For Bill, the main change was that he had left his old school and the people in it to start at a new one, usually an unnerving prospect for a young teenager. Bill, however, had developed little connection with the teachers or kids at Newtown, and the days that he attended school were something he merely endured because he had to. Going to the new school, which backed onto Prince Alfred near Railway Square, didn't change much at all.

It was less than a mile to walk there in the morning and the best thing about it was how close it was to town and the bustle of the markets. This is where he chose to do most of his learning instead. It was unusual for Bill to form new friendships, but he managed to do just that, falling in comfortably with a couple of other boys who also spent most of their school days at the markets.

The first day of the new summer in 1947 was eventful for both Tom and Bill Davis, though for very different reasons. Bill didn't make it through the school gates that day, instead meeting up with two other absconders. They walked with a strut, bags tossed over their shoulders, laughing and joking along the way and attracting glares of disdain from the respectable people they passed.

They continued with their antics amongst the stalls and shop fronts of the markets, being shooed away several times by the stall keepers. One man took objection to them loitering close to his fruit stall, afraid that they were scaring away potential customers.

The run-in with this stall-keeper became a source of amusement for the young larrikins, and as it rolled on, the boys used it as an opportunity to act out the scheme they had hatched earlier in the day. While two of the boys began wrestling in a mock fight to draw in the attention of the targeted stall-keeper, Bill helped himself to a tray of apples and filled his shoulder bag with them.

After a couple of minutes, Bill took off in one direction while the other boys ran off the opposite way, all of them meeting up as planned in Belmore Park near Railway Square. There they shared the spoils, laughing and celebrating their stunt. Bill's mates had more plans for the day and wanted him to join them for their venture towards the historical part of Sydney near the harbour, known as The Rocks. For Bill, though, he had had enough for one day and was content to stay in the park when they headed off.

The fruit was the first thing that he had ever stolen, and the morning had been exhilarating. Now, from where he sat under a huge fig tree, biting into a crisp apple, he looked to the far edge of the park where he saw two makeshift camps of homeless people. They sat between a few shady trees with the entirety of their physical possessions spread out on the ground.

It reminded him of the years at Happy Valley, when he was just a small child. He stood, tossed his bag, which was still half full of fruit, over his shoulder and walked towards them. People in collared shirts and fancy frocks hastened their footsteps as they walked past the homeless squatters, though Bill could feel their pain. He got close to one dishevelled man, whose face was wrinkled like a crumpled piece of paper, and he lifted the bag from his shoulder. 'You can have these apples, if you want,' he said. 'I don't need them.'

The man looked through his dusky eyes, perplexed with the offer. 'Jesus! I haven't had an apple in a long time.'

Bill emptied his bag, leaving eight shiny red pieces of fruit on the ground. 'I'll just leave 'em here... You can share 'em around.'

The man raised his hand, a gesture of thanks. 'Haven't got a smoke, have yer?'

~

While Bill was up to mischief with his mates, his father was putting in another hard day's work until 'smoko', when he'd have a break and enjoy some bread and cheese. The afternoon always seemed to pass more quickly, and finally, when the workday was finished, he was tired and thirsty. That afternoon, he walked out of the stifling factory into an afternoon under a heavy grey sky that rumbled with thunder.

Recently, he had taken pleasure in stopping at the Duke of Cleveland for a beer on the way home. It was a short walk of about twenty minutes from there down Cleveland Street to his home. Up until then, he hadn't felt ready to see the door that Hazel appeared from fifteen years earlier, and so he would backtrack through Redfern, taking an extra twenty minutes.

There was an added attraction for Tom to stop in at The Duke that day, for it was the first time the Indian national cricket team had ever toured Australia and there was a test match in Brisbane. He sat at the bar, nodding to one of the familiar faces downing a beer, and listening to the game being broadcast from a wireless that sat between them.

Tom had little interest in the cricket, but he remembered how his father loved the sport. Being there and hearing the commentary reminded him of Charlie. That day, as Don Bradman approached another hundred runs, he remembered back to his first days living at Happy Valley, when he and Charlie gathered near a group of men at Haymarket in town, listening to Don Bradman score a hundred against England. Now, as the other men in The Duke cheered and raised their glasses as the great batsman yet again went past triple figures, he remembered his father and the day they bought their first bag of rabbits.

He only ever had the one drink at The Duke after work, and that day as he left to go home, the dark sky told him that he'd better hurry if he wanted to stay dry. It made sense to head directly down Cleveland Street, and that's what he did. He was buoyed by the company of the men in the pub and braced himself to walk past the O'Brien house for the first time since before the war.

He had anticipated this moment for years now, the scene playing out in his mind where Hazel's mother would be initially abhorred to see him but then listen to his story and what he had been through. Then in his fantasy, the old woman would relent and tell him all about Hazel and where she was.

As the heavy sky threatened to dump on him at any moment, he paused outside the O'Brien's and put both hands on top of the old metal gate. He breathed the air in deeply as the first fat drop of rain smacked on his shoulder. Then another as a crack of thunder trailed a bolt of lightning that stabbed the ground somewhere close.

He breathed in slowly once more and began to push the gate to walk inside when the neighbour's front door opened and an attractive woman of about forty years of age appeared. He stopped what he was doing as she hurried the few steps to the letterbox before scurrying back to the shelter over her door.

'Oi,' she said, 'who is it, you'd be after?'

'Well, that'd be Hazel... Hazel O'Brien, but she probably hasn't lived here for a while... so I suppose it's her mother I'd be looking for.'

The woman pulled out a cigarette from the pack she had tucked under her blouse. 'Gone,' she said, striking a match and drawing in the smoke. She was obviously ready to chat. 'The girl left years ago; it was all very hush-hush. Her mother, the silly old biddy, wouldn't let her out of her sight, poor thing.'

'Don't suppose you know where she went? I'm an old friend... from before the war. Tom's the name.'

The woman smoked, leaving red lipstick on the cigarette, and looked up and down at Tom. 'Mm, I can imagine you in uniform.'

'Trying to forget those days. Do you know where they went?'

'The old bitch, pardon my French, well she took her off to some home for girls like her... ooh, a year or more before she left with the rest of her kids.'

'So, they don't live here anymore?'

For the moment, the rain was holding off and the woman took the few steps back out towards the front fence that separated her from Tom. 'Isn't that what I just told you?'

'Yeah, you did. So, where'd Hazel go?'

'To that home in Darlinghurst,' she continued, leaning towards him, 'where girls in disgrace go.'

'Darlo?'

'Funny, eh?'

'Why is that funny?'

'Ah, the old cow used to carry on as if they were so righteous; church every Sunday and bad words about everyone else about the place - made a few enemies, she did. No wonder her old man took off.'

'Where's the family now?'

'That's just it... took off in the middle of the night a couple of years ago, before the war ended. The talk about the place is that she hadn't paid rent for a year or more and they were coming for her... left furniture and all sorts of things behind.'

'Darlinghurst, you say.'

'Ah, that was years ago, way back in the depression days. God knows where she is now.'

She looked at Tom closely as if something had just caught her attention. 'I think I've seen you around before.'

'Don't reckon, missus.'

'Hmph.'

She looked to the dark clouds that had gathered over the Sydney Cricket Ground as another rumble of thunder sounded in the sky. She looked Tom up and down until she locked eyes with him. 'You're about to get drenched. How about a cup of tea and a cigarette inside till it passes?'

'Don't smoke, missus,' he replied.

'We'll see about that. My name's Marlene.'

~

It had been years since Tom had been with a woman. As soon as Marlene led him through the front door, she turned and pushed him heavily back against the door, slamming it shut. She leaned into his groin and rubbed it with her thigh. The tea and cigarette were put on hold as she took him by the hand into the front bedroom.

Thunder roared and the downpour was so heavy on the roof that it drowned out the sounds of their lovemaking. The summer storm was quick and intense and as the drops began to lighten, Marlene fell asleep nestled into Tom's chest. He was already regretting what had happened.

With the arm that wasn't trapped under her he rubbed his eyes and moved just enough to disturb her from sleep. With that she sat up and moved to the edge of the bed, giving Tom the opportunity to do the same. 'I'm not sure what to say,' he managed, 'I wasn't expecting that.'

'Don't worry, sweetheart,' she answered as she stood and retrieved a dressing gown from the cupboard. 'Doesn't mean anything; I just think we both needed it.'

The last thing Tom wanted was a cup of tea but thought it would be the right thing to do. 'That cup of tea sounds like a good idea.'

'Ha!' she scoffed. 'Don't think so. I need to tidy things up here; my old man will get home in an hour... Don't reckon you'd like to meet him.'

'Whoa, didn't know about that,' he said. 'I guess I'd better fix myself up and leave.'

'Don't get me wrong,' she said with a wry grin and walked over to where Tom was pulling up his trousers. 'That was nice but...'

'But?'

'It was just the once,' she said kissing him on the forehead.

'Just the once,' he said smiling.

~

For days, following the dalliance with Marlene he struggled with guilt and questioned the authenticity of his plans to find Hazel after being so easily tempted. At work he kept to himself, and the others were comfortable with his quiet presence in the background.

He often woke in the mornings roused from his dreams of Hazel. On those days, he would think about her all through the day while he shovelled the mix and loaded it in the hot factory. He became preoccupied with his plan to find her though he didn't have much to work with. All he knew was that about fourteen years prior, she had been taken to a home in Darlinghurst for disgraceful girls, whatever that meant. He began to find out where these places were.

~

One Saturday, having sourced the location of one such institution in Darlinghurst, he dressed himself as respectfully as he could and set off on foot. He felt frustrated that, until then, he had no idea St Monica's existed and that Hazel could have been so close to him for all that time before he set off for the Middle East.

As he walked, he began to wonder what he would say and who he would say it to. After all, to those at St Monica's, he was just some stranger off the streets with no right to any sort of information about who had come and gone through their doors.

When Tom arrived at the large building, it presented as an intimidating fortress. He fell into contemplation, wondering if he was a step closer to finding her and whether their fractured lives even had a chance of being put back together.

There was a bench on the opposite side of the street, and for now, he would wait there and think through his next move. The bench was in the shade of a huge fig tree overhanging from the park and he was grateful for the cool place to sit.

He sat and decided to wait for someone who was about to go into St Monica's or for someone to come out and ask for their help. For more than an hour he sat, standing from time to time and walking up and down the pavement only to return to the bench.

It must have been getting towards the middle of the day when he saw a suited man accompanied by a woman whose age he could not estimate for she was mostly hidden beneath a black and white tunic and habit. The pair walked up the steps to the main doors of St Monica's, causing Tom to jump to his feet and dash across the street, a car braking suddenly to avoid him and its driver beeping a horn in frustration.

The man and the nun turned abruptly, taken aback by the unintended intrusion. 'Excuse me,' gasped Tom, 'I'm hoping you can help me.'

'Yes, Sir,' said the suited man. 'How so?'

Tom stood at the bottom of the four steps and looked up to them. He could see that the nun was of considerable age, perhaps in her sixties. 'I'm trying to find someone I once knew,' he explained, 'from before the war.'

'And how is that our concern, Sir?' said the man.

'If you have a little time, I can explain.'

The man and the nun stepped back down to where Tom was standing.

Tom introduced himself, though felt too uncomfortable to extend his hand to either of them. He told them about his days during the depression and his time with Hazel. The nun's eyes widened at the mention of her name. She listened intently; her eyes fixated on every word Tom said.

Sister Julianne remembered many of the girls who had passed through St Monica's, but none more so than young Hazel. The girl's determination and spirit had found a special place in the Sister's heart. After Hazel left with her baby for the grounds of St Steven's, Sister Julianne had made it her business to follow her progress, albeit from an inconspicuous distance.

Tom did his best to explain what he was trying to do, much to the annoyance of the suited man who clearly had more urgent matters in his mind. Anticipating her colleague's lack of interest, the nun spoke up. 'Would you excuse us for a moment, Mr Davis?' she said. 'I would like to talk to my colleague... I'm sure you understand, this is quite a personal situation, and we must be careful.'

'Of course, missus... sorry,' he said, 'I mean madam... er Sister.'

'Haha, Sister is fine,' she replied.

The suited man and the nun ambled down the street while they spoke.

'So, what exactly are you suggesting, Sister?' asked the suited man.

'You know as well as I do that the operations of St Monica's are not for public knowledge, especially information about the girls of the past and what ever happened to their infants.'

'Why are you telling me the obvious?'

'I have concerns for the young man. Who knows what he has been through. I am suggesting that it might be more appropriate for me to talk to him and explain things. I will surely have a softer and more understanding way with him.'

'Perhaps what you say is true.'

They returned to Tom.

'Can you help me then?' he asked.

'Mr Davis, as you know, we must be very careful with anything we tell members of the public. I am rushed for time presently, so I have asked Sister Julianne to explain things clearly. I bid you good afternoon.'

The suited man stepped up to the large door and extracted a key to gain entry.

'Mr Davis,' began Sister Julianne, 'what was just said is true. We must be very careful...'

'So, you won't help me?'

'Sir, it is now my turn to speak. I have been a sister at St Monica's for more than forty years...'

'Okay,' he interrupted, 'Do you remember her?'

'Please, let me speak,' she said. 'During that time, we have helped many a young lass from respectable families, who have found themselves in trouble. I must say that some are more memorable than others. The girl you speak of, Hazel O'Brien... I did have a soft spot in my heart for her. Can you describe her for me? Just so I am sure we are talking about the same girl.'

'Hazel... she was beautiful, long reddish - blonde hair and dimples. And she spoke with the tongue of someone who had come from abroad, from Ireland.'

'We are indeed speaking of the same person, Mr Davis. She was in my prayers for a good many years, but I must say that I am not at liberty to tell you where she went...'

'Please,' he said. 'You have told me something already, please don't leave it at that.'

'What I am trying to say, Mr Davis, is that Hazel was one of the few girls to ever leave here with her baby.'

'What? She had a baby? Where did she go?'

'I am not able to tell you much more, Mr Davis', she continued with a wry smile, 'much more except that Hazel and her little baby girl left a mark in my heart and I was filled with joy when I heard that she was doing so well at St Steven's.'

'St Steven's,' said Tom hanging off every word, 'where is that?'

'Well, that is just common knowledge, but I doubt that you'll need it.'

'I beg your pardon?'

'This is what I was trying to explain, Mr Davis,' she said. 'St Steven's and St Monica's have somewhat of an affiliation, so I came to know quite some time ago that Hazel and her little girl left there and were taken in by some members of the St Steven's community, The Byrnes.'

'When, Sister?'

'Well, let's see... I know that it was before the war broke out. As I was saying, she has always been in my thoughts, and I believe in my heart, that you being here today is God's answer to my prayers.'

The nun then proceeded to tell Tom the whereabouts of the Byrnes's house, a prominent family in the Catholic Church community.

'Young man,' she said boldly, 'I dare say that you will be able to take it from here.'

Tom grabbed her hand and shook it in appreciation. 'How can I ever thank you, Sister?'

'You have already done that by being here today, an answer from the Lord above,' she said, 'just one thing though...'

'Anything.'

'You worked this out by yourself, didn't you?'

'Sister?'

'Smart young man you are, didn't need to hear anything from me.'

'Er... of course,' he said smiling and continuing to shake her hand. 'Thanks for your time; I wish you had been able to tell me something.'

11. Reunion

'Yes, can I help you?' asked Arthur.

Tom stood at the door wearing his same best clothes he wore to St Monica's. 'Good morning, Sir. My name is Tom Davis. I was once a close friend of Hazel O'Brien, though we lost touch before war broke out.' He spoke quickly, and there was a slight tremble in his hands. 'I have been trying to find her to say hello and my information is that she may be residing here.'

Arthur frowned and looked down his nose at Tom. 'Oh, I see,' he said. 'If you don't mind waiting, I'll see if she is available.'

'Thank you, Sir.'

Arthur stepped back and pushed the door closed. *Who is this stranger and what does he want from Hazel?*

The sun belted down on Tom's back and although only a minute or so had passed, it felt much longer before he heard footsteps approaching from inside the house. His heart pounded so heavily that he found it difficult to gain a deep breath.

The footsteps grew louder until they stopped just on the other side of the door. Slowly it opened inwards, and then, after so many years and the hundreds of nights of dreaming about this moment, Hazel was standing there.

'Tom? Is it really you?'

For a moment he could not speak. Her hair had darkened since he had last seen her, now light brown rather than reddish blonde, and lines radiated out from her eyes, a legacy of what life had thrown at her. She was in a yellow dress, appropriate for the well-to-do suburb they were in, and she filled it with a much more womanly body than he remembered of her. He stared once again at the most beautiful woman he'd ever seen.

'Tom?' she said again. 'I can hardly believe it!' Her words were soft and carried the tune of the Irish brogue that had always captivated him. The years since they last spoke to each other dissolved away.

'Hello, Hazel,' he said at last. 'It's been a while.'

He held out his hand and she accepted it with one and then two hands, holding it firmly. She smiled warmly, the gesture telling him that the effort in getting to this moment was not wasted. 'You look just the same, Tom, just a bit older and, dare I say, a wee bit more handsome.'

It was now 1948, fourteen years since their last encounter, and he wanted to tell her everything he could, for so much had happened since 1934. 'I wasn't sure that you would want to see me. I've wanted to see you again, before the war and then all through it.'

It was surreal, as if in hearing his own words he was listening to someone else. 'I understand that we are both much older and everything has changed, I know that, but I had to see you.'

The sight of her standing there and looking every bit as though she belonged in this leafy streetscape of two-story houses made him cringe as he recalled the conditions they shared at Happy Valley. Even his house at Surry Hills was a far cry from what he was seeing, and for a moment in his mind, he began to back-peddle. *How could I think she would even consider giving this up for me?*

'Oh Tom, so much has happened, to be sure,' she said, letting go of his hand. She took him by the arm and led him along the pathway to the front gate and away from any ears that could be listening. 'I know that I do owe you an explanation; I'm not proud of what I've done to you and...'

'It's okay, Hazel,' he said. Bill is a fine young man now. He's had to go through a lot, but he's a good lad.'

'Does he know about me, Tom? Does he know that I left him?'

'He's fine,' he assured her, 'but he doesn't know a thing about you... not yet anyway.'

'Dear Tom, I can hardly believe that you're here,' she pushed on. 'Do you have it in your heart to forgive me?'

'Nothing to forgive, Hazel. We were just kids ourselves.'

Hazel looked over her shoulder to the house.

'Will you tell me more sometime? I must get back to my chores.'

'Yes, of course,' he said. 'And you? Will you tell me everything as well?' He left the question hanging, testing the water as to how much she would divulge.

'Tom,' she said, 'I have much to say, and there is something you must know.'

'Go on.'

'I have a daughter; we have a daughter.'

Tom's thoughts flashed back to what Sister Julianne had told him. Now, upon hearing that the child was his, he felt dizzy with happiness. He could not find the words to express his feelings, and instead he grabbed Hazel's hand and squeezed it gently to convey his joy.

'Oh Tom, there's so much to tell each other. Can we meet somewhere else perhaps, not here?'

Tom felt a surge of adrenaline throughout his body. They would meet again and just maybe that would be the beginning of something bigger. 'Is tomorrow, Sunday, too soon? I will be back at work the day after.'

'Oh, that will be grand.'

'Perhaps this time tomorrow then?'

'Grand. And Tom,' she continued, 'I'll bring Nancy. I don't want to leave her behind, and I want you to meet her.'

'Er... yeah, but...'

'She doesn't need to know anything, not for now anyway. You can just be Tom, the rabbitoh from the Great Depression... who was a dear family friend. We can talk proper when she goes off for a walk, just can't be leaving her here while I'm away.'

'Hazel,' he said with concern, 'is everything okay here?'

She paused, nodded, and returned to the house.

Even though she hadn't felt well for some time, there was something about a Saturday that would put Rose in a good mood. Usually, she had the company of both Tom and Bill for most of the day, doing some shopping and catching up on chores about the place. The routine was comforting for the three of them, adding stability to their lives, and towards the later part of the afternoon, Rose would heat up the oven to bake a piece of mutton and roast some vegetables. The smell of the roasting meat was an announcement that another week had passed.

Bill would play his part doing whatever chores were asked of him, usually clipping the patch of grass next to the concrete path, sweeping out the small square back yard and then taking any garbage to the bins in the lane behind. He loved that part of the week, when he would spend time with his grandmother, doing the best he could to make her happy. Once his chores were done, he was free to catch up with his new school mates.

That Saturday, the one when Tom had found Hazel, Bill ate a sandwich his grandmother made for him, and drank a glass of milk on her insistence, before he reached over to her cigarettes on the kitchen table.

'Well, just one... but don't tell your father. Now, before you go, come here and give your grandma a hug. Don't be late for tea tonight.'

As Bill was setting off for the afternoon, his father was returning, and the two crossed paths just outside the front gate.

'You off now, Bill?'

'Yeah, back a bit later.'

'Done your chores then?'

'Just finished and had a bit of lunch too.'

'Off to see your mates? Might want to bring 'em round one day, introduce us.'

'Aw... don't reckon, Dad. We just hang around and have a bit of fun; then we all just go home.'

'Well, stay out of strife then.'

'See ya.'

Bill was in a hurry to get away. His group of lads had grown in recent times, and now there were six of them who created havoc through certain inner-city streets that had become their domain.

Inside the house, Rose was in the kitchen, cutting some bread and slicing some cheese and tomatoes. She was feeling very tired, but pushed through it, not wanting to be the focus of any attention. Tom was already on her case about the weight she had lost, but she insisted that it was because she had a lot on her mind - namely Bill. Something had changed in him.

'Hello, Ma,' said Tom coming through the front door.

'Just in time,' she said before coughing several times. 'Ooh excuse me. You're just in time to have some lunch with your mother.'

'You might need something for that cough.'

'It's just a tickle in the throat,' she scoffed. 'It's been a busy morning. How about we have a spell after lunch? Then you can give me a hand getting the roast ready for tonight.'

'Sounds good, Ma.' He ran his hands under the kitchen tap to wash up, wiped them on a tea towel and walked over to sit at the small table.

'Did you get done what you had to do?' she continued as she coughed again.

Tom hadn't told her about visiting St Monica's.

'Well yeah, I did,' he answered. 'Let's have something to eat and a cuppa and I'll fill you in.'

Rose busied herself once more in the kitchen, teased by the prospect of some news.

She poured the hot water into the pot, covered it with a tea towel and put it on the table in front of Tom. 'Give it a couple of minutes and pour some, eh Tom?' She followed that with a plate of sandwiches and sat down with her son.

'Thanks, Ma.' Tom took a large bite, chewed frantically and then spoke. 'Well since I got back, I've been trying to track someone down.'

Rose put her sandwich back on her plate, trying to think who it could be. Tom left that first part of the conversation hanging as she processed what had been said, and then her eyes suddenly widened.

'I haven't told you who it is yet, Ma.'

'I don't think you have to... Don't tell me it's...'

'Aw come on Ma, you can say her name...'

'Not Hazel!'

'Guess what,' he went on. 'I found her! I saw her today and...'

'And what?'

'I'm going to see her tomorrow too.'

Tom was befuddled with the silence at the table as Rose picked up her sandwich and took another bite. 'Aren't you going to say something?'

'What do you want me to say? That I'm happy you found the mother of your child, the woman who deserted you both, years ago?' There was emotion in her voice, and she coughed again to clear her throat.

'Jesus Christ, Ma,' he said sharply. 'We were just kids ourselves, you could be a bit more forgiving.'

'Does Bill know anything?'

'Not yet, I'm not sure how much to tell him... I know that you've been like a mother to him, that doesn't have to change at all.'

'Think very carefully how much you tell him, Tom!'

Silence once again fell over the table, and he could sense his mother's wrath. He had been hungry, but the disappointment of the conversation had quashed his appetite and he swallowed the food as if it was a duty. He had invested all his energy into finding Hazel, not considering anything in the past that would upset his mother and son if he found her.

'There's a bit more to it as well, Ma.'

She stared at him expressionless.

'She has another child, a girl fourteen years of age. I'm pretty sure she is...'

'Don't say it, Tom! Don't say she's yours. She can't be!'

Tom slumped in the chair. 'She can be, Ma. It makes sense. Hazel and I were together at Happy Valley; it would have happened before she left us.'

The second announcement came as another blow to Rose. A myriad of thoughts and consequences cascaded through her mind, not least the very real possibility that Hazel, someone she had been happy to have out of their lives for many years, could once again be part of them. She tried to take a deep breath and pulled a white handkerchief from her pocket to cover her mouth as she coughed.

'Ma?'

'Oh, be careful, Tom,' she said, trying to digest the revelations. 'Please think about what you're doing, think about poor Bill.' She coughed and looked into her handkerchief, quickly screwing it up so that Tom wouldn't notice the red spots.

'It's okay, Ma, we're just going to meet. There are things she needs to know about Bill, and I need to know things about her daughter. We owe each other that much.'

'Tom, we've just got you back. Don't do anything silly now. Remember how much she hurt you, hurt all of us?'

'Everything will be alright, Ma.'

~

Nancy noticed the lift in her mother's mood after seeing an old friend, and it wasn't lost on Arthur either. Hazel could feel his eyes upon her whenever she was in his presence and sometimes caught him watching her when he thought she wasn't looking.

The next day, Nancy helped her mother make breakfast for the Byrnes and finish the chores that had accumulated over the past few days. By late morning, they were in their room getting ready for Tom's arrival.

'Mum,' said Nancy,' do I really have to go with you today? Why do I have to meet your old friend?'

Hazel tried to bring her daughter into the mood. 'It'll be fun,' she said. 'You'll like him, and we'll be sure to have a treat.'

Nancy rolled her eyes.

'And you're growing up so nicely, Nancy,' she added. 'Here, let's both of us, put on a little makeup!'

Hazel read the situation perfectly; her daughter warmed to the idea of getting herself all dolled up. They came down the steps looking beautiful just before mid-day to wait near the front gate for Tom. Arthur had been sitting and reading in the adjacent living room. 'Where are you two off to, dressed up like that?'

'Mr Davis, the man who came yesterday, an old family friend... He'll be calling just as soon as can be,' said Hazel. 'We're going on a little excursion to take some refreshment.'

'Have you finished the washing and drying?' he said. 'You know we can't have Ester doing it.'

'It's all done,' said Hazel. 'You need not be concerned. Your lunch is waiting for when you want it, and we'll be back in plenty of time to get your supper.'

There was a knock at the door that ended the exchange with Arthur. 'We'll be off then,' said Hazel, opening the door to see Tom in a collared shirt and trousers carrying a leather bag.

'I was thinking we might take a stroll to Centennial Park,' he said. 'I've brought some fruit and biscuits and I think there will be a stall near the lake.'

'That sounds lovely, Tom,' said Hazel, stepping out and closing the door to Arthur's prying ears. 'This is Nancy, my daughter. Say hello to Mr Davis, Nancy.'

Tom stared at her dimples. He'd seen them before, on his son's face. 'Hello Nancy,' he said, taking her hand. 'Please call me Tom.'

For a short while, conversation was polite and proper as they slowly settled into each other's company. They walked through the gates of the park and across the fields that had been planted out with colourful flower gardens around the lake.

The afternoon became a picnic of sorts, finding an enormous tree just off a walking track, which shaded them while they unpacked the food. They also chose this spot because nearby, up a gentle slope towards the boundary of the park, was a vendor sure to be selling ice creams and sweets to make the outing more special.

As the talk began to flow, both Tom and Hazel remained guarded in what they said, mainly for Nancy's benefit, and it wasn't until she was sent off to find out what was being sold at the stall that Hazel broached the subject of their son.

'Is he a good lad?' she asked. 'What does he know about me, Tom?'

Tom sat with his back against the trunk of the tree while she sat cross-legged on the soft green grass.

'He is indeed. He'd do anything for his grandma; she's been like...'

'You can say it, Tom. She's been like a ma to him. She always was as I remember it, even when I was there with you at Happy Valley. It was like he wasn't even my baby.' Her words tapered off quietly as the memory extracted sadness from deep within. 'And me? What does he know about me?'

'I'm sorry, Hazel,' he answered, 'He thinks that you ... he thinks that you died when he was a baby. He used to ask about you...'

'And what did you tell him?'

'I'm sorry, Hazel,' he said. 'We, I, well I was so bitter that you'd left us, I couldn't even say your name...'

'And?'

'I told him that your name was Helen and that you had come from the country. It's what he still believes.'

The words hung in the air for a while before either of them could speak. 'Perhaps... not perhaps, definitely, I think... that's how it must be. He would hate me if he knew I left him.'

'I'm sorry, Hazel. I didn't want any of this to upset you. As I said, I was bitter when you left... I hated what you did but... well so many times, especially at night during the war, I thought about you. I began to understand why you left. It must have been very difficult for you.'

'Tom, it was never easy,' she said. 'Please, we must keep it as he thinks it is. If I get to meet him, I'll be the old family friend you once sold rabbits to. I can never have him know what I've done.'

'There's so much to tell you, Hazel,' he continued, his words beginning to break up with sadness. 'My Da never made it back. My

119

sisters have gone off and Ma, well, she does what she must do to get through each day.'

Hazel looked up the hill to where her daughter was returning from. 'Nancy is on her way back; there's so much I want to tell you too, but it will have to wait.'

'She's a beauty,' he said, turning his head to see her walking back, holding some treats in her hands and wearing a broad smile. 'It does feel strange though, you know... her being...'

'She is, Tom,' said Hazel, finishing the sentence for him, 'She's your daughter.'

'But to her I'm...'

'Yes Tom, you're the family rabbitoh, from before the war, way back in the Depression.'

~

Over the rest of summer change was upon each member of the Davis household. Bill, now approaching his fifteenth birthday, had consolidated his association with the larrikin mates he made from school - not that they presented themselves there very often. The opportunities that lay within the streets of Sydney were far more attractive. On more than one occasion, they had lifted goods from shop fronts and made a get-away run, only to team up later to celebrate their success.

Rose as always, was in tune with her grandson and could tell that he was up to no good. Her cough had become much worse, but more worrying was the increasing amount of blood she was bringing up with it. She kept that part of her life to herself and soldiered on with her work about the house, making sure that Tom and Bill were well fed and always had clean clothes on their backs.

One day at the beginning of autumn, she was out in the small backyard beating the dust from a mat when she heard a commotion in the laneway behind them. She wondered what the ruckus was just as the tall wooden gate at the back was shoved open and Bill rushed in. He slammed it shut behind him and slid his back down the wooden palings to sit against them. He was shocked to see his grandmother standing there looking at him, and he put a finger to his lips. Moments later they heard heavy boots pounding the tar, running past their back fence.

When he was sure that the threat was gone, Bill stood and walked towards the house and right passed Rose, leaving her gobsmacked. She dropped the mat she was working on and followed him inside. 'What on earth have you been up to, William Davis?' she barked. She tried to say something else but began coughing violently, bits of blood spluttering on the hand she had over her mouth.

'Grandma?' said Bill, turning in his steps and forgetting about what had just happened.

'I asked... you... a ... question,' she said, coughing more but determined to get to the bottom of her grandson's antics.

'Come and sit down, Grandma,' he replied. 'I'll get you some water.'

'You listen to me, Bill,' she persisted. 'Were they police? It sounded like it.'

He stepped closer and took her arm, leading her to the lounge chair. 'What's the matter, Grandma? You're not well, you need a doctor.'

She sat, trying to suppress her cough. 'I'm only... going to say... this once, Bill.'

He fetched a glass of water from the kitchen tap and sat beside her with it. 'Go on then.'

'I want you to stay away from those ... lads you... spend your ... time with.'

'But Grandma, right now I'm worried about you.'

'If you're ... worried about me... you'll stay away from them.'

'A doctor, Grandma,' he pleaded.

'You stay away from them... and I'll see a doctor.'

'Orright, Grandma.'

~

While Bill and his grandmother worked their way through the newfound issues in each other's lives, Tom was on what had become another regular visit with Hazel and Nancy. He had grown fond of Nancy too. Sometimes her mannerisms or her facial features in a certain light caught him by surprise and reminded him of her mother. He wanted her to know that he was her father, but that that could never be.

Hazel and Tom became enthralled with the weekly instalments of each other's lives since Happy Valley, though they had to be careful with what they said when Nancy was around. Hazel would tell Tom something of her days at St Monica's and, in return, he would reveal something about the people he had met in the army, and over time, they learned a lot more about each other.

There were parts of their lives however that remained unspoken. For Tom, the dark and gruesome details of warfare were never to be shared with those who hadn't suffered through it with him. Whenever conversation touched on the war, he would remember certain things and stop talking, withdrawing into himself.

Hazel had a dark side too and a history she wished she could change. Although she told Tom plenty about her life, he was never to know anything of her relations with Arthur Byrne. Tom could sense, however, that things were not quite right.

~

On the day that Bill ran home from the police and found his grandma unwell, Tom was returning in a bus with Hazel and Nancy from Bondi Beach. They walked from the bus stop, through Centennial Park to grab a cool drink from what had become one of their favourite places.

While Nancy went to the vendor, they sat under the same tree in the shade. 'Please don't get me wrong, Hazel,' began Tom, 'I love Nancy coming out with us, I really do.'

'But...'

'But at her age, does she really want to be with us all the time? Wouldn't she rather be with friends her own age or even just stay at home and do... you know... girl things?'

The question caught Hazel by surprise, and she shuffled herself away from him. 'I think it's a bit mean, what you're saying,' she said. 'I thought, especially as she is your daughter, that you'd want to be seeing her.'

'Ah, Hazel, I meant what I said. I do like her being with us... but I do wonder if she hasn't got other places she'd rather be.'

Hazel went quiet and looked down to the ground.

'Hazel?... What is it?

'Oh Tom,' she began. 'Where we are living, it looks so nice, but we don't get on very well with the Byrnes.'

Tom's eyes widened. 'Has something happened?'

'One day,' she began, 'if we continue to...'

'Do you mean if we continue to see each other?'

'Yes,' she said, her eyes welling up. 'One day I'll have a bit more to tell you.'

He wanted to know more but knew that for now she had said enough. He shuffled over and put his arm around her. 'Nancy will never know that I'm her dad,' he began. 'I know that, but there's something I want you to do, Hazel.'

'We've missed out on so much already, Tom. What is it?'

'Sounds silly, when I think of it...'

'Go on.'

'I know that I wasn't around when she was born...'

'That couldn't be helped.'

'But it would make me feel a little bit like I was... if...'

'Come on, Tom. If what?'

'Would you write my name on her birth certificate? Even if we're the only ones who ever see it... It would make me feel that we belong together.'

Hazel put her hand on his and leant over to kiss his cheek as Nancy bounded down the grassy slope carrying cups of ice cream.

'Oh, look at you two!' she said in delight. 'One for each of us, better eat them before they melt, I've got your six pence change too, Tom.'

Hazel squeezed his hand before letting it go and took the ice cream from her daughter.

It was a lengthy but relaxing walk from the Byrnes' residence near Centennial Park to his house in Surry Hills. There was a cooling breeze at his back, and as he thought about the day, a smile grew across his face. He felt closer to Hazel than he ever had before and was convinced that he could provide a home for her and Nancy.

He knew that there would be friction between Rose and Hazel, and he started to think about how he could make it work. His smile became a grimace as he thought it through. There was the resentment from Hazel towards Rose about her dominance over Bill when he was a baby, and Rose had made her feelings about Hazel very clear. Would they even be able to maintain the facade with the two kids anyway?

By the time he got to his front gate, he was in a state of torment. As he pushed open the front door to walk inside, things were about to get a lot worse.

'Dad!' called Bill from the living room down the hallway. 'Dad, you better come here.'

He rushed to where Bill was sitting with his arm around his grandmother.

'Stop... fussing,' she struggled to say between coughs. 'I'll be... alright... in a...'

'Jesus,' said Tom, 'is that blood?'

'Just... give me... a moment,' said Rose.

'Bill, you know where the doctor is... at the back of the surgery. Remember we went there a few months ago?'

'Over on Elizabeth Street?'

'That's it. Run there and tell them what's going on with Grandma while I wait with her!'

Rose passed away a week later in South Sydney Hospital at Zetland. While Bill grieved deeply for the loss of his grandmother, Rose's death stirred up so much grief for Tom that the demons sleeping inside began to make their presence felt once more.

Tom's workmate, Jack, recognised the signs of someone grieving from his own time fighting in New Guinea and he suggested that Tom borrow his car and go away for a few days. At first, he declined the offer, but after thinking about it for a while, he thought it might do both him and Bill some good. Maybe it could be a chance too for Bill to meet Hazel.

Hazel was apprehensive when he suggested that they spend a few days away together. However, as she contemplated the opportunity of getting to know Bill a bit more, she accepted the invitation. It was a bold move, but one they both wanted; they just hoped that they could pull it off without either of the children ever discovering the truth.

~

Tom and Bill collected Hazel and Nancy from the stately Moore Park home before first light on a crisp autumn morning. The early start was Hazel's request, wanting to be gone well before any of the Byrnes had risen for the day.

When she announced that she was going away with Tom for a few days, an unpleasant encounter with both Arthur and Ester followed, and after that she tried to stay out of their way. The Byrnes had increased Hazel's workload significantly and made sure that she had no doubts about her lowly place in the household's hierarchy. She knew that her time remaining with them was limited.

Hazel was anxious leading up to Tom's arrival that morning for another reason. She was about to see Bill for the first time in fifteen years and desperately wanted him to like her. She hadn't forgiven herself for abandoning him, but now she had a second chance of sorts, one in which they could possibly share some type of loving relationship. Bill would never know that he was about to meet his sister too, and Hazel hoped that the two of them could be friends.

For Tom's part, there was much to contend with, none of which he could talk through with his son. Bill had been withdrawn and angry since the funeral, and to be going on a trip so soon after with people he didn't know, made him even more disgruntled.

Tom too was battling his own feelings of loss on several levels. His parents were gone far too soon, and that cut deeply. Now he had found his own family, the mother of his son and daughter, and at last they were about to be united. What hurt was that they would never be able to celebrate that fact. Instead, the mother was an old friend with her own daughter, and he was a man who once sold her rabbits. He wondered if this could ever be more than a sad situation.

It was a drive of more than four hours up the Pacific Highway past the industrial city of Newcastle, to Sapphire Point on the coast. Leaving early, they made good time, making only one comfort stop along the way. Hazel was desperate to make the mood in the car bright, and with the adrenalin pumping through her blood, she kept chatting. She had hardly slept the night before, the prospect of seeing her first born after so long, holding her in an agony of doubt.

When she laid her eyes on him, her heart skipped a beat and she couldn't help but hold her breath. There he was right in front of her, her own flesh and blood. She fought hard against her instincts to wrap her arms around him and tell him how sorry she was.

True to her nature, the only way to deal with the anxiety was to talk a lot and ask everyone questions, most of them trivial, but useful in dissipating her suspense. Bit by bit, she continued to prattle on, and gradually the barriers between everyone in the car began to be dismantled.

'And tell me young man, oh, I should say, Bill, how did you get that scar on your cheek; not that it looks unsightly. I'm sorry if it sounded that way, hardly noticeable...'

'Bit of a disagreement with another lad, missus,' he said.

Tom looked at his son in the back seat through the rear vision mirror. 'The less said about that, the better.'

'Ooh, I think I've opened my big mouth,' said Hazel. 'Well, I should say that you're a fine strapping young man, Bill... and please call me Hazel.'

Nancy looked at her mother the way embarrassed teenagers do. She then looked at Bill, who was sitting next to her, shook her head and rolled her eyes. Bill noticed her pretty face, and for the first time in a long while, a smile grew from the corner of his mouth.

Part Three: Three Different Women
1st February 1966

12. Respite

Bill pushed the window up so the cool breeze from the ocean rushed into their flat, one of four units on the third floor of the red brick block. He walked to the other end of the unit to open the kitchen window for the hot air to escape.

The place was small, a two-bedroom dwelling with a view over the streets of Maroubra to the beach. Bill thought it big enough for the two of them since most of the time they were either at work or out somewhere.

He was now a man in his early thirties and would always be home an hour or so before Nancy, when he would languish on the couch, smoke a cigarette and have a cold drink. It was a time for respite from the day.

The noise from the small black and white television in the corner filled his head so he didn't have to think about things, at least until after he'd drifted off to sleep for a while. He gulped a glass of cola, belched, and lay back on the lounge with eyes that were heavy from the day's work. A jingle for the introduction of decimal currency sounded out from the television and made him even drowsier.

"In come the dollars and in come the cents, replacing the pounds and the shillings and the pence, be prepared folks as the coins begin to mix, on the 14th of February 1966."

The monotonous tune lulled him softly, and soon he was asleep.

~

Living in their Maroubra flat had been the result of a long and convoluted route over many years. It began after Bill's grandmother, Rose, died just a couple of years after the war. His father, Tom, and Nancy's mother, Hazel, had introduced the teenagers to each other on their first ever trip to Sapphire Point.

The four of them got on well and enjoyed the few days away getting to know each other. Tom and Hazel were grateful for the pleasant holiday and were totally oblivious to the chemistry of attraction brewing between Bill and Nancy.

Tom and Hazel married in 1949, and with their children they presented as a loving, blended family. As they grew into adulthood, both Bill and Nancy pursued their own relationships with other people though an undeniable connection, deeper than purely platonic, remained between them.

Before the move to Maroubra, Nancy had been in a long-term relationship with a man who worked in the same government office block as she did, in the city. To Tom and Hazel, it appeared as though Nancy was happy and settled in her Paddington unit, and it was just a matter of time before she would be married.

For years, Nancy did as much as she could to make the relationship work. It wasn't enough however, for beneath everything, she continued to hold feelings for Bill, and eventually cracks began to appear in the relationship with her boyfriend. When they broke up, it was Bill who offered her comfort and support.

Soon after that she was hit by another devastating blow. After feeling unwell for some time, Hazel was struggling through the afternoons and evenings to keep things normal without making a fuss. She had been very tired in recent weeks, and despite feeling the need to rest, she continued to soldier on each day, pushing through her malaise to get things done.

One evening, while peeling potatoes in the Surry Hills kitchen, she simply dropped like a stone, the victim of a failing heart. The sound of the bowl crashing on the hard floor and the thud of Hazel falling made Tom rush to her and scoop her up in his arms. He yelled her name time and time again, pleading for her to open her eyes as he bargained with a god he had little time for to keep her alive.

A surge of dread filled his soul, as his dear Hazel slipped away. The split moment in time that took away Hazel's life also marked the beginning of Tom's demise, for life lacked meaning without her in it.

Hazel's death shattered Nancy, and Bill felt for her. She'd lost her mother and her closest friend. They had been through so much together during their years of living with the Byrnes that a strong and loving bond had grown between them.

Bill spent more and more time with Nancy at Paddington, and although he had a reputation for being a hard man, he cared for Nancy as a loving big brother would. What made this more complicated, however, was having to suppress his desire to be with her more intimately. The feelings were mutual, and as one day rolled into the next, the attraction they had for each other continued to build.

Sometimes when Nancy was at her lowest and feeling unhappy in the unit that held bad memories, Bill would put his arms around her to provide comfort and reassurance. Nancy would return the embrace with gratitude for him being there and soon, such physical affection became a frequent part of their lives.

Bill sometimes stayed overnight, sleeping on the made-up bed in the living room, always the first to wake when the sunlight beamed through the window each morning. With that, he would rattle around the kitchen to make sure that Nancy had something to eat when she woke up before he would leave for work.

One evening, after cleaning up the dinner dishes and then watching a bit of television, Bill began yawning on the lounge as he tried his hardest not to doze off. Noticing this, Nancy announced that she was going to bed so he could get some sleep. In what had become a routine, she leant over to kiss him on the cheek to say goodnight. Without thought, Bill turned his head slightly so that their lips met.

Weeks of frustration came to a head as they each sensed the desire in the other. Nancy fell back on the lounge as Bill followed, kissing and caressing her. Later that night, Nancy lay in his arms feeling a strange contentment that had been eluding her until now.

Bill was torn in how he felt; his desire to be with her was as strong as ever, though at the same time, he was confused by guilt because this was the woman who since their teenage years, had been his stepsister.

After that night, neither Bill nor Nancy fought their urges to be with each other, and when they spoke about it, they could see no reason to stop themselves. Despite this, they both remained uncomfortable about telling Tom anything about their loving relationship.

With everything that had happened, Bill suggested that they make a new start somewhere else, maybe close to the water. He'd always wanted to live near the beach, and he thought that getting a place at Maroubra would lift Nancy's spirits.

Just six months after Hazel's death, they moved into their new flat. As far as Tom was concerned, it was a sensible move in which siblings were simply sharing a place to save money.

Sometimes Nancy caught a bus after work from the city to Surry Hills to see Tom on her way home. They worked it out so that Bill would visit him on alternate weeks, and in that way, they kept a check on how he was going. On Bill's visits he would sit with Tom and talk, usually over a pot of tea, and when Nancy went to see him, she would put together some form of a meal that he would pick at.

For a year or so, it seemed that despite his sadness, Tom was holding it together but as another year passed and he gradually became more dishevelled, both Bill and Nancy knew that life for Tom had become even more of a struggle.

The Sydney summer of 1966 was relentlessly hot. Each day, the humidity would build and make the skin sticky until the evening sea breeze came to make things more bearable. Late one afternoon as Bill dozed on the couch, Nancy got off the bus as usual and made her way up the hill to their block. She was more tired and looked forward to getting to the top of the staircase that led to her front door.

'Not that jingle again,' she said as she walked inside.

Bill coughed and snorted as he woke. He rubbed his eyes. 'Hi,' he said with a yawn. 'Yeah, it gets stuck in the head... "in come the dollars and in come the cents..."'

'Oh Stop, please!'

'Yeah, fair enough,' he continued, sitting up to make space for her. 'Want me to get you a cold drink before I go and see Tom?'

'That would be nice,' she said as she flopped down beside him.

'You okay?' he asked.

'Just tired, I suppose... Feel a bit off though.'

'Have you eaten anything?'

'Nah, I'll be fine,' she said. 'If I get hungry, I'll find something. You go and see your dad.'

It was just dark enough for the streetlights to come on when he left the flat and got into his red Ford sedan. Despite its reasonable late vintage, only six years old, it was in a dilapidated state when he bought, it and that's why he got it so cheap. He knew to park it at the top of the hill near the block of flats just in case it wouldn't start. Predictably, that's what happened again that night and he got it going by first rolling down the hill and then taking his foot off the clutch to turn the motor over.

'Go, you bastard!' he mumbled as a splutter of smoke came out the back. He considered whether he'd call in on a mate along the way. It might be a chance to line up another job shifting some merchandise that had apparently 'fallen off the back of a truck'. It was easy money, and way more lucrative than slogging it out in the warehouse every day. It was getting dark though, reminding him of the hour, and he decided to put that on hold and go straight to his father's.

When he got to Tom's house, his father was once again flat and despondent. Bill let himself in through the front door. 'G'day, Dad. How about I make you a cuppa?'

Bill looked around the old house. The once-white curtains had yellowed, and dirty dishes sat in the sink. 'How about we get you out of here for a bit, go down to the Shakespeare for a beer?'

'Aw, dunno,' said Tom, 'don't feel like going out anywhere.'

'Yeah, come on, it'll do you good.'

It was easier to comply than argue, and with a bit more prompting, Bill got Tom into his car for the short drive to the Shakespeare Hotel where they sat on a couple of stools at the bar. For a weekday night, there were quite a few patrons in the smoky bar room, including a table in the corner with four young men who looked to be in their early twenties, each wearing jeans and with beards and longer hair than was normal at the time. Behind them was a door with a sign above saying 'Ladies Lounge' that opened to another room.

Bill ordered the drinks, content with the change in scenery. It didn't really matter if conversation was sparse; at least he'd gotten his father out of the house. As they clinked their glasses together and took a big sip, Bill noticed the door to the adjacent room open to some young women at a table, smoking and sipping from narrow glasses. One of them was at the door trying to gain the attention of the tallest of the long-haired men. She had long black hair, red lips and large brown eyes that punctuated her milky white skin.

'Just give me fifteen minutes; we're nearly finished,' the tall man said.

She raised her eyebrows in frustration and turned away, the door eclipsing Bill's view and releasing him back to the company of his father. It was obvious that the talk around the long-haired men's table was intense, and gradually it became much louder.

'America should have stayed the hell out of there!' said one of them.

'Same as Korea; it's their business and if the Soviets want to give them a hand, well so be it!'

'There's been turmoil since the Vietnamese kicked the French out and it's none of our business.'

'Any of our soldiers who go are just helping Prime Minister Holt grovel to the yanks.'

It was far from the quiet drink Bill had hoped for. The long-haired men got even louder, talking about the conflict in Vietnam. Tom noticed his son flinching, his nostrils flaring as he glared at them. 'Just relax Bill,' he said, 'let's have our drink and we can go.'

'But Dad...'

'Thing is, I'm not sure we should be sending troops either...'

'That surprises me coming from you. I mean, if it wasn't for you and the others like you, and the Yanks, we'd probably be speaking Japanese by now. What's the difference with these Asian commos on their march south, Korea and now Vietnam?'

'I know what you're saying, Bill. We had a close call with the Japs, that's for sure. We really needed the Americans to help us back then. But this is different.'

'It is different! It's more than just Vietnam. The Soviets have got the bomb and the commos including the ones in Vietnam, have got to be stopped... I'm a bit surprised that you don't reckon we should be a part of that.'

They both took a swill of beer.

'What you're assuming Bill is that these Asians are going to come our way... The Japs were, but dunno about this. It's complicated.'

'What if they are? Yellow hordes, you know, like before?' said Bill, finishing his beer and signalling the barman for another. He let out half a laugh.

'What's funny?' said Tom.

'Well at least I've got you out and you've got an opinion about something again.'

'Hmph,' grunted Tom, 'and what's more... another reason I've got my doubts about all of this is the poor bastards who get conscripted...'

'You don't like that?'

'Ah, they're only twenty years old, for Christ's sake, sent to a war I'm not sure about, and they're not even old enough to vote.'

'Yeah, good point.'

'Not even old enough to have a beer in a pub but they can be sent off to war. You can't tell me that's right.'

'Fair enough, I'll have to agree with you on that.'

At that point, one of the long-haired men started yelling. 'We've gotta make it uncomfortable for any one we see in a uniform!'

The hairs on Bill's neck stood up. 'Listen to those pricks!'

'Now it's my turn to agree with you, Bill,' he said. 'Bastards don't know what they're talking about.'

When the tallest of them got even louder, Bill was barely able to contain himself.

'In a couple of months, the yank president, Johnson will be out here. We've got to get organised, get as many as we can out in protest... This'll be our war!'

'Gather round people, where-ever you roam, 'one of them started singing, soon joined by the others as Bob Dylan's protest song gathered voice. They banged on the table and continued to sing. 'For the times, they are a changing.'

With the ruckus, Bill didn't notice the door to the ladies lounge open with the dark-haired beauty amongst the others trying to see what was going on. The men cheered as they finished and the tallest one made an announcement, 'Anyone in uniform... our enemy!'

That was enough for Bill's temper to break through its containment, and he slammed down his glass on the bar before stomping towards the bearded, long-haired men. Tom got to his feet, knowing that if there was going to be trouble and Bill was in it then he'd be in it too.

'Oi, you feathery prick!' snarled Bill as he placed both hands on their table. 'See this bloke behind me?'

The men were silent.

'I asked you a question,' he spat. 'Do you see this bloke behind me?'

'Yeah,' said the tallest of them, trying to maintain his prominence. 'What about him?'

'While you were probably sucking on your mother's tit, him and others like him were fighting so you could keep sucking. His old man too! Only he didn't make it back.'

'Hey, man...'

'Don't fucking "hey man" me!' he snapped. 'If blokes in uniform are your enemy... conscripts too... then you'd better be ready to take on blokes like me.'

At the ladies lounge door, the dark-haired beauty watched on, two things about the argument giving her satisfaction; she liked that someone was standing up to her arrogant boyfriend and, secondly, she was excited by the gruffness of the man who was doing it. Tom stood behind his son, hoping that the few heated words were now over and both parties would walk away. He hoped but knew it probably wouldn't end that way.

'I think, for your own good,' began the tall man, standing up, 'I mean, you're not exactly in your prime and the man behind you, well...'

There wasn't a lot of Bill in terms of body weight, but what he threw was fast and accurate, spreading the tall man's nose across his face. When two of his friends got up to retaliate, Tom's well-timed jab and Bill's uppercut returned them mercilessly to the ground. With that, the dark-haired beauty rushed in and lifted the tall long-haired man's head, holding him in her hands.

'Ooh,' he groaned, 'oh, Honey.'

'You are pathetic! It's about time someone did that!' she snapped and dropped him cold.

The publican had given the dispute time to sort itself out before he strolled over. 'Righto, you blokes, Get on your way!'

Tom and Bill adjusted their shirts and began to make their way out of the pub. 'Not so fast you two,' said the publican. 'You'd better help me tidy this place up.'

'Fair enough, Harry,' said Tom as he bent over to lift a fallen chair.

'Not you, Tom. Go and sit down. Bill can help me.'

'No worries, Harry.'

As the broken men and most of the young women from the other room vacated the Shakespeare Hotel in dribs and drabs, the dark-haired beauty languished behind and approached Bill. 'Are you alright?'

Bill's eyes widened as she spoke to him. 'I'll survive.'

'I'm Anne,' she said with the hint of a smile. 'You certainly made this a bit more interesting than the usual Thursday night.'

'Er, okay,' he said, taken aback. 'Er... I'm Bill.'

~

Back at Tom's house, Bill made some sandwiches from whatever he could find in his father's fridge and put the kettle on to make them a pot of tea. The feisty night had done his father good and for the first time since losing the love of his life, he showed a spark of interest in the world.

'Thanks for doing that, Bill.'

'What part? The sandwich, the beer or the blue?'

'Ha,' he chuckled. 'All of it.'

Bill poured the tea and sat a cup in front of his father on the small table in the kitchen.

'Yeah,' he grinned, 'I enjoyed it too.'

'And I think you've got an admirer. Pretty thing too,' said Tom. 'She wasn't one of them hippies, was she?'

'Ha,' Bill snorted as he sipped his hot drink, trying not to spill it, 'don't reckon. That's in America, the hippies, you silly bugger.'

'Nah, here too,' insisted Tom. 'Seen 'em on the tele.'

'It doesn't matter anyway, won't be seeing any of that lot again.'

It was after ten o'clock by the time Bill left his father's house. It had been an eventful night and he got home about an hour later than he had anticipated. He knew Nancy would be asleep and as he drove, he thought about what happened that night, happy that Tom was in better spirits.

He woke the next morning to the sound of Nancy heaving in the bathroom and figured that she must have been much sicker than he had thought. He threw off the bed sheet to go and check on her.

'You sound terrible, Nancy,' he called at the door to the bathroom, 'Can I get you anything?'

'I'll be alright,' she managed, suppressing the urge to throw up some more.

'Can I come in?'

'No,' she spluttered, 'just give me a moment.' She flushed the toilet and went to the tap to splash water over her face.

'I don't think you'll be going to work today,' he said as she opened the door.

'Nah, I wouldn't last,' she said, 'would you be able to...'

'Yeah, just go and lay down,' he said, following her into the bedroom. 'Give me the number and I'll go down the street and call them. Will you be alright on your own today, need a doctor?'

She didn't answer and instead wrote out the phone number of the government office block she worked at and handed it to him. 'When they answer, ask for extension two... Talk to Mr Jones... and I don't need a doctor - I'll be okay soon.'

She knew that she didn't need a doctor because she was certain of what was happening to her: two weeks late with her monthlies, and now the terrible nausea in the morning. She wanted to tell Bill but was scared about how he would take it.

'Are you sure?' he said. 'You look terrible.'

'Bill, you better come and sit down on the bed with me.'

'Jesus,' he said, 'what's going on?'

'Bill, I think I'm...'

'What?'

'I think we're having a baby.'

'What? Maybe it's just a bug,' he said. 'You know... maybe you ate something bad.'

'Bill,' she said, 'I'm pregnant.'

'Jesus Christ,' he mumbled, 'a baby... I'm going to be a...'

'That's right,' she said watching the news sink in, 'You're going to be a father.'

For days after the news of impending parenthood, Bill walked with an extra spring in his step. In their flat at night, after each day was done, they talked about baby names and making a nursery. Sharing their lives with a child would take their relationship to a joyous place.

In the small hours when the world was dark and quiet, Nancy's mind would wander. She felt that Bill would be a good father, but where did he go on those nights he had special business to attend? The more she dwelt on it, the more she began to wonder if Bill was ready for this.

The early hours; the silence when it feels as though the rest of the world is asleep; the darkness when the mind unloads. She knew her pregnancy would have consequences with her job. Although there were rumours that the law might change, allowing married women to remain employed, she doubted very much that the same would ever be said for those who were with child. She needed Bill to be at his best.

~

Closer to the city, Anne Johnson sat on the small couch of her share flat, skimming through the pages of a hard cover textbook. Every so often she reached for a notepad and jotted down a point of importance. It was still morning; she had plenty of time before her next modern history lecture at university.

There was more room in the flat since her boyfriend moved his things out just the day before. He had spent several days feebly attempting to re-establish his dominance in their relationship after being belted by Bill, but Anne was having nothing of it. She felt as if the shackles had been removed; she was enjoying sharing the space with just one other female student.

She made tea and assembled a bowl of nuts and raisins in the small kitchenette. She yawned and stretched backwards, exposing her midriff as she stared at the 'Make Love, Not War' poster that covered a large part of the wall in the small living area.

Anne's ex-boyfriend belonged to a group of friends that fed off each other's antics, which did little more than inflate their sense of self-importance. At first, they were an outrageous attraction to her, a constant source of amusement masquerading behind their pseudo-involvement in political issues. They hid behind pretend activism, concealing their inadequacies when compared to other small-but-committed groups on campus.

Anne began to see through their façade when they began ridiculing one such group of students who had joined Charlie Perkins on the Freedom Ride protest over discrimination against Aborigines. The ride, which happened a year earlier throughout rural New South Wales, drew a great deal of attention not only from those at Sydney University but more broadly across the population.

Anne was initially attracted to her group because what they stood for flew in the face of what her domineering father had planned for her. As far as he was concerned, Anne was to gain an education in the big city as well as an appropriate amount of worldly experience before returning to the sheep station where she would settle down with the son of a neighbouring grazier.

As far as she was concerned, she had escaped a prescribed life of privilege, devoid of romance and adventure. The only thing she missed from her old life was a seasonal worker who her father employed during the busiest time of the year. He was an excellent horseman, and although quiet in nature, his gentle humour had found a way into her heart. When her father became wise to the chemistry between them, he was given his marching orders and left suddenly in the dark of night, never to return.

Her new life in Sydney had so far followed her father's script, albeit he would never have approved of the company she was keeping. It was easy for her to have been impressed by her boyfriend's clever conversation, and his displays of behaviour that bordered on brazen protest over society's issues.

In the past months however, she had grown tired of university life, especially the clique she had become part of. It bothered her that the gross injustices in the world were little more than sources of intellectual debate for these well-to-do students, their birthright granting them exemption from many of life's harsher realities.

Her mind flashed back to a few days prior, when two men she had never seen before confronted her pompous companions at the Shakespeare Hotel. What was it about the man who stole her attention that night? He appeared considerably older than she was, but that only added to his aura of worldliness. She could tell from the several scars around his handsome face that he'd seen his fair share of life.

The morning was ticking over, and Anne knew that she needed to get back to the books. She couldn't afford to fail another subject if she wanted to finish her studies by the end of the year and get out into the world. She dropped back onto the couch, retrieved the heavy book and tried to focus. *Did he say his name was Bill?*

~

More than a week had passed since Bill found out about the pregnancy, and too long since he'd been to see his father. He'd spoken to Nancy about telling Tom the news, for it was only a matter of time before he would find out one way or another.

'Do you think we should go together to tell him?' he asked one evening after Nancy arrived home exhausted after work.

'I don't think I'm up to that,' she said, sitting on the lounge.

'Orright... probably best if I see him on my own.'

141

'I think so,' said Nancy. 'So, you'll tell him?'

'Yeah, reckon so,' said Bill, 'but I'm not sure how he'll take it.'

'Mm, hopefully he'll be happy about it,' said Nancy. 'It might give him a boost knowing that he'll be a grandpa.'

Bill roll-started the Ford so it spluttered to life. He passed the detour which would have taken him to the pub in Redfern where his associate in dodgy business would be. *Can't afford to get m'self into any strife now... more than just me to think about.*

He let himself into his father's house as usual, calling out a greeting on his way through the hallway. Tom was still in his work clothes and predictably sitting on the couch in front of the small screen. His eyes were glazed over and he was not paying any attention to it. On the small table next to him were three used cups and a small stack of plates. It was obvious to Bill that the better mood he had left his father in a week earlier had not lasted.

'G'day, Dad.'

'G'day.'

'Wouldn't mind a cuppa; how about I put the kettle on? You want one?'

'Go for your life,' he answered. 'Yeah, I'll have one I suppose.'

'I'll make a pot then. You been okay?'

'No good complainin'.'

Bill went about making the tea and tried to get some conversation out of his father. 'Nancy thought about coming over too, but she's worn out after work,' he said. 'She needed a rest. But it's kind of good that we can have a chat by ourselves. That was a funny old night at the Shakespeare.'

'Hmph,' grunted Tom, 's'pose it was.'

'We can go back again tonight if you want.' Bill carried the pot of tea over to the table and picked up the dirty dishes on his way back to the kitchen. 'Jesus Dad, you need to wash up a few things when you've used them.'

'Yeah, fair enough.'

Bill rinsed out a couple of the cups and returned with them. 'Here you go, drink this and I'll fix us something to eat. Then we can go to the pub if you want.'

'I'm pretty tired actually.'

'Up to you,' said Bill. 'Actually, I've got something I want to tell you... it's good, I reckon.'

They sat and blew the steam off the top of their cups and Bill steeled himself for what he was about to say. Tom took a small sip of tea.

'And what would that be?'

'Mm,' he muttered, waiting for the right moment, 'there's no roundabout way of telling you...'

'Well go on then!'

'Yeah, orright...it's just that... Nancy... well Nancy and me...'

'What?'

'We've grown close over the past couple of years.'

'So what?' said Tom. 'She is your step-sister.'

'I mean we've grown very close...'

'What does that mean?' said Tom. 'How close?'

'Dad, we're a couple.'

The silence in the room was unbearable as far as Bill was concerned. Tom put his cup on the table and sat back in his chair stunned. The secret he was happy to take to his grave had finally caught up with him and now there was no escaping its repercussions.

'For Christ's sake, Dad, say something!'

Tom withdrew into himself, and for the first time since Hazel had died, he was glad that she wasn't there with him.

Bill hoped that once it sank in, his father would be okay about it. 'Dad!' he repeated. 'Did you hear what I said?'

Tom slowly shook his head back and forth and raised a hand to rub his eyes. 'You can't,' he said. 'You just can't.'

'Why not?' Bill snapped. 'She's just my stepsister, not a real one, so what the hell does it matter?'

'It's just not right,' snapped Tom. 'It just doesn't look right.'

'Who cares what it looks like?' said Bill, winding himself up. 'I don't care what other people think and neither should you. If Nancy and me... Well if we happened to meet some other way all those years ago... some other way without you and Hazel involved, well, then you'd be happy about it.'

'Jesus, Bill,' said Tom. 'It's not as simple as that.'

'Of course it is!' yelled Bill.

'I'm telling you, there's more to it for Christ's sake!'

Bill felt the blood rush to his head. There was no point in holding back with the rest of it.

'I don't know what the problem is,' he began, 'but I may as well tell you now, there's more to it.'

'Jesus, Bill! What else?'

'We're having a baby,' he said. 'You're going to be a grandpa. We thought you'd be happy about it.'

Tom's head dropped into his hands.

'Say something, Dad!'

'Christ... you can't... you just can't!'

'We are!' said Bill. 'Listen to me, Dad! We are having a baby!'

'There's things they can do, you know... to make it go away.'

'I can't fucking believe what I'm hearing! Why are you saying this?'

'Bill,' said Tom, knowing that he now had no choice but to disclose his dark secret, 'you can't have the baby...Hazel... Nancy's mum... she was...'

'She was what?'

'She was... your mother too.'

It was Bill's turn to recede into silence.

'And I'm Nancy's father.'

Bill was stunned. He felt himself trying to wake from a bad dream. *Nancy is my sister, my full-blooded sister and we're having a baby... What does that make us? All this time my mother was with me... Hazel was my mother and they didn't tell me... My life has been a fucking lie... Nancy's life has been a fucking lie... They knew and they didn't tell us... and now this.*

He stood and took dizzy steps towards the front door.

'Bill!' pleaded Tom, 'you've got to try and understand...'

He turned to look at his father. 'Both of you... you never said a word... and now...'

'We couldn't. If you let me try to explain... Come back and sit down and I'll do my best to tell you.'

'How can I believe anything now? We've been living a fucking lie!' he snarled. 'And tell me one thing without any bullshit: did Rose know?'

'Bill...'

'So, she knew too.'

'Come back for a minute, will you...'

'You've got to be fucking joking'.

'Maybe tomorrow... when you cool down, maybe we can talk it through then.'

'Not fucking likely,' he said. 'You and me... I think we're done.'

Heavy steps up the hall and the slamming of a door. Tom leant forward into his hands, closing his eyes to a barrage of quick-fire images, a mental rush of his life to that point. He recalled that same feeling of heartache once before, that throbbing pang in his chest years ago, when he said goodbye to his young son on the platform of Railway Square as he set off for war. Since then, so much had happened and for merely fleeting moments in his life, he'd felt the love of a family's pieces put back together around him.

Now, after all that time, it had come down to this.

13. Dismay

Bill had never been one to put on a facade, but as far as he was concerned, that's exactly what he now had to do. The burden of carrying the secret had been passed onto him and he felt betrayed and helpless as to what he would do. The only thing he knew for certain was that he had to protect Nancy, and that meant she was never to know. Just maybe, the baby wouldn't be a freak, and no one would ever know, and in time he'd be able to wipe the reality from his mind.

In the days following his last visit to Tom, he made excuses to keep away from Nancy, for he knew that the more he was with her the more likely it would be for him to drop his guard and tell her everything. He made excuses that he needed to go and check on his father because he wasn't well, and then he would roll away in the Ford, only to park near the rocky headland at Maroubra where he could smoke and stare out to sea.

With the abrupt change in Bill, it was obvious to Nancy that something was wrong. The only thing she knew was that Bill had told Tom about the baby and he wasn't happy about it.

About a week later, he drove to the pub in Redfern to see a contact about a job. He needed the distraction, and as it happened, his services were made use of that very same night; an easy job simply moving a haul of beer from a cellar room in the inner suburb of Erskineville to a storage shed in nearby Stanmore. The adrenalin through his blood did the trick in shifting the focus of his torment, if just for the night. Nancy, acutely aware of the time he got home, lay quietly feigning sleep, for she was in no mood for confrontation.

In the sleepless hours that followed, her thoughts began to put together the patterns of his recent behaviour. She wondered that by getting home at four in the morning he had been with another woman.

A couple of days later, she asked Bill to visit Tom with her. He managed to put her off by saying that he and his father had a big argument, and they needed a bit of time together to fix things up. He would do this alone, and it would take a while. She was told not to wait up.

Who is she?

~

It was early winter, and the first distinct chill blew in from the west. The bite in the wind said that there had been some early snow at the top of the Blue Mountains. Bill and Nancy stayed inside their flat, watching a new show on the television about a hero kangaroo called Skippy. Neither of them had any interest in it though the show took the place of any conversation.

He hadn't given her any clue about the truth of their relationship, but the change in his demeanour persisted and created a tension that fuelled Nancy's misgivings. At times they exchanged a little bit of small talk, mostly comments about the kangaroo they were watching on the screen and something about getting some food for their Saturday tea. When Nancy ventured to take the conversation a bit further and talk about the baby, the conversation was shut down immediately.

The theme song of Skippy played, and Nancy got up from the couch and went to the kitchen. As she put the kettle under the tap to fill it, they were both startled by three heavy knocks on the door. Bill's instincts immediately put him on the defensive, thinking that the police had caught up with him for some of his recent activity.

'You expecting anyone?' said Nancy.

'Nah,' he answered. 'Better see who it is.'

He opened it to see two big policemen, making him think that his fears were about to be realised.

'William Davis?' asked the older of the two, a giant of a man about fifty years old.

'Yeah, Bill Davis.'

'Son of Thomas Davis, 79 Edwin Street, Surry Hills?'

'Yeah, that's right.'

'Sir, may we come in please?'

'What's happened? Is he alright?'

'Can we come in please?'

Bill and Nancy were held in suspense over the next few minutes as they were told of Tom's neighbour, Mrs Green, who hadn't seen him for more than a week. She had noticed that his mail had not been collected for days. When she knocked on his door to check on him there was no answer. It was she who called the police out of concern.

The explanation from the policeman seemed to drag on interminably. When the final blow was delivered Nancy let go a tortured shriek and Bill sucked in a breath and held it, knowing that if he let it out, he would break. His mind flashbacked to his last encounter with his father and it felt as though a knife was being thrust into his heart.

The smaller policeman explained how, upon gaining entry to the house, they found a notepad with Bill's name and address on it. After leaving them with some procedural information the policemen departed and shut the door behind them.

Bill and Nancy sat together and embraced each other for the first time in weeks. Tears streamed down Nancy's cheeks while Bill clammed up as men like him did, forcing the pain deep down. Outside, the cold rain smacked against their window.

~

With the bulk of the academic year behind her, Anne Johnson decided to knuckle down to some hard work and get her degree finished as soon as she could. She put her time into learning as much as possible, consolidating what she gained from lectures and tutorials with as much research in the library as she could fit into the day.

In her down time, she sketched and painted, and each Thursday she would go with her flat-mate for a drink at the Shakespeare Hotel. She was comfortable there, finding it to be a relaxing haunt, especially now that the long-haired bunch and the girls they associated with had moved on.

Meanwhile, at Maroubra, Bill was feeling the strain. Losing his father while they were on bad terms had taken its toll, and living a lie with the person he cared most about in the world was slowly tearing him apart. He craved his father's company for so many reasons, one of them to ask why he'd done what he'd done. He wanted to be close to him and the best he could do was to go back to the Shakespeare, where they last shared each other's company in good spirits.

He sat at the same bar stool. There were a few drinkers either side of him and some empty tables back from the bar. He lit up a cigarette and looked at the table in the corner, the one where the ruckus with the long-haired men happened. 'Hmph,' he grunted.

'Haven't seen you for quite a while; not since the disagreement you had with those blokes in the corner,' said the publican, pouring Bill's beer. 'Sorry to hear about your father.'

'Yeah, thanks, Harry.'

'I knew he'd been struggling since Hazel,' he pushed. 'You were good to him though.'

Bill guzzled the rest of his beer. 'Another one thanks, Harry.'

The publican recognised the signs of someone who wanted to shut down a conversation or at least change the subject. Bill breathed out smoke and motioned with his head towards the door that opened to the ladies lounge.

'Anyone in there tonight?'

'Just a couple of girls from the uni, same ones here every Thursday. They used to wait in there until the fellas were finished in here... You know the ones,' he laughed.

'So, they haven't been back?'

'I should be going crook on you for losing me some customers,' he chuckled, 'but they didn't drink much anyway, already doped up before they got here. Better off without 'em.'

'But the girls keep coming?'

'Yeah, they're supposed to have fellas with them,' said Harry, 'you know the law, but I turn a blind eye.'

'Stupid law anyway.'

'Ah! It's all gunna change anyway,' said Harry, enjoying the talk. 'Did you hear about those two women up in Queensland? They chained themselves inside the public bar at the Regatta Hotel. They reckoned they had every right to be in there, not just stuck in a lounge.'

'What happened?'

'The cops saw the funny side of it, I think... cut 'em loose and sent 'em home. But they'd made their point!'

'Yeah, just a matter of time.'

The publican moved across the bar, pouring beers for drinkers and taking their money. The door to the ladies lounges was pushed open, and standing there to catch the publican's attention was the black-haired beauty.

'Same again, Anne?' he called out.

She nodded and was about to let the door shut again when she noticed Bill stubbing out his smoke and draining his glass. He saw her, and when she smiled at him, the eye contact sent a bolt of excitement up through his spine. She motioned with her hand for him to approach her and he stood up from his stool to walk over.

'I remember you,' said Bill. 'Not sure if I should be apologising for that night with your friends.'

'Ha!' she said, 'they're not my friends. I remember you too. Bill?'

'Yeah.'

'And I'm Anne. So, Bill, where's your mate, the older fella who was here with you?'

The question stopped him for a moment. He baulked before finally speaking. 'Well, the other fella... he was my dad, but... he died just over a month ago.'

'Oh, Bill,' she said, 'I'm sorry, I didn't mean to...'

'It's okay,' he said. 'Can't pretend it didn't happen. It's just hard to talk about.'

She reached through the door and placed her hand on his arm in sympathy. 'You can come in here and have a drink with us if you want... We can't come out there, but you can come in here.'

He looked into her young eyes. 'Yeah, well maybe just one.'

At first, he felt out of place in the carpeted room, sitting at a round table with two young women he knew nothing about. Anne carried the conversation and soon it became clear to Anne's flat mate that she was superfluous to how the night was progressing, so she decided to leave.

'I'll go with you,' said Anne.

'What for?' she said. 'It's only one street away, I'll be fine.'

'Well, I won't be late,' said Anne. 'Early lecture tomorrow.'

Bill stood to say goodnight before resuming his seat, now alone with Anne. Her youthful exuberance was like music to his ears, and for the time being, the problems in his world were somewhere else. He answered questions about himself but kept the responses brief.

Time was passing quickly, and their talk loosened up over a couple more drinks. When she felt that there was some type of connection forming between them, she asked him the question he was afraid of hearing.

'I do have someone,' he answered. 'It's not a good situation and it won't last.'

'Well why are you still together?'

'I won't lie,' he said. 'We're having a baby. If it wasn't for that, we wouldn't be together... couldn't be together.'

'What do you mean, couldn't?'

'We just can't,' he said. 'Once I know that the baby will be okay and that she'll be okay... it'll be over.'

A deathly silence fell upon them. Bill was not regretting what he had said, for it was the truth.

Anne looked at him and saw a man who had been through a lot.

'Let's change the subject,' he said.

'Sure.'

'Okay... so what do you study?'

'I'm getting near the end of an arts degree.'

'Like drawing and painting? You mean, like an artist?'

'No, no,' she giggled. 'I mean, I do like to paint, landscapes and portraits mainly, but that's my hobby.'

'What then?'

'I study history mainly, political history.'

'Ah, wars and stuff like that?'

'Pretty much.'

'So, you got opinions then? Like, Vietnam?'

'I've got lots of opinions,' she said, enjoying the questions, 'and a few beliefs too.'

'Okay, what do you believe in?' he asked, escaping more from the turmoil of his life.

'Some rules first,' she said.

'What kind of rules?'

'I can tell you what I believe in, and you can tell me what you believe in, but we don't have to agree with each other.'

'That sounds fair enough.'

'So, if I don't agree with you, it doesn't mean that I don't like you... just don't agree about everything, that's all.'

'Yeah, same with me... I probably won't agree with you about lots of things.'

'Like what?'

'Probably Vietnam,' he said. 'I believe we should be there alongside the Americans - especially after the Second World War.'

'You and most of Australia,' she said. 'I'm not so sure though. Have you seen stuff on television? Real film from the war, almost as it's happening. It's awful.'

'Yeah, war on tele,' said Bill. 'I remember my father telling me about the news-reels of the war... People saw them at the movies... that's how they found out what was going on... Now it's in our homes.'

'In America, they're protesting more and more about it because they can see what's happening... It'll be like that here soon too,' she said. 'What about conscription, our twenty-year-olds being sent there to fight. Do they even know what they're fighting for?'

'Maybe that's something we can agree on,' he said and thought of what his father had said. He pulled out a cigarette, 'You want one?'

'Thanks.'

Bill struck a match and cupped his hands to protect the flame. She took a puff and he used the same match to light his. 'Poor bastards get sent there, doing what they think is right or doing it because they have to. Then people like your long-haired mates give them a dog's life back here.'

'They're not my mates,' she snapped. 'I told you that.'

'Yeah, sorry,' he said. 'What else do you believe in?'

'Free love,' she said, looking at him straight in the eye and waiting for a reaction.

'What does that mean?'

'Remember our rule?'

'Rule?' he asked. 'Not to get angry if we don't agree?'

'That's the one. Well then, I believe in free love,' she said again. 'People should be able to express their love, not necessarily always to the same person.'

Her words stopped him. He had never spoken to a woman before about anything they'd discussed that night. What they had divulged to each other was more intimate than he could ever have expected, and it caught him off guard.

'Have I shocked you?'

'I wouldn't say shocked,' he said. 'More like surprised.'

The night had delivered more than the escape he was seeking; he had connected with a beautiful woman at least ten years his junior and he felt contrasting impulses. He was attracted to her, but his head told him that his life was already too complicated and now was a good time to run. This woman was a delightful distraction, that was for sure, but when he closed his eyes, he thought of Nancy. He knew that whatever happened soon, she was going to be hurt and that tore at his heartstrings.

'I better think about getting myself home,' he said. 'I've got an early start tomorrow.'

'Me too,' she said. 'It's been nice talking to someone like...'

'Yeah,' he said with a chuckle, 'someone like...'

'Someone who has lived,' she said, 'someone who has a few battle scars to show for it.'

Bill was uncomfortable with the backhanded compliment. 'Yeah, it's been good,' he managed. 'Are you okay to get home?'

'Yeah, didn't you hear my flat-mate? It's just one street away.'

Bill stood and put out his hand to shake hers. She smiled, a warm surge moving through her body. No one had made her feel that way since her secretive liaisons back at the family farm. There had been other men since, a few clumsy lovers at university but none who had connected with her like that... until now. She took his hand and leant over, planting a kiss on his cheek. 'If you want to talk some more, you know where to find me.'

With that, she took the several steps to the door that opened onto the street and was gone. Bill was left standing and wondering what had just happened. He went back into the public bar and signalled for Harry to pour him one last drink.

~

Nancy continued to have a hard time with her pregnancy and felt sick most mornings. The anguish went far beyond her physical state though, for the prospect of soon having no job and then bringing a child into the world with a man who had become bitter and distant created constant suffering. She was increasingly convinced he was seeing another woman, for in her mind there was no other explanation.

Bill continued to seek respite from his place at Maroubra by going to the Shakespeare Hotel, always on a Thursday night. He couldn't tell Nancy about Anne, even if in his mind he had done nothing wrong. Anne was his sounding board, and he looked forward to his time with her, escaping from his worries at least for a few hours.

She had become genuinely concerned for him and in that way, they grew as friends. Bill had been honest with Anne, and she was convinced of his genuine affection for Nancy and how he wanted to be a good father to the baby. But he wouldn't elaborate upon the reasons for his doomed relationship and that frustrated her. She felt a twisted comfort when he told her again that when the time was right, he would leave Nancy. In the meantime, the pent-up desire she was feeling for him was growing.

Bill would return to Maroubra feeling better for his time away, and it was easy for Nancy to pick up on his more tolerable demeanour. She took it as a sign that he'd had a fine time with another woman and once again the mood in their flat would ice over.

Bill and Nancy grew distant, despite the small flat they occupied. They continued to share chores and meals and even sleep in the same bed, but communication was minimal at best; the electronic dialogue from the television replaced their own.

One day in late October, Bill got home from work to find Nancy already there. The window was open, and the lace curtains were waving in the breeze that was flowing through the room. She was spread across the couch in front of the television, her well pronounced bump pointing up to the ceiling. Despite their usual lack of interaction, Bill had to ask if everything was alright.

'We'll have to be careful with our money from now on,' she said.

'Yeah, we usually are,' said Bill. 'Why? Has something happened?'

'I can't work anymore,' she said, 'not like this and probably never again.'

She moved her legs to the floor and sat up.

'We've got problems, Bill. I don't know what we'll do.'

He was silent as the consequences of their predicament began to catch up with them.

'Haven't you got anything to say?'

'Yeah, sorry,' he said. 'No more work, eh?'

'They won't let me stay on with a belly like this!' she said. 'I know they're already talking about me, saying all sorts of horrible stuff.'

'Like what?'

'Horrible stuff,' she said as her face twisted in an effort not to cry, 'and it's not as if I have a ring on my finger to make it all respectable either.'

'I'll get some more work somewhere,' he said. 'You don't have to worry; I'll get us more money.'

'I do worry, Bill,' she said, the cracks in her defences beginning to open. 'What about us?'

'What do you mean?'

'When was the last time you kissed me? You never come near me anymore! You were happy about the baby at first and then everything changed and it's like you can't stand the sight of me.'

'It's just...'

'What, come on, get it out.'

'It's just a lot to get used to.'

'And that's it? I can tell you're lying, Bill!'

'Nah...'

'You are lying,' she said. 'I know you've met someone! You're seeing someone else and now you don't want to be with me! Why don't you admit it?'

Her words hit the mark. He couldn't say anything for the moment, knowing that part of what she said was true. Even at that moment he thought of Anne, anticipating the next time he could escape into her company. For now, he grabbed the fact that he had not been physically unfaithful and clung onto that.

'I haven't been playing up.'

'I don't believe you!' she snarled. 'I know that we're as good as finished.'

'Look, Nancy,' he said, trying to gain some voice. 'Let me explain.'

At that moment the few seconds of silence felt interminable while he wracked his brain for words. After months of tenseness, the subject of their relationship had been broached.

'Say something!'

'Just give me a chance,' he said. 'I'm gunna be honest with you...'

'Well?'

'I haven't been playing up but...'

'But what?'

'There is someone I've been seeing,' he blurted out. 'We just talk about things...'

What he said turned her anguish into a rage. 'What do you mean, you just talk about things! You don't talk to me!' she yelled, 'I'm not sure what's worse... sharing your secrets with this floozy or sleeping with her!'

'But...'

'How long has this been going on?' she yelled. 'Since you got me pregnant?'

He was trapped and knew there was nothing to say that could fix this. He got up from the chair and took heavy steps to the window where he could gaze at the glimpses of ocean between the rooftops. He steeled himself for more.

'Where did you meet this trollop? Where do you have these conversations?'

At that very moment he wished that his father was alive so he could tear strips off him for the bind he now lived in. He cared deeply for Nancy but that didn't matter anymore; there were things that had to be fixed.

'Look, Nancy,' he snapped, turning around to face her. 'We've got things to work out, so when you calm down, we can talk about it.'

'How dare you!' she yelled. 'Calm down? After what you've just told me?'

'Just listen to me!' he yelled back. He could remain on the defensive for only so long. 'Whatever happens to us, we can't stay here. You just said yourself, money is going to be tight.'

'What then? You going to get up and go? Leave me and the baby to fend for ourselves?'

'I never said that...'

'You may as well have...'

He walked back to sit on the chair again, close enough to Nancy to indicate he had more to say and wanted to be heard. 'Tom's house is empty... I've been thinking, maybe we should move back there.'

Nancy was quiet, startled by what he had just said.

'Together? We would live there together, like a family,' she said with a glimmer of hope. 'And you would stop seeing that woman?'

He didn't reply. The silence said it all and she sighed heavily, shaking her head.

'So, what's the point of it then?'

'Money,' he said. 'It won't cost anything. It would be convenient for both of us.'

'It's disgusting... but what choice do I have?'

'It might be alright,' he pushed on thinking about what he'd just said and how it just might give them a way out of the mess they were in. 'We could get help too. Mrs Green, you know, Tom's old neighbour, she'd love to help us with the kid, and it'll be good to have people around like her, someone we know.'

'I don't know...'

'Like you said Nancy, it's not like we have much of a choice.' The pieces of their predicament were coming together. 'You know what else? What if Mrs Green... Thelma Green... what if she looked after the kid, I'd pay her for it.'

'What!' she shrieked. 'We haven't even had the baby and you're trying to unload it.'

'Hear me out, Nancy! We still see the kid, but she looks after it, I pay her.'

'You're disgusting!'

'Think about it.'

'No! There's nothing to think about.'

'As far as anyone would know at your work, you wouldn't have a kid. You could go back to work.'

'They already know at work.'

'Some other work then. Somewhere they don't know you.'

'What makes you think Thelma Green would be interested anyway?'

'Maybe she wouldn't be,' he said, 'but she never got the chance to have a kid herself, so who knows?'

'I don't know,' she said. His plan, as terrible as it was, offered a hint that there might be a solution to her woes. 'I'd be able to see the baby all the time, after work I mean.' She pondered for a moment before realising how horrible his idea was. 'No, it sounds terrible; we're talking about our baby!'

'Okay,' he said. He'd made his point. 'We don't have to talk about it anymore, not right now anyway.'

It was the most they had spoken in a long time and Bill rubbed his chin in contemplation as he went into the kitchen to put the kettle on. Their cohabitation could not be sustained forever, but that could be worked out later. His shoulders felt a little lighter.

~

If Bill was thinking straight, he would have walked just a couple of blocks to the Maroubra Bay Hotel and given Nancy a couple of hours to herself before getting back. They both needed time on their own. But it was Thursday, and he was drawn to the Shakespeare Hotel.

By the time he parked outside the pub in Devonshire Street, the lights of the inner suburbs were starting to glow in the dusky twilight. He pushed through the door to the public bar, nodding to Harry the publican as he pulled out a cigarette.

'Usual, Bill?'

'Thanks, Harry,' he said, nodding towards the ladies lounge. 'She in there?'

'Yeah, mate. Are you going to be a gentleman and get her a drink too?'

He held out an open hand of notes and coins and Harry took what was required.

'How much are you taking, Harry? Drinks gone up, have they?'

'You can't buy one for her and not one for her friend too.'

'Hmph,' he grunted with a wry smile.

'Go on then,' said Harry. 'I'll bring your drinks in.'

Anne had her back to him when he pushed through the door to see the two women at their usual table. The friend whispered something to Anne and she turned around and smiled as Bill approached. He saw something extra in her face, something more alluring this time. He sat between the women as the door pushed open again and Harry carried drinks to their table.

'Thanks Harry. Cheers girls,' he said, picking up his beer and touching glasses with the others.

'You seem a bit more relaxed than usual,' said Anne.

'Yeah, well, maybe.'

'Are you going to tell us why?'

'Not just yet,' he said. 'Don't really feel like talking about it.'

Anne's friend watched their body language and intense eye contact. 'I was only waiting with Anne until you got here, Bill.'

'You were sure I was coming then?' he asked.

'I was,' said Anne with a grin.

'At least finish your drink before you go,' said Bill.

They exchanged some talk about their past weeks, and by the time Bill had finished smoking his cigarette, Anne's friend had finished her drink and left.

Anne was happy to carry the conversation up to a point now they were alone, but when there was no response to several questions it became clear that his mind was elsewhere.

'So, you're going to wear a dress to work tomorrow?' she asked.

'Yeah,' he replied. 'Wait, what did you say?'

'I'll keep talking if you want,' she said, 'but only if you listen.'

Bill took a long sip of his drink, placed the glass back down and extracted a packet of cigarettes from his shirt pocket. 'Yeah, sorry,' he said, holding out the packet for her to take one. 'What were you saying? I'm all ears.'

He struck a match and held it for her to light her cigarette before lighting his own.

'You're acting a bit strange tonight,' she said. 'Are you alright?'

'Hmm... we had a blue,' he began. 'I knew it was coming, but after that I reckon it makes things more certain about us.'

'You're not making sense, Bill.'

He smoked for a moment, thinking back over the harsh words from Nancy. He knew that she had a right to be angry when he told her about Anne. 'I told her about you.'

'We haven't done anything,' she said, 'not like that.'

'That's what I told her, but it's like... well, I can talk to you about certain things that Nancy and I can't talk about. She was angry about that.'

Anne was silent.

'The thing is,' he continued, 'we both know that it's over between us. Once the baby is born, I'll make sure that it's looked after and that Nancy is too. Then that's it, I'll be gone... eventually anyway. She knows that.'

'It must be hard for you, but I think it's probably harder for her.'

The conversation had reached a point that he was not prepared to take any further. 'I've told you everything,' he said, 'everything that I can. Can we talk about something else?'

'Whoa,' she murmured. 'If you say so. It's obvious that there's a line I can't cross.'

He wanted to finish the discussion, tie it up and get past it, even if it meant fabricating something that wasn't quite true. 'Listen,' he said, preparing a lie so he could put the conversation to bed. 'I care about her, but I just don't love her, and she doesn't love me. Getting together was a mistake and I'm not even sure if I'm the kid's father.'

'Ooh,' she said, 'I'm beginning to understand.'

'Good,' he said. 'Want another drink?'

'I think I need one.'

He went next door to get the drinks, and as far as he was concerned that conversation was over. In his absence, Anne couldn't deny her feelings of happiness now that she was convinced that it was only a matter of time before he would leave Nancy.

Bill returned and the room was quiet and empty apart from the two of them. Anne moved her chair so they were closer and put her hand on his. It felt rough and worn, an extension of this man who excited her, someone who was an anomaly to the rest of her life.

He felt a thrilling surge through his body from her soft touch and lifted her hand to his lips. 'I'd be lying if I said I don't think about you.'

Anne leant into him and pushed her lips onto his. 'Bill,' she whispered into his ear, 'we've waited long enough.'

14. Torn

Leon was born on the second day of 1967. Nancy wanted the name because it meant 'lion' in ancient Greek. Lions were her favourite animal since receiving a soft lion toy as a present when she was a baby. Choosing the name was a small victory on her part, giving her the illusion that she had some sort of say in what was happening around her. The reality, however, was that Bill didn't care what the baby's name was and so it was an easy concession to make.

The delivery was straight forward, a stark contrast to the family dynamics the child was now a part of. Bill's involvement went as far as getting Nancy to the hospital when her contractions became intense. He stayed with her for a while and then went back to the family home in Surry Hills where they now lived.

Nancy was content in the company of nurses and doctors where she was given respite from her life at home. She was mesmerised by her beautiful baby boy, cherishing the time she had with him before he was returned to the nursery with the other babies.

The time she had alone gave her a chance to ponder her immediate future. She was not looking forward to going back to Surry Hills knowing that she would be sharing motherhood with Thelma Green. She wondered how much of her son she would eventually lose to the woman.

Bill's second and final visit came on the day he took mother and child home. Their communication was civil but cool, more business-like than that of new loving parents. Nancy was on the vulnerable side of the negotiations, having already given up so much that she was now left floundering in the wake of the decisions made by Bill.

When they left the maternity ward and got to the car, she sat on the front bench seat of the red Ford and cradled Leon in her arms. Thankfully the motor turned over without incident and Bill drove them back to Surry Hills where, in just a few days' time, Thelma would assume her role in the arrangements. This was a necessary part of Bill's plan after persuading Thelma to be involved at such an early stage.

~

Bill barely engaged with his son. He was holding the secret passed onto him from Tom close and remained determined to protect Nancy from ever knowing. If everything panned out as he intended, the baby would stay with Thelma. He would simply be her neighbour, a close family friend.

He knew that the financial arrangement would have to be satisfactory for Thelma, especially if the baby had special needs. Nancy would assume her life as a family friend of Thelma's too, free to work as she liked and live independently. Bill's plan was set to come together, a clinical arrangement devoid of Nancy's well-being.

Bill would find his salvation because the child was secure, being raised by Thelma as her own. In his plan, one day he would resume his life without Nancy and without the gross blemish upon it, that indelible stain created by his parents. He could never forgive his parents for hiding the truth for all those years.

Now it was up to him to somehow make things right. One day Nancy would have a new life somewhere else, and as much as it hurt him to think about it, with someone else. What his plan lacked was foresight of the heartache sure to be enmeshed in their lives from then on.

~

It was with great trepidation that Nancy, baby in arms, walked through the front door of the house. When she was told that Thelma would be getting to know Leon from the earliest moments, she held him more closely, her hands trembling around the tiny infant. Words failed her, and her heart throbbed in pain as the most intimate parts of her life continued to be dismantled around her.

The house had been rearranged during her brief absence. Bill had set up the smaller of the two main bedrooms for himself leaving Nancy the bigger room to sleep in and nurse the baby. When she got to the third bedroom, she glared at several of Thelma Green's belongings sitting in the corner. Disempowered, she plummeted further into despair.

~

When Leon was just days old, Nancy was affronted by her inevitable fear, the sound of Thelma Green knocking on the front door and being met by Bill who ushered her into the house. She held onto Leon tightly. *Why did I ever agree to go along with this? Dear Jesus, how can I pass over my baby to this woman?*

The walls were closing in on her as Bill approached and prized the child from her arms.

'Meet Leon,' said Bill passing the baby to the buxom woman.

It was too much for Nancy and she fled the room sobbing. She was trapped, slinking further and further into a miserable existence and with no sign of it ever getting any better.

The following days were painful, overwhelmed with a grief that she had effectively lost her baby son except for the times when he would latch onto her nipple for nourishment. She existed in a daze, detached from all around her.

~

Just three weeks after Leon was born, Thelma had insisted Nancy express some of her milk into small glass containers that she kept in the refrigerator. 'It will be useful to have the supply, if you're not up to feeding him.'

As the sun set on another summer's day, Thelma waited until Leon had been fed by his mother who was by now very weary. 'You would do well to have a rest for a bit,' she said, 'a good lay down and nod off for a while. I'll take good care of Leon.'

Nancy's heavy eyes could barely stay open, and she passed the baby over to Thelma, falling backwards on her bed. 'Just a few minutes,' she managed. 'Then I can take him back.'

When she opened her eyes and realised that she was the only person in the house, she became frantic. Bill was not home from work yet, and the house was eerily quiet. She sat upright and swung her legs onto the floor, standing so quickly that she became dizzy. She rushed into each room of the house, looking for Thelma and the baby.

'Leon!' she called out. 'Thelma, where are you? What have you done with my baby?'

She scurried back into her room, pulled out a pair of slip-ons from under the bed and raced to the front door. She stopped in her tracks as it opened from the other side. 'Bill!' she gasped, 'Leon's gone... she's taken him!'

'Whoa,' he replied, putting his hands up to stop her running off. 'Just settle down, everything is alright.'

'Did you hear what I said?' she pushed on, trying to shuffle her way around him to get outside.

'Stop for a moment,' he said. 'Calm down and I'll tell you what's going on.'

Her heart sank as once more she realised that this latest blow was merely another detail of
Bill's tangled web of organisation. 'So where is he?' she said, 'Where is Leon?'

'Come and sit down and I'll explain.'

'Why am I finding out everything after it happens?' she yelled. 'And what if I don't agree to it? He's my son too!'

166

Her pulse was still racing when she walked back to the small living room and sat down. Bill went to the kitchen and filled the kettle while he thought about what to say.

'I'll make a pot of tea,' he said, 'then we can talk.'

The tears she was trying to contain began to flow. Bill brought the tea into the living room and passed her a cup. She didn't take it, so he put it on the table and prepared to speak.

'We've been over all of this. Thelma will take Leon to her place a lot more from now on, but she'll bring him over each day for you to feed.'

Nancy stared as if into an abyss. She couldn't remember the intricate details of what was being played out right at that moment, nor could she recall agreeing to any of them, but now she felt totally defeated. Tears ran down her cheeks.

'Remember Nancy,' he continued, 'I'm doing this for both of us. The boy will get everything he needs, and you will have a fresh start. You'll be able to do whatever you want.'

She was at her lowest point, beyond caring what would become of her. All she could think was that she couldn't live there any longer. She looked at Bill as words formed in her mouth. 'You say that I'll be able to do anything,' she mumbled, 'except the only thing that matters... to be a mother to my son.' *I can't stay here any longer. I love you Leon, but I must go. I'll be back as soon as I can.*

~

Anne sat nestled into the couch of her small flat and flicked through the classified advertisements of a newspaper. It was February and she was only mid-way through the long summer university break of 1967. It was important to get some casual employment so she could stay there without having to ask her father for more funds. She had always found it easy to obtain work, her good looks and personable manner finding favour with the middle-aged, male cafe owners in the city.

Sometimes, Bill would spend the night with her, and when he did, Anne could sense he was escaping his tumultuous homelife.

Her time with Bill was not always harmonious. At first, he had been such a lustful temptation, someone from a world so different to hers, and their encounters thrilled her. Recently though, his once-intriguing peculiarities had begun to annoy her. He would have been there again that night, had she not made excuses to be alone.

Running her finger down the page, Anne used a pen to circle a job advertisement. She planned out the remainder of her week, giving herself two more days to pin down a job and hopefully be earning money by the end of the week.

It was getting late in the day, and with the sun now past her window she got up to open it and let the air in to cool the place down. She was content with her own company, looking forward to a quiet night and making progress with a streetscape painting before going to bed.

~

Bill Davis's name was often exchanged in hushed voices between men of a certain network who collaborated in various pubs of the inner suburbs. Recently, his services had been in demand, mainly because of a huge haul of cigarettes and whiskey that had been lifted from the maritime ports of Sydney, avoiding government taxes and charges. His role in the distribution was straight forward; over the course of successive nights, he'd collect large quantities of the goods from one place and then drive to another part of the city where they'd be dropped off. For this service, he was paid very well.

Closer to home, he was making progress organising his life after Leon's birth. It would not be very long before Thelma would assume the role of being the baby's mother, leaving Nancy the opportunity of resuming life as a single woman.

One night as Nancy sat zombie-like in front of the television with no noise coming from her mouth but for an occasional whimper, he worked in the kitchen preparing the evening meal. He now called it 'dinner' instead of 'tea' as they had always done before, one of the habits he'd picked up since Anne had become part of his life.

He boiled potatoes and sizzled sausages in a frying pan as he tried several times to talk to her in the adjacent room. The silence frustrated him until he snapped that her dinner would be ready soon and he didn't really care if she ate it or not. The silence was intolerable, and he wanted to be elsewhere.

He sat down to the small table at one end of the kitchen by himself and swallowed a few mouthfuls before standing up and leaving it behind. He'd had enough. He grabbed his car keys from on top of the refrigerator and headed for the door. The Shakespeare Hotel once more would be his sanctuary.

~

The Bourbon and Beefsteak Bar opened in October of 1967 in the cosmopolitan and red-light part of Sydney known as Kings Cross. As soon as the sun went down, William Street became a gallery of brightly coloured neon lights and bars, each clambering for a share of the bustling crowd that had been drawn to the infamous strip.

With the war in Vietnam in full flight, The Australian Government had made an agreement with the United States, to provide a welcoming destination where American servicemen could spend their rest and recreation. The bright lights of Kings Cross shone like a beacon and attracted many thousands of American soldiers seeking an outlet in the crowded footpaths and nightclubs of this alcohol and sex-fuelled part of Sydney.

Bernie Houghton, an aggressive Texan with links to organised crime and Sydney's underworld, saw the opportunity to make a lot of money by providing American-style drinks and food in a hub that would attract the soldiers who were on leave. When he opened the Bourbon and Beefsteak Bar, its popularity soared, and it was obvious that he'd created a money spinner. With that came opportunities for young women, especially attractive ones such as Anne to gain work.

The lure of the bright lights was exciting, and after working in mundane cafes of the city, she gravitated there in search of something more enthralling. Her days at university had come and gone, and although she now had a degree qualification to her name, she decided there would be plenty of time later in life to make use of it.

She had maintained her interest in global events, and working around the American troops on rest and recreation made her feel connected to the world. She now belonged to the busy and colourful tapestry of Kings Cross, and with Bill's help, it was not difficult to move her belongings to a small one room apartment in a narrow street off Oxford Street.

After the move, she had been seeing less of Bill and that suited her fine. As far as she was concerned, he was like an intense spice, good in small quantities. Under these occasional and fleeting arrangements, she enjoyed his company and the moments of physical pleasure that came with it. For the rest of her time, she relished her freedom, particularly working her shifts at the Bourbon and Beefsteak.

Thelma was taking good care of Leon, though because of his developmental delay, he required much more care than had been anticipated. Thelma thought it reasonable for Bill to increase the amount of money that he was paying her, and he was in no position to argue about it.

Nancy had been gone for weeks, and with that another part of Bill's grand plan had come to fruition. He had assisted her in finding a place in the nearby suburb of Erskineville and paid her first month's rent; enough time, he thought, for her to re-establish herself in the workforce as a single woman. In his mind, he had done what was necessary.

When she moved away, her depressed state of mind tore at his emotions. He tried to suppress these feelings, and he hated himself for hurting her, convinced, however, that he was taking the only course of action available.

The nights he enjoyed the most were when he would meet up with Anne. She was happy to see him once or twice each week, feeling that she was in control of the relationship. They spent their time together enjoying the nightlife of Kings Cross. Bill was quick to pick up on the seedy nature of many who frequented the place, tantalised by the questionable opportunities he sensed laying just under the surface.

Flamboyant figures from Australia and from abroad had capitalised on the fertile ground for development of night spots with colourful names such as the Pink Pussycat, Kit Kat Club, Whiskey-a-go-go, all competing for their share of the revellers and the cash they were prepared to part with.

Sammy Lee was one such Canadian-born developer, having toured Australia many years prior as a musician, when he recognised a thirsty demand for exciting nightlife and the opportunities that came with it. Returning to Australia years later, he pushed forward with his dreams and opened several bars and night clubs around Kings Cross.

'Les Girls' was the most famous of his operations, where patrons enjoyed dinner and a show of athletic men dressed in feathers and glittering frocks, their faces made up with eye shadow and bright lipstick as they danced to the effervescent music of the time.

Anne had heard a lot about the dancing and miming transvestites or drag queens as they were known. After Bill met her when she finished her shift at the Bourbon and Beefsteak one night, she took him to Les Girls to see for themselves what all the talk was about. He was reluctant to go at first, but he hadn't seen her for more than a week, and so he agreed to go to make her happy. The colour and music of the show created an infectious mood of celebration, and while Anne appreciated the flamboyancy of the female impersonators, Bill became intrigued by the antics of the characters on stage.

The festivity of the night went back with them to Anne's apartment, and despite the late hour, their energy manifested itself firstly in playful banter about some of the characters they had watched that night. Anne reached into her small refrigerator to retrieve a box of white wine. 'Have you seen these before, Bill? There's about six pints of wine in this.'

'Where did you get that?' he said from the couch, the one piece of furniture in the room.

'The pub at the end of William Street sells them,' she said, pouring wine from the box into two glasses. 'They'll be selling them everywhere soon, I reckon.'

'I don't usually drink wine,' he said, 'but I'll give it a go.'

'I think you'll like it,' she said, 'and what about the show tonight? I know you didn't want to go, but I think you enjoyed it.'

'Hmph,' he muttered, with the hint of a grin. 'Certainly was different.'

He moved closer to her. 'Thanks for taking me.' He leant in and put his lips to hers. The night had been unlike any other he had experienced; the buzz of the nightlife and feeling exhilarated from the pizzazz of Les Girls had stirred his instincts and Anne was aflame in response. They touched and stroked each other, Anne moving her mouth over his face and onto his neck before her hot breath in his ear had him at her mercy. She stood and took his hand, leading him to the single bedroom. Outside, the sounds of the night washed over them.

~

December of 1967 was hot and stifling for reasons other than temperature and humidity. Bill's house was devoid of life except for his own company, and for the most part he was thankful for the solitude. Work in the warehouse filled a large part of the day, and it wasn't unusual for a night or two each week to be spent executing some moonlit activity of illicit nature.

After work, he often felt as though Thelma was watching for him to get home, for often she would arrive soon after he walked through the door. Her visits were built around complaints, usually about the lack of help she was getting from the child's true parents.

Bill insisted, that with a bit of luck, Leon, who was now just short of his first birthday, would soon begin to catch up to where he should be. Thelma wasn't so sure about that and wanted Bill to find out about special care options for the boy. He reluctantly agreed that he would investigate it but despite her insistence, he never did.

Bill's visits to Nancy had become less frequent and of shorter duration. He would tell her snippets about Leon without alarming her. His descriptions flattered the baby's well-being, consolidating the impression that Thelma was providing care of a standard far greater than they themselves, would be able to offer.

One Sunday evening just before Christmas, Bill was savouring some quiet time at home, glad that he was being left alone to watch some television. It had been hot, and he was enjoying the breeze from the south through his window while he poured beer from a long-neck bottle into an icy cold glass that he kept in the refrigerator. It had been a day of national trauma and news of Prime Minister Holt's disappearance was read out by a solemn newsreader who explained that a search was continuing in the waters around Cheviot Beach in Victoria, where he had been snorkelling.

As grave as the news was, his attention was abruptly shifted when he heard a tapping on the front door. He knew that it wasn't Thelma, for her knocking was always fast and heavy. He was startled when he opened the front door to see Anne, and he was even more concerned when there was no hint of her usual carefree demeanour.

'Can I come in?'

'What? Yeah, of course! What's happened?'

They walked through the hallway to the living room, and without saying a word, sat on the couch.

'You're making me nervous,' Bill said. 'So come on, out with it.'

She rubbed her eyes with her fingers and prepared to tell him what he needed to know. 'Bill, I wasn't sure for a while,' she began, 'but now I am. I'm pregnant.'

The ceiling felt as though it was spinning as the words reverberated through his mind. He was cast back to the first time he was told such news, and his heart thumped with anxiety. For the best part of a year his structured plan back to a normal life had been roughly falling into place; it had not been easy, and people had been hurt, but it was slowly coming together. Now, he felt everything around him was a house of cards and it was beginning to tumble down.

'You sure it's mine?' he mumbled, grasping for straws.

'How dare you!' she snapped.

'I mean, you've told me about this free love thing.'

'You make me sick! How could you say that?'

'I thought you were being careful,' he said.

Anne stood up abruptly. 'Well, thanks for the support!'

'Wait a minute,' he said. 'Sorry, but I had to say all that, had to ask.'

She stood and waited to see if there was anything else he had to say, something perhaps that would give her some comfort.

'You keeping it?' he asked.

'Not just me,' she snapped. 'I know that I'm not the motherly type, but we're talking about a life here! We...We are keeping it!'

Bill felt that familiar heavy blanket of burden drop onto his shoulders.

'It's not a baby yet.'

She glared at him, unable to find words strong enough to tell him what she thought of him. 'Just what I expected,' she spat and turned to walk away. Moments later the front door slammed shut.

Bill looked blankly at the television screen, not hearing a thing the news reader was saying.

'Divers continue to search for any sign of Mr Holt... It matters not on which side of the political fence your allegiance lies; a nation tonight holds its breath hoping for the best... but preparing for the worst.'

15. Guilt

During the final months of Anne's pregnancy, Bill was pulled in many different directions. He felt as though he could splinter into bits at any moment. It was useless to keep blaming his father and Hazel for what they did; they were long gone, and by now he had the insight to accept the mess he had created. It was he who put Thelma in charge of Leon's upbringing at the expense of Nancy's motherhood. He was the reason Nancy had broken down with despair and now he had put Anne in this situation.

It wasn't only his time and attention that was demanded of him, for each of the people he had compromised needed financial support to get by. In response, he often spent the small dark hours earning cash for his shady services. Fortunately, it paid well.

By the time the last trace of autumn warmth gave way to the chills of winter in 1968, he felt some respite, at least from Nancy's demands. She knew nothing about his girlfriend's pregnancy, and for the time being he would keep it that way. Nancy was strong, and despite grieving the loss of motherhood, she regained her determination to become her own woman again, so that hopefully, when she was better equipped, she could be involved in Leon's life.

Putting her experience to use, she began searching for work, and after just one week, she found what she was looking for at a city government office block. Her motivation to do well was strong, and in her mind, she pictured the day when hugging her son was not such a far-fetched idea.

As far as Anne was concerned, she needed much more from Bill. Her condition was by now obvious to the eye, and as a result she lost her place at the Bourbon and Beefsteak Bar. With her cash reserves dwindling fast, and the resolution set in her mind that she could not return to the family farm, she needed Bill to take responsibility for his baby, and her.

Armed with determination fuelled by desperation, she arrived at Bill's house unannounced on a dark winter night in June. It was only through good fortune that he was home to open the door to her rapid knocking.

'We need to talk,' she said to the dumbstruck man.

'It's late,' he responded. 'What's going on?'

'I can't tell you out here.'

'Ah, sorry,' he said. 'Come in, come and sit down. I'll make some tea.'

They walked in silence through the hall and past the kitchen, to the living room that smelt of cigarette smoke, and sat down. Bill went to the kitchen, filled the kettle and returned to Anne.

'Has something happened?'

'You sound like you're totally oblivious to what's happening, Bill. You can see for yourself; look at me.'

He did as he was told and nodded slowly. 'Not long now, eh?'

'No! It's not long now and what are we going to do about it?'

In the background the kettle whistled, giving him an escape for the moment, but only a brief respite from what was to come. He walked to the kitchen and made the tea, hoping the pause would break the tension in the room. He juggled two cups full of hot liquid and returned to the living room with them.

The break in the discussion failed to temper Anne's mood. 'I'll say it again, Bill. What are we going to do about it? In case the penny hasn't quite dropped, we…you… are having a baby.'

He was cornered with nowhere to go. His older child and the tangled relationships around him had been all consuming, and while Anne's pregnancy was the next big thing in his life, he hadn't been able to focus on it. that is, until now. There he was with the future mother of his child, sitting in a house of which he was the sole inhabitant. He knew that returning to her family was not an option for her, and it was almost without thought that words tumbled from his mouth. 'I'll take care of you,' he said, almost mumbling. 'You and the baby can live here.'

Anne felt a hint of relief. At least she would have shelter. Only a few years earlier, she was one of the privileged few, living on a rural homestead, secure with the provision of everything she could possibly want; that is, except for the freedom to live and love on her own terms. Bit by bit, her journey of self-discovery had led her to this desperate point. 'There's more,' she said. 'There has to be more to it.'

'What else?' he struggled to say. 'What else is there?'

She looked him in the eye. In all truth, she had no desire to spend the rest of her life with Bill. On the contrary, she couldn't imagine herself with him for more than a year or so. But as she sat there attempting to put some structure into her life, she knew that some formal agreement would be her security. 'You and I will pay a visit to the registry office tomorrow.'

'What? I have to work.'

'Not tomorrow, you don't,' she pushed on. 'There's paperwork and things to sort out.'

'For what?'

'For us to be married.'

~

During the final weeks of Anne's pregnancy, Bill knew that he had to face Nancy and tell her of his marriage to Anne and that she was having a baby. He understood this should have been done a long time prior, but he hadn't yet felt there was a good moment to do it. Finally admitting to himself that there was never going to be a good time to tell her, he steeled himself to get it done.

The only saving grace he could think of was that Nancy had become quite independent and had managed to put some order and purpose back into her life. He figured that once she knew, he would put a little more distance between them until she got used to the idea.

To say that the news did not go down well would be an understatement of gargantuan proportions. Nancy had been clinically managed by him when she was having his baby, ultimately resulting in Leon being given away. Now, so soon after, Bill was marrying another woman and having another child. It made her feel cheap and discarded and she would never forgive him.

The scolding he received was intense and as her bitter tirade went on, Bill could only stand there in the living room of her home and cop it. He knew he deserved every word of it, and the least he could do was let her give it to him without interruption.

In the days after, her anger was fuelled by every recollection she had about her life with Bill. She channelled her energy, making the decision that she would be strong and never again subject to such treatment. There was just one crack in her defence; she still had feelings for him.

~

Two weeks later, on the 10th of August 1968, Samuel Davis was born. Anne's labour had been as straightforward as it gets, but when a nurse passed her new son to her, the tiny person that would forever change her life, she burst into tears.

Bill had managed to get some broken sleep in the waiting room through the night and with the early morning sounds of trolleys being pushed about the ward, he was woken by a nurse who told him he could soon see his wife.

He made a trip to the toilet room where he splashed some water on his face. He put his lips under the tap, swishing the water around in his mouth to wash the stale taste of tobacco away. With his fingers he did his best to brush his hair before coughing to clear his throat and looking at himself in the mirror. Satisfied he was reasonably presentable; he made his way to the ward and to Anne.

'Hi,' she said feebly. 'Have you seen him yet?'

He bent over and kissed her on the forehead. 'Nah, not yet. Soon.'

Sleep deprived and unnerved by the movement of nurses in crisp uniforms in and out of the ward, he felt like a fish out of water. Anne's postpartum demeanour was soft and sweet, such a contrast to the weeks leading up to the birth. 'He's beautiful,' she said. 'You'll see for yourself.'

He pulled a chair closer to her bed. 'I will.'

She held up her hand for him to hold. 'I'm really tired now, Bill.'

'I'll let you sleep.'

She smiled with her eyes half closed and thought of another Sam, the worker on her father's rural property who was sent packing when her relationship with him was exposed.

'Go and meet Leon's brother,' she said.

Her words stunned him for a moment. For months now, their relationship had been tumultuous to put it mildly and it was nice to be sharing an affectionate moment. 'Leon's brother,' she had said so softly. The words swam in his head, his thoughts flicking back to his older child, one he had so far kept at a distance, and a wave of guilt washed over him. Anne's sweet words about Leon touched him. He wondered what Leon was doing at that very moment.

With that, he felt a deep sadness that he could never be a father to Leon, the way that he was about to be to Sam. His remorse went further, thinking about Nancy and how he could never be to her like he was at that moment with Anne.

Bill walked out of the ward and to the nursery. Still, he thought of Leon, who was clearly developing slower than he should be. He vowed that the little boy who needed more love and attention than other infants of his age, from now on, would receive just that. Bill would become the uncle that dotes on a favourite nephew, ensuring that the child would want for nothing.

A minute later, he stood with several other men, peering through a glass window to the inside of the nursery where two rows of babies were arranged in mobile cribs. Some of them were shrouded in pink blankets, others in blue, and Bill's eyes flicked across the names displayed on small name plates at the top of each crib. A young nurse inside the viewing room made eye contact with each of the new fathers, moving one baby and then another closer to the window for them to see. When it was his turn, Bill caught her attention, and she raised her eyebrows as if to ask which baby was his. He pointed to a baby under a blue blanket in a crib with 'Baby Davis' written on a small sign.

The nurse wheeled his new son to the window where he could see him. It had been a morning of strange and unfamiliar feelings, and right then yet another one took over. 'Your mother is right,' he said through the glass. 'You are beautiful. Hello little man, if it's okay with you, your mother wants to call you Sam.'

16. Regret

Sam was just eight months old when he caught his mother by surprise. It was a little after dark one night in early March of 1969, and she had him lying on a blanket in the middle of the living room floor. She continued wringing the nappies she had just washed in the laundry tub at the back of the house. It had been a day just like the day before and probably just like the next.

A good day now was when she didn't think too much about things, especially her university days or when she worked amongst the colourful night lights of Kings Cross. These thoughts would send her plummeting into despair. Her reality now was the house she felt contained in, a baby that needed her and a husband who was hardly ever there.

Walking back inside the house, she panicked when she looked at the blanket with Sam not on it. Frantically, her eyes flitted around the room until, with relief, she was surprised to find him behind the couch making a determined effort to continue exploring. It was a huge milestone in the baby's development, and once again his father was nowhere to be seen.

Bill's role was to provide, and to do this, there were several places he had to be, each of them demanding a part of him. Nancy's semi-detached house at Erskineville was one such place, and he would visit her each week to relay information about Leon and to check if she needed anything. Nancy would always despair after his visits, hearing bits and pieces about Leon and vowing to herself that one day she would be with him again.

181

Bill would leave each week having attempted to convince her of the fine job that Thelma was doing, emphasising how well equipped she was to provide everything that Leon needed. Anne felt a deep sympathy for Nancy's situation, and although she didn't begrudge his visits to see her, she was never comfortable with it.

On the night when Sam first crawled, Bill was at Thelma's where he watched her hold Leon's hand to help him put a knife through a cake she had baked. Bill hadn't told Anne where he was, choosing to keep that part of his life as separate from her as he could. Thelma drew a smile out of the little boy and Bill saw the threads of love between the woman and his son.

'Good boy,' she said as the knife was pushed through the cake.

'Ma, Ma,' he said, the first words that Bill had heard him say.

For Bill, it was a sign of progress in Leon, and it gave him hope that his son would be okay, especially with Thelma looking after him. He didn't go straight home after leaving Thelma's that night. Much to Anne's frustration, he'd forewarned her that he would be late again; off to do a bit of night work, as he called it.

Bill's work for the night was quick, simply providing the link between the distributor and receiver of two large boxes. He wasn't privy to the contents, and he didn't care, more than happy with the significant amount of money he was getting for his services. If he had thought about it long enough, he would have realised that there must have been some serious goods in the boxes to warrant his cut of the profits. Along with that, there were sure to be significant consequences if anything went wrong.

It was just after midnight when he stepped into his house. He hoped that Anne and Sam would be asleep so he wouldn't have to explain anything. If she wasn't, there was sure to be a barrage of questions.

He crept down the hallway, hoping to quietly slip off his clothes and slide into bed without notice. He was wracked with fatigue after so many broken sleeps and meeting the demands of the complicated life he had created.

'Another late night, Bill!' came the sharp words from the dark living room just past the kitchen, where Anne was sitting on the couch feeding Sam.

'Huh?' he responded. 'Didn't see you there.'

Suddenly he was wide awake, Anne's words making him more on edge than at any other time that night.

'I don't suppose there is any point in asking where you've been.'

'Night work - just trying to make ends meet.'

'Just as I said,' she scathed, 'no point in asking.'

'Look,' he said, 'I'm really tired and I've got to get up for work early; I need to get some sleep.'

She stood up still cradling the baby, and walked to the room that the cot was in, gently lowering Sam in and tucking him under a light blanket. She returned to the living room to face Bill. 'Do you think you're the only one who is tired? At least you get out of this place; I'm left here suffocating inside these hideous walls.'

For weeks, the realisation of what her life had become haunted her. She was an intelligent woman with a university degree to show for it, an achievement that not many other women had made. She had also given up her work in the most vibrant part of Sydney. There, her cheerfulness added a special touch to the celebrations of the drinkers and party goers at the Bourbon and Beefsteak. So many of them insisted she get them their drinks, and quite simply, she made it a happier place. That was then.

A couple of times over the past month, she had dressed Sam up as nicely as she could and packed a bag with what she needed for a day out. She would take a bus ride and then walk to Kings Cross to hopefully catch up with friends and show off her beautiful baby boy. Reconnecting with these people, those who had accepted her into their lives boosted her spirits. Alas, most of her friends lived a nocturnal lifestyle, and therefore the visits were short. She would return to Surry Hills, to her dirty nappies, with a head full of loneliness.

On that night, when Bill got home late after his night job, he was facing a woman who was struggling with her existence and their relationship. He braced himself as she began to unload. He knew what was to come, and in his present state of exhaustion, he was trying not to be baited into an exchange.

'You're out all day and most nights too!' she spat. 'And when was the last time you ever spent any time with your son?'

He thought of Leon earlier that evening, for he was his son too, even though the child would probably never know it. 'I can't talk about this now.'

'When can we talk about it?' she pushed. 'Tomorrow? The day after that? Ever?'

He felt the rage creep up through his body.

'You used to seem so interesting, so rough and tough like you could handle anything. Now you look like you don't care about us at all.'

The bile was stewing in his gut. Soon it would take over and he would lose control. He had to get away from her before he exploded, so he took a few steps into the bedroom.

'That's it, walk away,' she snapped. 'Leave us alone again; you spend more time with Nancy than with us!'

With that final taunt, he turned and glared at her. 'You know nothing about what I'm going through... I have to see her; there's things she has to be told! It's not easy for her and it's not easy for Thelma either... She does a great job with Leon and doesn't give me any grief about it.'

'Maybe you'd be better off with Thelma then! Or Nancy!' she yelled back.

She had hit a nerve and he took a couple of menacing steps towards her, unwittingly picking up an empty flower vase from the kitchen bench. 'You don't know when to stop! Now I'm telling you... shut your mouth!' His rage was bursting out and he was losing control. He had to channel it somewhere; he lifted the vase high in the air before smashing it down on the hard floor.

The baby woke and started crying and screaming. Anne rushed into the room and lifted him out of the cot, nursing him close to her breast.

'Jesus,' said Bill, the burst of fury out of his system, 'I can't do this anymore.'

He walked back up through the hallway and out through the front door, pulling it shut behind him. Moments later, Anne heard the old Ford start up and drive off.

'Shh,' she whispered, 'everything is alright Sam. Shh.'

They had reached a point, and she knew that from there, there was no turning back.

~

For months after the big argument, they continued to live quite separately, the arrangement made easy by the few occasions that Bill was in the house. When he was there, the mood was icy, and the conversation was minimal.

Politically too, the world was also in a state of agitation. The mood was tense between America and its Soviet adversary as both strived to consolidate their ascendency in the space race. These events intrigued Anne and were a welcome distraction to her own life. She liked to keep up with the global developments, and when she had any time, she would read about them or watch reports on television.

Since the carve up of Europe at the end of World War Two, the competition between the two powerful nations for supremacy had fuelled one conflict after another. For Anne, she loved keeping abreast of these world events, and she craved companionship to talk about such things. She knew that Bill had no interest in what was happening across the face of the planet and further, into the skies above.

She had grown lonely despite her attempts to engage with the familiar faces of her street, people who had formed their opinions that she was not like them and didn't fit in there. She remained isolated and apart from the company of baby Sam, she had no one she could really turn to.

It was now July 1969; less than a month before Sam would have his first birthday, and as the mood of the Cold War continued to be played out in space, Apollo 11 was en route to the moon. Anne wanted to share this moment in history with her baby, to tell him what wonder and excitement was happening in the world and not to have him weighed down with the drudgery and torment of her marriage to his father.

This would become her project, the thing to keep her sane, at least for now. Over the next days, leading up to the greatly anticipated and wondrous moment when Michael Collins, Buzz Aldrin and Neil Armstrong were due to land the famous rocket on the moon, she constructed her timeline of that period in history, the global events and political conflicts that led to the space race between the Americans and the Soviets. She worked on it with passion, making changes and redoing it until it was perfect.

She decided that when she finished it, she would store it with Sam's birth certificate and immunisation book for safe keeping. In years to come, Sam would open the envelope and share the moment when humankind reached Earth's lunar satellite.

The following Monday, on the 21st of July, about lunchtime, the streets in Sydney were empty as the masses scrambled to find television sets that could offer a glimpse of what was happening in space. Anne was sitting on the couch with Sam on her lap, watching the crackly black and white images of Neil Armstrong taking bounding steps in slow motion across the surface of the moon.

'Oh Sam,' she said, 'what an amazing time in history.'

The baby smiled and made noises with his mouth, happy and secure with his mother. The historical moment left Anne buoyed, and for the first time in a long while, she worked her way through the afternoon's chores in a lighter mood. From time to time, she interrupted whatever she was doing to return to the kitchen table and add a comment or drawing to her project. She was inspired by what she had just watched on the small screen, being reminded of what the world could offer, and at that moment decided that, somehow, she would get back out and become part of it.

That night, in the darkness of the small hours, Anne lay wide awake in the spare bedroom. Thoughts swirled in her head, fantasies of how she was going to leave. She knew she could easily find work again and support herself, remembering how popular she had been with the revellers of the night club. Her bosses had made it clear that, when she was ready, she would be welcomed back. She thought of doing some more painting as well, recalling the satisfaction of days gone by when she finished a portrait or a landscape. With those happy thoughts she drifted off into a deep sleep.

When she next woke, she was thankful that Bill had left the house for the day. Dragging herself out of bed, the first thing she did was to check on Sam who was just beginning to stir. The morning ritual had begun and after changing his nappy and giving him some breakfast, she would do some washing by hand and then a bit more housework.

Later, if it was warm enough, she would go into the backyard and hold Sam steady on the old red tricycle, guiding him around the small rectangle of space. He loved that.

Until then, she had work to do in the laundry, and while she did that, she put Sam on the living room floor to crawl around. She thought of the day before and the exhilaration she felt upon watching the moon landing. She dried her hands on a towel and went to the kitchen table to write more things on her time-line project, but it was nowhere to be seen.

Carrying Sam, she looked in each room and on every shelf until she was satisfied there was nowhere else to search. Feeling annoyed, she put Sam on the floor while she continued with the morning's sequence, filling up the kettle and slicing some bread. It was then that she saw it, the edge of her paper project hanging over the top of the refrigerator.

She retrieved it and started checking that it was okay and not marked or torn. She was angry at Bill for putting it there without telling her; surely, he would have seen it was important. Something else troubled her though, something that told her how precious her paper project had become. She felt her heart thumping and fought to hold back tears.

As if receiving an epiphany, it dawned on her that, at some point in recent days, she had made her decision to leave. This project was to preserve a loving and special moment, a part of her that she would leave with Sam. She knew that she couldn't take him with her. Since their fight on the night of the broken vase, she had tried to suppress certain things that had been said. *Perhaps Sam would be better off with Mrs Green.*

In her room, she picked up the art paper with the timeline on it and sat on her bed looking at it. Reaching for a pen, she began writing across the bottom of the page. *'My darling Sam, this is how the world was just before your first birthday. I will always love you, Mum.'* She slid it into a big envelope and put it in the drawer with Sam's other important documents. Moving to the living room, she picked up her child and hugged him, tears streaming from her eyes. 'I'll always love you, Sam.'

~

For months after Anne's tearful walkout, Bill was uneasy in his own home. He was not heartbroken about her leaving, but he did feel at a loss with his solitary existence in the house that held so many memories, both bitter and sweet. His company now was the crying and baby talk of his son, a few moments each day with Leon and a lot of help from Thelma.

Anne's final act on behalf of the family was to spend an emotional hour with Thelma, passing on all the knowledge she had about Sam's habits and peculiarities, talking and almost pleading until she was sure that the older woman had taken everything on board. When she closed the door behind her and left for the last time, Anne believed in her heart that her baby was better off.

Thelma revelled in the additional responsibilities she now carried for Bill's sons. Through her married life, she was never blessed with children, and when her husband didn't return from the war, that was never going to change. Now she was charged with caring for two boys, the eldest being with her full time and now the youngest with her from early in the morning until an hour after Bill returned home from work.

Life as he knew it had changed for Bill. For one thing, he was the first and only port of call for Sam's needs during the evenings and providing for the infant had been a steep learning curve to say the least. He was doing fewer jobs at night, and on the occasions he was needed, he extended the arrangement with Thelma for Sam to spend the night with her.

~

One day in November 1969, on the first Tuesday of the month, Bill stayed home from his day job for the first time he could ever remember. He hadn't slept well for months, and fatigue and exhaustion had crept up on him, so much so that he didn't stir until Thelma came knocking on his front door.

Sam had been crying for some time, hungry and in need of a dry nappy and he had slept right through the noise. When he answered the door drowsily, she came storming in, pushing Leon in his pram, and going straight to attend Sam's needs. 'Do you know it's after eight o'clock?' she yelled. 'You won't be very popular with the boss!'

'Yeah, never done that before, never slept in like that,' he said. 'Bugger it, I'm not going in today.'

'You crook or something?' she called out, having freed Sam from the wet cloth and comforting him.

'Dunno,' he mumbled, walking into the kitchen to fetch a glass of water. 'Maybe.'

'I think this little boy should still come with me.'

Bill did his best to come to terms with the new day. 'Can you wait here for a minute?'

'Why?'

'Just for a couple of minutes,' he continued. 'I've got to get to the phone box on the corner and ring the boss, better tell him.' He dashed out the door.

'Don't be long,' she called after him.

By the time Bill returned, peace had been restored and Sam was sitting on a blanket in the living room, happily trying to feed himself and making a mess in the process.

'I'm back now,' Bill called from the front door.

'I hope your boss didn't think you were staying home because of the Cup?'

'What?' he said, returning to the kitchen to fill the kettle. 'Ah yeah, its Melbourne Cup Day. Nah, don't reckon. But now that you mention it, I might get a bet on... There's a bookie I know down at The Duke. Hang on, what's it called now? Not The Duke, "The Bat and Ball"... Anyway, might get a wager on with Percy.'

At that moment, Sam, now covered in banana, rolled onto his belly and began crawling towards his father. 'He gets around pretty well now!' said Thelma. 'And you know what else?'

'Nah, what?'

'He's starting to be a chatter box,' she said proudly. 'Dada, one, two. You heard him say any of that yet?'

Bill shook his head while he put some leaves into the teapot and filled it with boiling water. 'Careful, Sam,' he said, as the baby scrambled to his father's legs. 'Whoa, wotcha doin'?'

Sam perched himself against him and, for the first time, started to pull himself up. 'Dada, to, to, to,' coming from his mouth.

'Now you have,' chirped Thelma. 'Did you hear that? He called you Dada and said number two!'

'Number two, eh,' said Bill, reaching for his tobacco pouch while Sam hung onto his leg. 'He's picking a horse for me. I'm putting some money on whatever horse number two is.'

'You do that,' said Thelma. 'In the meantime, I'll take this boy and get back to my house... lots to do. And I might need to remind you...'

'No, you don't,' said Bill, cutting her off. 'I've got your money. You don't have to worry about that.'

It was the best Bill had felt in months and months. After having the first solid sleep in a long time he was relaxing on the couch by himself, drinking tea and smoking cigarettes while the radio sounded out from the kitchen. Eventually he got himself ready to make his trip down to Cleveland Street to find his bookmaker. He decided that he'd have one or two beers while he was there and be home before the famous race jumped.

Having parked the Ford around the corner from the pub, he made his way around the back to where Percy was surreptitiously at work.

'G'day, Bill.'

'Percy,' said Bill. 'How's business?'

'I'll tell you at the end of the day. Haven't seen you 'round much lately... Keeping to yourself?'

'You could say that' said Bill, holding out cash in his hand. 'Twenty on number 2.'

Percy grabbed the notes and scribed the bet onto a small card, handing it over to Bill. 'Twenty dollars on Rainlover, eh... there you go. Hoping it can win it again, eh?'

'Anything's possible, Percy.'

By lunchtime, with a few beers in his belly, Bill was feeling relaxed. He drove back home to switch on the radio and stretch out on the couch. Despite the good sleep the night before, it was the first time in ages that he had relaxed for any amount of time, and with the effects of the alcohol, he was soon snoring.

He must have been asleep for about an hour when he stirred again, disturbed by the euphoric call of a broadcaster calling Rainlover's narrow win over Alsop in the great race. At first, he thought he was dreaming, waking groggily and in unfamiliar circumstances. Then, as he looked around the room, the events of the day gelled in his mind, and he remembered what he had done. 'Rainlover, you beauty!' he said out loud. 'Easiest day's work I've ever done. Thanks, Sam.'

His day off and earning such lucrative dividends marked a change in his frame of mind. On the next couple of mornings, he was awake and alert as the first rays of sunlight beamed through the bedroom window. He'd come a long way in his short time as a single father and without thinking too much about it, he would have the infant out of his wet nappy and into a dry one before he had rolled his first cigarette for the day.

On the Friday of that week, with Sam content to play on the floor, he moved about the kitchen with the last bit of a cigarette hanging from the corner of his mouth. Soon he would take his son to

Thelma's house before going to work for the day. It was the last day of the working week, when he would usually visit Nancy to tell her about Leon.

He did this as a routine on his way home from work, before stopping off to buy several longneck bottles of beer and some fish and chips to take with him. In the past, he had visited Nancy with some trepidation, anticipating a sequence of questions he could not answer and invariably with plenty of heated exchange. More recently though, the sharpness of their encounters had dulled and the two of them began sharing some decent conversation once more.

Bill was more comfortable about his place in the scheme of things, feeling that both children were healthy and cared for, and with that, he figured that he'd done a few things right. He knew that it was Thelma who was holding his life together, but he felt the ends had justified the means. At work on that Friday, there were moments in which he had a flicker of warm anticipation about seeing Nancy at the end of the day.

It wasn't a long drive from the warehouse to her place at Erskineville. He always got there before she did, so he waited in his car outside her house, taking the opportunity to rest his head and catch up on some sleep. It wasn't long before Nancy tapped on the driver's side window to break his slumber.

She went ahead, unlocking her front door and leaving it ajar so that Bill would come in when he was ready. Typically, the kettle was her first port of call and she started to make a pot of tea; their weekly encounter having now become sufficiently amicable that they could have their meeting over some form of refreshment.

It wasn't long before Bill followed, walking into the kitchen where he pulled up a stool next to the bench. Without asking, Nancy poured the tea. 'Another week done and dusted,' she said. 'So, what have you got to tell me?'

He said nothing for the moment, instead blowing the steam from the top of his cup. He noticed that she looked more relaxed than she had been in the past, and then hating himself for it, took a fleeting glance at her shapely bust line. 'He's been good,' he said, 'starting to make some words and move about on the floor.'

'What words?'

'Ah, well more like baby talk, lots of goo-goo stuff,' he said, 'and he's getting around on the floor pretty well now; pulled himself up on the lounge so it won't be long before he starts taking a few steps I reckon.'

Nancy nodded as she listened to what had happened in another week of her child's life without her. 'What else?'

'He's got a good appetite, eating plenty,' he continued, and then poised himself to take on the elephant in the room. 'Nancy, I reckon you still hate me for bringing in Thelma to do all of this...'

'I just don't think I had much of a say in it.'

'You may not believe me now,' he went on, 'but at the time, I thought it was for the best... for you too...'

'I don't want to get into all of that again, Bill,' she said, 'except to say that you did things very differently when you got Anne pregnant.'

'And how did that end up?' he snapped. 'At least you and I are still talking.'

'What do you mean? Has something happened?'

'I guess I should've told you a while back,' he began. 'She's gone, took off months ago.'

The announcement left them both silent for the moment, each filling the void by drinking tea. Finally, Bill added some more. 'And look at us,' he said, 'sharing a pot of tea. And just so you know, Thelma really is doing a good job; it's been hard for her too, you know he's not quite right.'

They sat in more silence. Nancy topped up their cups and he nodded to thank her. The mood was placid, the most pleasant their company had been since before their relationship had exploded into bits. Only recently had he begun to consider the misery inflicted upon Nancy by not having any contact with her son. He figured he owed her something that could make it a bit better.

'You want to see how Leon is getting on for yourself?'

'What? When?'

'Whenever you want,' he said. 'I think it would have been too hard for you before, you know what I mean? Spending time with him and then walking away.'

'I'm not sure,' she struggled to say. 'Yeah... maybe... I think I do; I think I'd be okay with it now.'

'Kind of like an aunty,' he said. 'I'm already like an uncle.'

'Let me think about it,' she said, placing her hand on his, on the hand of a man whose wife had left him.

Her touch ran through his body, throwing his mind back in time and stirring up memories of when they were together. 'Whenever you're ready,' he said. 'I'll talk to Thelma. It's just an idea, but maybe this time next week if you want; give you some time to get used to the idea.'

'You know what?' she said. 'I'll do it, this time next week.'

'Okay then,' he said, savouring the brief physical touch. 'I'll come past like normal, pick you up and take you to my place.'

'Yeah,' she nodded, already feeling the anticipation, 'next week.'

~

Nancy spent the week in a similar mood to a child waiting for Christmas morning, though not without extended periods of anxiousness in wondering how the evening with Leon would pan out. She fought any gratitude to Thelma for raising her boy, a child who needed so much extra attention.

Bill, however, was already regretting what he had done. He knew that he had been overwhelmed by the mood of their most recent encounter, swept away by the rekindling of feelings that he had tried to make certain were finished. He would steel himself from now on, to make sure their connection didn't bring Nancy any closer to knowing the truth. She deserved to be spared that.

Despite his reservations, the following Friday evening brought with it an air of expectancy. Bill had collected Nancy as promised and they made two other stops on the way home, firstly for beer and wine and then for fish and chips. They shared the refreshments, and the conversation flowed in the hour or so they had to themselves before Thelma was to get there with the boys.

'Come on through,' called Bill when he heard Thelma at the front door.

'You could come and give me a hand!' she yelled back, carrying Sam on one hip after he'd made a strong effort in walking part of the way, and holding Leon's hand after he had managed for the first time to walk all the way.

Bill walked quickly to the door in response. 'Yeah, sorry,' he said, realising the difficulty she was having. 'I should've come over to your place to get them.'

'Easy to say that now,' she said with a huff as she walked towards the living room where Nancy was waiting.

'Hello, Mrs Green,' said Nancy.

'Good evening, Nancy,' she replied stiffly to Leon's real mother. 'About an hour; we can't have him out too long - he goes down to sleep by eight.'

While Bill took Sam from Thelma, Nancy approached her and bent over to make eye contact with the much larger boy. Her heart was thumping heavily, and she struggled to keep her eyes dry. 'Hello, Leon.'

The little boy looked around and smiled when he saw Bill holding Sam.

'I'll be off then,' said Thelma. 'About an hour, eh?'

The next hour was sobering, especially for Nancy. Sam wanted to play for a while as Bill began getting him ready for bed, leaving Nancy to get re-acquainted with Leon. She had no idea what to expect and got down on her knees to move around with him on the floor. She held his hand while he leant up against the lounge chair to grab the soft toy she had brought for him.

As the time became nearer to Thelma's return, she lifted Leon up onto the couch where she could sit and hold him on her lap. Leon raised his hand and touched her face, firstly her mouth and then her nose. In a moment of connection, she hugged him with all the love she had inside. 'Do you remember me, Leon?' she whispered. 'I love you.'

It had been an intense hour, and when Thelma was heard at the front door again, Nancy hugged her boy again, a tide of emotion rising in her chest. 'It's time to go, my beautiful boy,' she murmured as the tears trickled down her cheeks. 'Until next time.'

A moment later, it was all over. She sat on the couch next to Bill and immersed herself in the hollow feeling, the aftermath of the reunion. 'That was alright, wasn't it?' she said sobbing, 'but I have to see him again.'

Bill did what he promised himself not to do and put his arm around her. 'Maybe we can do it again next week, if you're up to it... Aunty Nancy.'

She nodded slowly, comfortable sitting there with Bill. After a moment of quiet he spoke. 'We didn't think this through very well,' he said.

'Why? What do you mean?'

'We need to get you home.'

She looked at him, feeling the moment beginning to take over. 'I could stay if...'

'I'll put Sam in the car,' he said, mustering his last bit of strength to stop the conversation going in that direction.

It was a strange mood in the car on the way back to Nancy's house. She had been through a roller-coaster of elation and despair, all in one short evening. After such a long and acrimonious stretch of time with Bill, it felt good that she was now with him, being offered some strange form of comfort. Bill too had been affected by what had happened that night, his dormant feelings for Nancy having been dug up.

He pulled the car up outside the narrow row of houses that included Nancy's rented semi. The night was over, yet hanging on was a mood of expectancy that refused to die. Neither said anything, the silence of the moment carrying them along until it was broken by a soft whimper from the back seat.

'You'd better get him home,' said Nancy.

'It went well.'

'Thanks, Bill,' she said and leant over, as if delving back into a moment of their previous life together, kissing his cheek.

With that, a rush of emotion flooded him. His eyes gravitated to the narrow strap of her frock on her shoulder - how he longed to pull it down. There was a time when there would be nothing wrong with what he wanted to do, but that was before Tom had told him the truth. He sat there burning for her, feeling as though he was coming home to where he should never have left.

He looked into her eyes, his primal instincts working over his sense of what was right, slowly choking and obliterating it. Leaning in, he put his lips to hers as she hungrily responded. 'You can come in, if you want,' she panted. 'Bring Sam; he can sleep on the lounge chair.'

Nothing was said, just the cutting of the motor and closing of car doors. Inside the house, with Sam blissfully unaware of where he was, Bill fought the voices of reason in his head and peeled the straps of her garment so that it fell to the floor. *She must never know.*

She unbuttoned his shirt and ran her mouth over his neck and chest. There was no turning back.

~

The next morning, back in the sanctuary of his own house, Bill lay on his bed wallowing in regret. No longer could he blame Tom and Hazel for how his life had panned out, for now he knew what he was doing, aware of what it meant and the damage it would create.

Part Four: Sapphire Point
27th December 1980

17. Summer

Sam remembered the moment his father became old. Christmas 1980 had come and gone and there was just a week of January remaining before he would have to go back to school. The day had been like any other at this time of year on the coast, beginning early when the heat and the drone of cicadas made it impossible for an adventurous boy of twelve years to stay in bed after first light. With his mate Leon, they were gone just as soon as they'd scoffed a bowl of cornflakes. The sea was calling them.

For Bill though, it was another long morning to endure. He'd taken his walk to pick up a bottle of milk and a newspaper from the shop before it became too hot. If he took it slowly, reading the paper and drinking tea would take him through to lunchtime.

At first, he had been eager to get to the coast this year, needing a break from the parallel lives he was living in both his house at Surry Hills and also in helping Nancy with her place at Erskineville. He was also pleased to be giving Thelma a break, taking Leon off her hands for a while. The boy had been difficult in recent months, frustrated by the changes of early adolescence.

Now, however, after a week in the modest weatherboard holiday house, he was keen to get back to Sydney. As one day rolled into the next, things had felt different from how they had been just the year before. He thought of home and what needed to be done, and the longer it took for him to get started, the further he was falling behind. He stepped into the small weedy yard, enclosed by broken fence palings that separated it from the bushland beyond, and relieved himself on the thorny, scraggly lemon tree in the corner.

The job that he'd been told about was straightforward, a storage room full of cigarettes and with precious little security. His cut would be significant. The dilemma was that he had told Nancy he was finished with that sort of thing, and when he said it, he meant it. But things were different now, and he needed the money. Anyway, what she didn't know wouldn't hurt her.

At one point, he thought about crossing the road to the Ocean Spray Hotel, where he knew familiar faces would be gathering to drink, smoke and swear until they felt that all was once again well in the world. They'd be talking about fishing and football and having the same argument about the missing baby from Ayer's Rock, or Uluru as it was called by the first nation's people there. The two men on holidays from the western plains would be telling the others again how they'd seen dingos pick up whole lambs in their jaws and make off with them. A baby would be easy for a dingo.

Bill knew that he wouldn't be able to stomach it all again, more of the squabble from some of the men there who had an appetite for bloodthirsty speculation. 'Did you see the look on the mother's face?' one of them said yesterday. 'Cold as ice'.

'They were from some cult too,' another added, 'and Azaria means sacrifice in some bloody language.'

Over past summers, he'd become familiar with the same faces in the old pub where the crashing surf could be heard in the background and where they could see through the open, wooden-framed windows to the blue ocean that stretched to the white clouds on the horizon.

From time to time, the rumbling bar room voices would build, working towards a crescendo as raucous punters obliterated a race caller, riding a winner home. It was summer and they were escaping, at least for a week or two.

The pub could wait. Bill sat at a small table just off the kitchen, turned over a page and gazed mindlessly at the headlines. He had things to think through and the 'Spray', as it was known, was not the place to do it. By late morning, he succumbed to a mishmash in his head and lay on the sticky vinyl lounge chair in the next room and drifted into a restless sleep.

Several nights of broken sleep had caught up with him, and it wasn't until the early afternoon that he woke. His head was foggy, and he remembered that he hadn't eaten anything that day. He wouldn't wait for the boys; they should have been back before then anyway. He wasn't hungry, but he knew that he should make himself a Devon sandwich and wash it down with a cup of tea.

One sandwich was enough and again he sat in his white singlet and shorts that were damp from sweat and re-lit a half-smoked rollie, so that a cloud of smoke hovered above him. He put his weathered elbows on the table and gazed at the spread-out newspaper in front of him. The air was hot and thick, and a film of sweat tracked through the lines of his forehead to make a drop in his furrowed brow before falling like a tear onto the print. He moved his bare feet around on the floor, searching for a cool patch to rest them on, even if just for a moment.

Sam burst through the back screen door of the house with water dripping from his board-shorts onto the linoleum. He had run back from the beach as fast as he could. At best he was expecting a mouthful for being late, but more likely it would be a clip across the back of his head. He didn't mind either way; that was how his father kept things in check. 'Gunna come fishing with us, Dad?' he said, regaining his breath. 'After lunch, I mean.'

Bill turned a page, the movement pushing the waft of smoke away. 'You boys go,' he said not looking up, 'after you have something to eat. It's too hot for me today.'

Where was the rousing for being late? The boy felt sand drying on his burnt shoulders and brushed it off so that it sprinkled on the drops of salty water on the floor. 'C'mon, Dad,' he pushed. 'You didn't come yesterday either.'

'I'll give it a miss today,' he said. 'Make some sandwiches, there's Devon in the fridge.'

'Yeah, orright, want one?'

'Nah, I already had something; didn't want to wait any longer,' Bill mumbled through the smoke. 'Where's Leon?'

Sam opened the fridge and felt the rush of cold air hit his face. He reached into the back and grabbed a tall bottle of cola, shoving it under his arm to free his hands to collect a plate of cold meat and a tub of butter.

'He's still down there,' he said, using his shoulder to push the fridge door shut. He plonked the goods on the bench next to the sink. 'You know what he's like; sometimes it's impossible to get him out of the water.'

'He's not by himself at the beach I hope.'

'Don't worry. He's in the rock pool. You know, the one this side of the river, where it's safe.'

'Hmph,' murmured Bill. 'There's more bread in the cupboard; take a sandwich for him when you go back.'

'Okay. Sure you don't want one?'

Bill turned another page, fanning the last trail of smoke away. 'Nah, but pour us a glass of that, eh.'

Sam grabbed a couple of glasses from the cupboard and emptied the soft drink into them. He guzzled one and took the other to his father. 'Grrrer... er... er,' Sam belched and screwed up his face as a pain from the icy drink shot through his skull. 'I swear, sometimes I feel like just leaving him there. It's too hard to get him away from his friends.'

Bill looked up with the first indication of interest he had shown since his boy got back for lunch. 'What friends?'

'Aw, you know what I mean,' Sam said laughing. 'He'll have names for the starfish and the sea urchins he's playing with. When I left, he was sitting in the rock pool covered in kelp, happy as a pig in shit.'

'Just make sure he eats something and make sure he goes with you, fishing I mean. Don't leave him on his own for too long.'

'He's okay, Dad.'

'Just make sure he's with you; you know he's not right.'

Sam smeared a layer of butter, which had begun to melt over some bread. He slapped a few slices of Devon on it, capped it off with another slice of bread and took a big bite. He chewed and swallowed, then shoved the remainder of the sandwich into his mouth, causing his cheeks to bulge while he made another sandwich for Leon.

'Fill up the kettle,' said his father, his eyes flitting across the paper in front of him. 'Switch it on before you go, eh.'

Sam pulled out a brown paper bag from the kitchen drawer and pushed Leon's sandwich into it. He grabbed a few more slices of bread for mullet bait; he would throw them into his fishing bucket outside. Chewing frantically, he swallowed what he could, sucked in a deep breath through his nose and swallowed the rest. 'I'll catch us some mullet,' he said, 'down at the river. Cook 'em up for tea?'

'Yeah, go on then,' said Bill as he picked up the pouch of tobacco next to the newspaper. He pinched a small wad, the makings of his smoke, and peeled a small white paper from its pack, resting it on his bottom lip while he worked the tobacco. 'Just make sure Leon's okay,' he mumbled from the corner of his mouth, 'and get back before the streetlights come on.'

'I know the rules,' said Sam as he filled the kettle from the tap at the kitchen sink and flicked the switch. 'We'll be back before then anyway. See ya.'

The screen door slammed shut as Bill ran his tongue across the glue of the paper and finished rolling his smoke. He struck a match and sucked in deeply, making the tip glow red while, on the bench the kettle began to bubble and hiss. He stuck his hand into a pocket of his shorts, pulled out a crumpled piece of paper and flattened it out on top of the newspaper. He stared at the name, 'Hoc' scrawled across the top and his new phone number underneath.

Thelma, the woman who had looked after Leon since he was a baby, had recently been making a lot of noise about needing more money to care for him. Over the years she had grown to love the boy deeply, albeit her care coming at a financial cost to Bill. It was a price he had always been prepared to pay.

Bill got up to turn the kettle off and pour the hot water over a teabag in a cup. *Ah, what the hell; I'll do it, need the money.*

~

The small fibro holiday house was one of five similar pale-green dwellings that occupied a stretch of the main street opposite a huge wooden hotel, the centrepiece of the small coastal town. On the veranda of the holiday house were a couple of chairs either side of a wooden table, and from there it was a good view to the hotel and the ever-present ocean behind it. Bill would sit there most afternoons, in his white singlet and shorts that exposed his gnarled limbs. It was a good spot to catch the sea-breeze as the sun passed over to leave a haven of shade.

Sapphire Point was a scruffy town. To kids like Sam and Leon, that was its attraction, for it was a place they could simply fall into each summer and pick up where they had left off. Sam was at one with the ocean and the sea and sometimes he would stare out to the horizon and think about the infinite space past it. He wondered about the endlessness of time while Leon, more than a year older than he was, made friends with little fish.

A footpath ran past the pub, general store and a few houses either side. Archie, a hunched and dishevelled old man, lived in one of the houses up from the pub, a weatherboard cottage with peeling, yellow paint and in need of repairs. The locals knew to leave him alone and give him plenty of space when he would venture from the front door and onto the cracked path in the middle of his weedy and overgrown front yard.

He was the town crazy old man', a source of amusement to the kids of tourists, some who would accept a dare to get as close as they could to taunt him, until he would shake his walking cane at them, swear and cuss and then open the broken front gate to stumble after them for a few steps.

Sam and Leon knew better though and always kept a distance from Archie's front fence when they walked past it on their way to a track that would take them down to the beach. Not that Sam was scared of Archie; if anything he felt sorry for him and would love to give him some fish one day when he caught plenty.

Time for the boys, was dictated by the sun, moon and appetite, and they were free to follow their instincts to explore and catch fish and crabs. After lunch on the day that Sam decided his father was old, he was desperate to get back to the sea and the rocks as quickly as he could, for the tide was turning and there wasn't long to explore the rocks before they'd be under water. In his haste, he crossed the road and ran past the pub, swerving on the footpath to give Archie's place a wide berth, before turning into one of the tracks. The water was getting higher on the beach and soon schools of mullet would be riding the currents past the rocks into the river.

While he was puffing heavily and trying to get his breath back, he saw Leon on the protected side of the rocks in the same pool he left him in. He stepped up onto a large rock platform just as the ocean roared and a wave crashed on the dangerous side that was open to the ocean, sending spits of water high into the sky that fell like rain on his face.

He could see that the water was up to Leon's chest now. High tide was not far away, and he needed to get his line into the water on the other side of the rocks where the water from the sea began its tidal flow into the river. He knew that the mullet would be making their run past the river entrance, but he told his father that he'd make sure Leon would be with him, and so the fish, for another frustrating moment, remained just out of reach.

'Hey Leon, I've got a sandwich for you,' he said as he dropped his rod and pulled the brown paper bag out of the bucket.

'There are lots today, Sam,' said Leon as if his friend had been there the whole time, 'lots of little fish swimming all around me. See 'em?'

Sam squatted down, his skinny hairless legs having a brief rest as he plopped backwards onto his bottom. 'I can see 'em. C'mon Leon, time to get out and have something to eat.'

Leon cupped his hands just beneath the surface of water. Small fish the size of golf tees swam into his hands as he lifted them up, the water draining through his fingers to leave them flipping and flopping in the air.

'Come on, Leon,' yelled Sam. 'Come and eat this sandwich!'

Leon slowly rose out of the water with his wet blonde locks draping down and dripping on his bronzed shoulders. He stood much taller than Sam and was already well-muscled and somewhat manly. He took the sandwich and shoved as much as he could into his mouth.

He followed Sam across the rocks, scrambling up and over the highest of them until they could come down on the other side where the sea-spray from the crashing waves fell as a cooling mist on their hot faces. They tramped down past where the rocks became buried beneath the sand, to the mouth of the tidal river.

Sam figured he had about an hour at best to catch some mullet, and he wasted no time pinching some bread from the middle of a slice and melding it into a small lump of dough around the hook. He cast the line just a few metres to his right and let the current take it slowly downstream.

The first few casts had small nibbles that made his rod tweak, and with each bite, he jerked the rod backwards to hook the fish, cursing each time the fish claimed the prize. Leon waited and watched, listening to the gasps of angst that trailed each miss. He too was anxious for the first catch, keen to play his part. 'Are the mullet being pricks again, Sam?'

'Yeah, mate,' he answered, 'maybe they're too small for the hook. I'll try further out.'

He waded out to where the water was knee deep, his feet sinking into the shifting sands, and threw the line as far as he could to the right. The sediments gathered around his ankles, sucking him down, making him pull each foot out to take a couple of steps backwards. Regaining his stance in the river, he felt the tug as the top of his rod bent down. 'Gotcha,' he yelped and wound in the first mullet of the afternoon, stepping backwards and dragging it up and out of the water to where his friend grabbed it gently, easily unhooking the fish and placing it into the bucket.

By the time the tidal flow began to slow and turn, they had eight fish in the crowded bucket. Sam, enlivened with the thrill of each catch, wanted one more to make it three each. Leon was mesmerised by the wriggling silver creatures that he unhooked and dropped into the bucket, watching them move in futile and desperate bids for freedom until they slowed and slowed with their gills gaping.

Standing in the shallows of the river, Sam felt the first breeze of the afternoon sooth his burnt and peeling shoulders. It was coming from the south and instinctively he looked back over the rocks to see the angry grey clouds building on the horizon. 'Hey Leon, feel the wind coming up? We better get going; that southerly is on the way.'

The wind picked up; cold and loud as they walked into it.

'We've still got three more days,' yelled Sam.

'I don't want to go back. I want to live here forever,' replied Leon, pushing his head down into the face of the wind.

Sam remembered his dad telling him a long time ago that one day they would live at Sapphire Point and never have to leave. But that was just him and his dad when he retired from working; Leon would have to stay at his place with Mrs Green; she wouldn't want him to go away forever.

'If my dad moves here to live one day,' said Sam, 'you know that you can come and visit us.'

'Not to live but?'

'Nah mate, not to live,' answered Sam, 'but you can come here for holidays.'

'You and your dad will live here forever?'

'Yeah, mate.'

'But I will live with Ma.'

'Yeah, but you can come here whenever you want.'

The sky darkened and rumbled just as the boys made it inside. The screen door snapped closed behind them as the first fat drops smacked on the tin roof.

'How'd you go?' said Bill. The newspaper was still spread over the table next to a freshly emptied ashtray.

'We got eight, not bad size,' said Sam. He showed his dad the contents of the bucket and then stuck his mouth under the kitchen tap to gulp water.

'Hmph, not bad,' said Bill. 'Come and sit down for a bit, boys.'

Sam hated it when he was told to sit down for no reason he could think of. He opened the back door, took a step out and threw the bucket onto the small patch of lawn. The rain was tumbling now, and a crack of thunder hurried him back inside. 'It's pissing down!' he yelled over the roar of the rain on the roof.

'That was the best day ever, Uncle Bill,' he said, 'and Sam says we've still got three more days.'

Bill looked down at the table, avoiding eye contact and reached for his tobacco. 'We might be going back a bit earlier.'

'When?' asked Sam, his shoulders slumping.

'Probably Sunday morning.'

'Why?' snapped Sam. 'That's the day after tomorrow!'

'Your Aunty Nancy needs a hand with something and there's other stuff I've got to do back home.'

'Why can't you help Aunty Nancy later? What difference will a couple of days make?'

'Haven't we got three more days?' said Leon looking at Sam.

Bill worked a pinch of tobacco and rolled it into shape on a small white paper. He rested it in the corner of his mouth and avoided looking at the boys' faces.

'Don't reckon,' snarled Sam. 'Only one.'

'But you said, Sam... you said three.'

Bill lit up, breathed the smoke in deeply and looked at Leon. The boy's bottom lip was quivering, and his eyes were glassy, and what Bill saw tugged at his heartstrings. 'Come on, mate. We've had a whole week here already.'

For Leon, the announcement that they were going home early was the second shock of the afternoon.

'You and Sam are going to live here forever one day, and I will live with Ma.'

'Who told you that?' said Bill.

'You told Sam.'

'Yeah, but that was never for sure...'

'You said, Dad! When you finish working, we'll come here and stay!'

'Jesus Sam, I said that years ago.' He spoke loudly over the sound of the rain. 'I said that when I was young and could go fishing and down to the beach all the time.'

'You shouldn't have said it! You shoulda said nuthin' if you didn't mean it.' He glared at his father, seeing a man who was too old to go fishing anymore.

Bill looked at Leon who by now was unable to contain the trickle of moisture from his eyes.

'Okay Leon,' Bill conceded. 'What about if we leave late on Monday, you can have the whole day here first and there's your three days.'

'Three days,' said Leon nodding, 'like Sam said.'

Bill breathed out the smoke and slipped his hand into his pocket to screw up Hoc's piece of paper; he would not be making a phone call that night. 'Yeah mate, like Sam said.'

As far as Leon was concerned, the crisis had been averted and the world was almost normal again. Sam, though, just had the jewel in his life, the promise of living here forever, ripped away. *We're only getting three more days because of what Leon said.*

He was angry with his father, and it was at times like this he wondered about his other parent, the one he never knew. For as long as he could remember he yearned to find his mother. Something had been planted in his infant mind that continued to fuel his desperation to connect with her, and now it was more important than ever. One day he would find her, and when he did, he would show her Sapphire Point, and she would stay there with him and never want to leave.

18. Secrets

Sam walked along the cracked footpath, kicking a tin can as he went. School was back for his final year at the local primary school. The air was already hot and sticky and there was a sickly-sweet whiff coming from the jam factory. He had to be precise with each kick; too much to the left and it would roll onto the road and get crushed by the traffic. Two more decent kicks and the can would be in Thompson's Park, where he'd wait for Stephen and Mark and walk the final three blocks to school with them.

He walked and kicked, dressed in the grey shorts and shirt of regimentation, his peeling nose the only remnant of the summer break. The narrow footpath and walls of semi-detached houses that almost came up to their front fences was once more his reality. It would take a week or so to get the melancholy out of his system.

The tin can rolled onto the grass. He hadn't finished with it just yet, and after he threw his school bag onto the solitary park bench, he bent down to gather some dirt and grass, shaping it into a mound. He placed the can on top, stepped backwards and moved in to kick the missile high and over the imaginary goal posts.

'Hey Sam!' came the shout from Stephen who was weaving his way across the busy road with Mark. 'I've got some smokes. Let's go behind those bushes.'

Sam picked up his school bag and followed the two boys. 'Where'd you get 'em?'

'I knocked 'em off my dad,' said Stephen. 'He won't know.'

He gave one to Mark and then held another in his outreached hand to Sam. In his mind, Sam pictured his father sitting at the small table in the house at Sapphire Point, engulfed in a cloud of smoke, looking old and defeated.

'Nah,' he said, screwing up his nose and shaking his head, 'I don't want one.'

'You chicken?' prompted Stephen.

'Not chicken,' he snapped, 'just don't want a smoke.'

'I reckon you are,' he persisted and struck a match to light his cigarette. The first one went out and he flicked it away to try again. With the second light, he sucked on the filter like he'd watched his father do and breathed it in. He coughed and spluttered and took another drag. 'Here you go Mark,' he said as he struck another match for his friend to follow suit.

Sam watched for a while and then went to fetch his tin can. 'I'll wait for ya,' he called out as he made another mound to kick the can from. After three or four kicks, the other boys were finished and the three of them walked off on the final leg to school.

'Wanna go to the tree park after school?' said Stephen as they strolled along.

'Yeah, sure,' said Mark, 'but I've gotta go home first. Are you going to come, Sam?'

'I can't,' he said, 'it's Wednesday.'

'So?' said Stephen.

'I have to go to Leon's on Wednesdays, remember?'

'Can't Leon come to the tree park with us?' said Mark.

'He's weird, Mark. You know, mental,' said Stephen.

'Yeah, but he's okay.'

'He goes to that special school,' Stephen went on, 'where the spazos go.'

'Shouldn't say that word,' said Sam. 'Mrs Green wouldn't let him come anyway... well, not unless she came too.'

'No way!' said Stephen.

By the time they walked through the school gate and into the bitumen playground, the morning bell was being rung. Sam enjoyed Wednesdays the most, mainly because they got to do art. The teacher called their art 'free expression', an hour or so when the kids could draw, paint or sketch anything they wanted about the summer holiday they just had. The school employed some special help for Wednesdays so that each class would have the benefit of a real artist in the room for the hour or so.

For Belinda-Anne Dawes, the day's work at Sam's school each week and another day at the local high school was ideal. It supplemented the meagre income she generated from selling her paintings, and she also loved working with the children and helping them to tap into their creativity. She tried not to have favourites, though it was difficult for her not to spend more of her time with the more promising students such as Sam.

For the kids, it was a treat to get a whole piece of white paper, bigger than two normal pieces, and the freedom to choose coloured pencils, thick ink pens or small pots of paint from the big table near the teacher's desk. The only rule was that they had to ask the teacher, Miss Hornibrook, for anything they wanted to use so things could be shared about fairly.

Miss Hornibrook was a thin woman who wore a colourful frock every day and always had her hair pulled up in a bun, emphasising her high cheek bones and dark-rimmed glasses. It was difficult to tell how old she was, but most of the boys, and one or two of the girls, thought her attractive. Sometimes, on the way home, Stephen would make Sam and Mark laugh, saying how he had dreams about her and woke up with a stiffy.

Stephen got busy straight away, pushing some pencils around his piece of paper, roughly outlining the laneway behind his house with some stick figures scattered around playing cricket, using a garbage bin as the stumps.

Mark, however, was having trouble getting started and needed some help. Miss Hornibrook bent down and began talking to him about Christmas and the holidays. 'Didn't you go to your cousins for a few days?'

'Yes Miss,' he answered, 'he lives in the mountains.'

'That sounds nice,' she gently probed. 'Did you go bushwalking or anything like that?'

'Oh, yeah! We went down a big track to a creek and there was a pool deep enough to swim in!'

'Do you think you could draw a line that's the track and a circle that's a pool? Maybe you could draw some stick figures in the water that are you and your cousin? If you could do that, it would be a good start.'

'Sure!'

Sam's thoughts gravitated to Sapphire Point, and it was easy to think of the soft sand beneath his feet on a trek to the rocks and the river. He sketched out a detailed plan and as Miss Hornibrook moved from one child to another to monitor their progress, Belinda-Anne paused behind Sam's desk, appreciating the detail and ability of one so young.

Sam didn't notice her standing there while he drew an outline of a man sitting at a table. The figure was gazing outward to the large building on the opposite side of the road, with the ocean all around it. He sketched out glimpses of the beach and a bunch of rocks towards the left of the paper that gave the impression of being far away. He looked at the small pots of paint on the desk, eager to use them.

'Is that where you went for a holiday, Sam?' she said, crouching down close behind and startling him.

'Whoa!' he yelped. 'Didn't know you were there, Miss!'

Belinda-Anne let out a stifled chuckle. 'Sorry about that. This is very promising, Sam. I'm looking forward to seeing it when it's finished.'

'Thanks, Miss.' The words of encouragement stirred him further into action and he drew the pencil across the page eagerly, outlining where he would shade the ocean and the sky in different blues and greens.

All around the room, kids were making shapes and messy colours on their pieces of paper. 'Careful Susan,' Miss Hornibrook said. 'You're making a mess on the table. Here, I'll give you some more newspaper to put under the paints.'

The teacher continued patrolling, stopping at every kid to exchange some words, mostly of encouragement and a few of suggestion.

As the morning lingered on, Sam began to add some detail to his work; the individual rocks he knew so well and tiny figures of two distant boys standing on them. He thought of Leon, only a week earlier, sitting in the rock pool and then waiting with the bucket while he caught fish. He didn't know why, but as he delved into his daydream, a dull throb panged inside his chest.

With no warning, he fought hard to control what was happening in his head, his eyes starting to seep as he remembered the storm and his father going back on his word. For a while, he stopped and just sat, staring aimlessly into his picture.

Moments passed before he lay down his pencil and reached for a paintbrush, the thickest one on offer. He poured some black paint onto a dish and mixed in a little white to make a stormy grey. Using his brush, he swirled the dark paint around and around where the clouds had been sketched. He thought of his father and Leon and slapped some more paint on the paper, this time more black than grey.

The sadness became stronger, more black swirls spreading across the page and engulfing the sky and beach. As tears trickled down his cheeks, Miss Hornibrook from the opposite side of the room saw his anguish and began to approach him, watching the black paint obliterate the man sitting at the table looking out to sea.

'Sam,' she said, crouching down close to him, 'what's the matter?'

'I need more black paint, Miss,' he sniffled.

'Sam, it's okay to feel sad sometimes; how about you come outside with me for a while.'

The other students were engrossed in their creations and paid them no attention. He stood and followed her outside. It wasn't the time to say much to her and if the truth be known, he was confused about his feelings and wouldn't have known what to say anyway.

'Do you want to tell me anything, Sam?'

'No, Miss.'

She made a mental note to watch over him for the foreseeable future while Sam gradually composed himself, took some deep breaths and dried his eyes.

'Do you want to go back inside, Sam? I'm sure Belinda-Anne would like to work with you. She thinks you're very clever.'

He nodded in reply, and as they walked back inside, he asked Belinda-Anne if he could have another piece of paper and start over again. 'Of course, Sam,' she said. 'I think we can afford that.'

'I'll draw something different,' he said, 'maybe some animals in a zoo. I went to a zoo once, a long time ago.'

That afternoon, while Stephen and Mark went to the tree park, Sam walked around the corner to Thelma Green's house. In his pocket, he carried an envelope that had been left, as it always was, in the kitchen drawer on top of the plates and saucers. It was his job every Wednesday to give it to Mrs Green the moment he got there. He thought of the other boys at the tree park, tempted for a fleeting moment to join up with them, even if only for a little while and then come back.

'Hello, Mrs Green,' he said to the imposing figure occupying most of the space in the doorway of where Leon lived.

'Do you have something for me?'

'Ah yeah,' he answered, sticking his hand into his pocket to extract the envelope. He handed it over. 'There you go.'

She took it and stepped aside to let him pass. 'Leon is in the shed out the back; you two have got about an hour before tea.'

'Okay.'

Mrs Green peeled back the top of the envelope and stuck her fingers inside to count the notes. *Good, it's all here, not like last week.*

The wooden shed took up most of the space in the yard, save a rectangle patch of concrete under the clothesline. Behind the shed were splintered wooden palings of a fence leaning over and threatening to tumble down. Weeds were growing out of the cracks in the concrete under the clothesline, the only plant life in the yard apart from an Oleander shrub in a pot.

'Hi Leon,' he said, pulling open the shed door, 'what are you doin'?'

'I'm making my clubhouse,' he said as he pushed a fold-up card table towards the wall. 'It's a club for people who like wild animals. I've got some chairs too. Wanna join?'

The shed had been built by Mrs Green's husband, before he went to war. It was a handy space to store things, he had said. In reality, it was a small sanctuary with a bed in it, a place that he could escape to when she got too much for him.

Sam half smiled as any irritation he felt for having to be there evaporated. 'Sure, I'll join,' he said, 'but there's not much wildlife around here.'

'I got these pictures from school. Ma gave me some nails and a hammer and said we could put 'em on the wall. They're of Africa, and one day when I'm grown up, I will go to Africa and see the animals.'

'Okay, Leon. They'll look good on the wall.'

'And I got some jars that we can put insects in. That's wildlife too, you know... but dead ones.'

Leon's excitement was infectious. 'There are cicadas at the tree park,' said Sam. 'I saw some dead ones on the ground, Green Grocers and Black Princes. Next time I go there, I'll get some, maybe even a Cherry Red.' He picked up one of the fold-up camping stools, opened it up and sat down. 'Nice clubhouse, Leon.'

Sam watched for a while as Leon positioned a cardboard picture of giraffes on the wall. 'Can you hammer this in while I hold it?'

Sam picked up a hammer from the floor and did just that. Taking a step back to look at it, he saw a hole in the wooden panel of the wall, near the table. 'We can fix that hole too, if you want, Leon.'

'No, no!' he exclaimed. 'That's my best surprise for you!'

'A hole in the wall?' chuckled Sam.

'Real wildlife!' said Leon, 'There's a rat I've seen come in there.'

'A rat?'

'Yeah, Sam,' he explained, 'but, you know how you reckon rats are pricks? Well, he's not a prick, not this one. This one is wildlife.'

'Aw, Leon,' said Sam, shaking his head in dismay, 'rats are rats.'

'Yeah, but this one is okay; you'll see when you meet him.'

~

The first week of the school year had slowly passed, and gradually the instincts to explore the sand and the sea abated. In reality, life could have been much worse, for Sam was granted a huge amount of freedom for a boy of his age, allowed to roam the labyrinth of streets and lanes provided he adhered to some basic rules: come home straight after school before he left again, go to the shop and buy bread and milk on Mondays, go to Leon's on Wednesdays, take the garbage out on Thursdays and to be home before the street lights came on every day.

There was one more weekly ritual that he looked forward to and that was his father bringing home fish and chips for tea on Friday nights. It was a celebration, another week done and dusted, a couple of hours of abandoning the nightly schedules of having a bath and going to bed before he was tired. Friday nights were more special because Aunty Nancy always came over and they would eat the fish and chips straight from the unwrapped paper, the greasy morsels spread over the laminate table while the television played in the background.

At the end of this first school week, the salty batter tasted extra special because in his bag was a note from school about a three-day trip to the snow in July. He was both excited and nervous about giving it to his dad, knowing that the trip would cost a lot of money, but for the moment he wasn't about to consider disappointment. *It's Friday night so he'll be in a good mood. Besides, there's six months to save up; it should be okay.*

Aunty Nancy had caught two buses across town like she always did, to be there before Bill arrived home with the food. She always brought a bottle of orange soft drink for Sam and Leon. To Sam, Friday nights were like a party with Leon coming over to share the special food and soft drink for an hour or so.

Then he was allowed to stay up late after his dad had dropped Leon back at Mrs Green's on his way to take Aunty Nancy home. He would watch television from the lounge, and it didn't even matter if he fell asleep there. On this Friday night however, things were a bit different because Leon wasn't there. He'd taken ill with a stomach bug and Mrs Green insisted he stay home.

Bill always had two longneck bottles of beer, and Sam knew that if he was going to bring out the note that night, the timing would be critical; after one bottle the feeling of wellbeing would have kicked in, but towards the end of the second bottle, the mood could dip, and it wouldn't be long before Aunty Nancy would be on her way home. Sam waited until there was food in their bellies and playful banter around the table before he fetched the note from his room.

As his father opened the fridge and reached for the second bottle of beer, he made the dash down the narrow hallway to his room where he pulled the crumpled note from his school bag lying on the floor.

'Hey Dad,' he quipped as his father poured the icy beer into a glass, licking the overflow of froth from its side, 'there's a school trip to the snow in July. Reckon I can go?'

Bill took a gulp of his beer and held out his hand for the note. Sam's heart pounded and his right leg trembled. The boy looked at Nancy, hoping that there was something she could say to make his father say 'yes'. Sam's eyes locked in with Nancy's and she gave him a smirk and a wink.

'Hey Bill, remember when your dad met my mum?'

He looked up from the piece of paper with a quizzical look. 'Yeah, what's that got to do with anything?'

'How old were we then? I think I was about fifteen and you were sixteen.'

'Sounds about right,' he said, 'a few years after the war... they had just gotten together; still don't know how they met.'

'We were thrown together like an instant family,' said Nancy.

'Jesus, we had some blues,' said Bill with a grin. 'Had some fun too, eh.'

Nancy laughed as she went to the fridge to get the cask of wine and top up her drink. 'Remember they sent us on that school trip to the mountains? It must have cost them a fortune.'

'Yeah, that camp was terrific! I left school pretty soon after that,' said Bill.

'Yeah, it was worth every cent, don't you think?'

Sam was listening to each of Aunty Nancy's carefully orchestrated words. Bill looked at the note again, swilled another gulp of beer and plonked the empty glass on the table. He rubbed his brow a few times and sucked in a stream of air that whistled through his pursed lips. He reached for the pouch of tobacco and pulled out a wad to start working it through his fingers. 'Yeah,' he drawled, 'reckon you can go, Sam.'

'Thanks Dad,' the boy yelped as he wrapped his arms around Aunty Nancy.

'Here you go,' said Bill, holding the note out for Sam to take, 'better put this somewhere safe.'

The boy grabbed the precious piece of paper and took off to his room where he filed the note in a drawer with the other precious things in his life: a penknife, a MAD magazine, and a large envelope containing his only thread of connection to his mother. In it was a beautifully constructed timeline of events leading up to Apollo 11's moon landing in 1969. Nothing on that folded piece of paper made any sense to him, except the words written at the bottom. *'My darling Sam, this is how the world was just before your first birthday. I will always love you, Mum.'*

He put the school note with these other precious things in the drawer and closed it. It felt funny being Friday night without Leon there to have fish and chips with them, and he flopped down on his bed, trying to imagine what snow was like.

Sitting at the kitchen table, Bill went quiet as he weighed up what he'd just committed to. He thought of the extra money he'd promised Thelma and he hoped that his accomplice, Hoc, had some work for him.

For the moment, they each retreated into their own minds, their own memories. Nancy thought of Leon, longing for the time when she could send him off on a school camp too, her heart sinking as she thought how unlikely that was to happen.

'Missing him tonight?' asked Bill.

'Yeah.' She tried to block out the guilt she still hung on to before it once again began to destroy her. She made herself think of other things. 'They did know each other, remember?' she said. 'When they got together, they already knew each other.'

'Who?'

'Your dad and my mum.'

'Don't reckon.'

'Years before the war... don't you remember? They told us.'

'Told you maybe,' snapped Bill, dismissing a detail he did not want to know about.

'He was a rabbitoh,' she persisted. 'He sold rabbits during the depression; Mum bought them from him.'

'Nah', he snapped. 'I was never told a thing about that. I mean, I knew he sold rabbits, went out and got 'em from the markets, but that's about all I know.' He topped up his beer too fast, causing white froth to overflow, and took a long swill. He wiped the foam from his mouth with the back of his hand. 'Should think about getting you home soon.'

For Sam, images were already gathering in his mind of shovelling snow out of the way so he could get into his hut and glide down white slopes on slender strips of wood. He emerged from his room and sat on the lounge to watch television.

Nancy gave him a peck on the forehead to say goodbye, and he slid down on the lounge to embed himself into the worn fabric, staring at the television screen as if it was a campfire feeding his daydream.

'Keep the door locked, Sam,' said his dad as he slammed it shut behind him. The boy heard the car doors slam and the motor of the old Ford turn over.

Hours earlier, the streets were choked with vans and trucks picking up and dropping off; now all was quiet with corrugated metal factory shutters all down and shut. They made their way through the myriad of lanes and back-streets until they turned onto the highway, the road to the inner southern suburbs and the streets of semi-detached brick houses that included Nancy's.

Bill rolled the car to a slow stop next to the curb.

'You coming in?'

'Not this week.' He picked up on the tone of her voice, how she sounded younger and forbidden.

'Better get going,' he said, noticing the strap on her shoulder and how it could easily be flicked off to let her frock slip down. He knew what was under it and it made his loins stir.

'Suit yourself,' she said and lent over to kiss his whiskered face. Fleetingly, she saw a younger and handsome man, the traces of those rugged good looks still there. A collage of snap shots flicked through his mind, mostly of when they were first thrown together as stepsiblings, the dusting of freckles across her nose, the silky brown skin that teased and taunted him. He turned his head.

He leant in to kiss her goodnight, their lips touching for one second too long. 'Well,' he mumbled, 'I won't be staying.'

'You never do.'

19. Snow

The room that Sam shared with two other boys was accessed by the third track on the left of the pathway that led to the meal room. It was a far-cry from the images he'd created in his mind of cabins with chimneys puffing smoke from them, nestled in a valley shrouded by snow. It didn't matter though, for he was excited to be one of the hundreds of kids from a number of city schools, camped there for the week.

He was glad to be sharing a dormitory with Mark although he would have liked Stephen to have been there as well. He loved the feeling of being grown-up and sharing a place with friends, just as he would do one day when he got older. Stephen's absence was ironic, for it was he who had planned and organised what they might get up to on the camp. He had been barred the week before as a punishment for sneaking into the girls' washrooms at school and painting the black toilet seats with vegemite.

The cold biting air was so crisp that it hurt to breathe in deeply. When he exhaled, a stream of white mist poured from his mouth. There was much to look forward to, especially sitting around the roaring campfires at night and drinking hot chocolate. Then there were the expeditions further up the mountains to where there had been a recent dumping of snow, and Sam was excited about it all.

There were times, though, when he wanted to be alone and immerse himself in the wild beauty all around. He'd grab moments when nothing much was happening and go off to explore. Behind the cabins and detouring from a gravel track through the scrub, he found a huge flat granite rock that was perfect to sit on. This became his secret place; from there he could look down into the valley below, bisected by a fast-flowing river that was fed by melting snow from higher up in the mountains.

On that rock, he was the only person in his world, and it made him feel free. On the third morning there, his bottom numb from the cold rocky outcrop, a strange feeling crept over him as though something, or rather, someone was missing. It was Wednesday.

~

'Why isn't Sam here, Ma?' asked Leon. 'He should be here today; we go to the Wildlife Club on Wednesdays.'

Thelma breathed out with a sigh. 'He's not coming today, remember? He's gone to the snow with school.'

Leon was miffed. He had been told that this week was going to be different, but it never properly registered with him and he'd made some new things for the club, things that he wanted to show Sam. He pushed through the back door and went into the clubhouse. Pictures of animals he had drawn through the week sat on the small table, ready for him to stick them up on the wall with Sam. That would have to wait.

He unfolded one of the camping chairs and sat down, his enthusiasm for club day all but gone, only to be sparked once more by the sound of scratching and a rustle just outside the small hole at the bottom of the wall. He stayed quiet, knowing that if he remained totally still, the rodent would appear.

Later that night, after they had eaten, Bill knocked at Thelma's door. He was still in his blue work clothes and was in a hurry to drop off the envelope so he could get home and put an end to the day.

'Can I say hello to him while I'm here?' he asked Thelma as she took the envelope from his outstretched hand. 'Don't worry, it's all there.'

'Quickly then, Bill. He's ready for bed.'

Bill knew his way around the dark house. He walked through the hall, which was decked with black and white photographs of Thelma and Herb on their wedding day, to the small living room where the light from the television was flickering in the dark space. The next door was to Leon's room where he was lying on his bed, looking at his hand-drawn animal pictures.

'Hi Leon,' said Bill. 'Nice drawings.'

'I like the giraffe best, Uncle Bill,' he answered, staring at the picture.

'Show us the other ones too before I go.'

Leon handed Bill the bunch of drawings, child-like sketches of elephants, lions and giraffes amongst tall grass and the flat-top trees of Africa. He looked at each drawing and thought of Nancy and what she had been forced to miss out on in her life. He tried to stop his face twisting in sadness and instead forced out half a smile. 'I like the giraffe best too, mate.'

It was just a short walk back through the winter air. The city lights glowed above the rooftops on the other side of the street. Bill was yet to eat anything that evening, though he wasn't very hungry; maybe he'd feel more like it after he had a shower.

It was quiet inside the house, empty without Sam. Maybe he would go and see Nancy, perhaps even stay the night, a chance for them to talk things through. Standing half undressed, his work shirt thrown into a basket of dirty clothes in the laundry, he picked up the telephone receiver and dialled her number. Almost ringing out, he thought about changing his mind when she picked up.

'Nancy O'Brien.'

'It's me,' he said. 'Fancy some company tonight?'

An hour later, Bill was in his old Ford on his way. It was strange to have a fresh set of work clothes bundled up next to him, and he was already questioning his actions. *I hope she doesn't start talking about Tom and Hazel again... or start talking about seeing Leon more often.*

Underlying these thoughts there was another urge, a stronger one to see her and feel her soft skin; they would be alone, and for one whole night it would be like it used to be, all those years ago when there was nothing wrong about it. *What part of tonight will I regret tomorrow?*

Their love making that night was intense and primal. They fell asleep in each other's arms and slept solidly before Bill stirred, feeling the need to leave. He sat up in bed, not sure if she was awake too.

'Been awake long?' she asked with a croaky voice.

Her words startled him, and he didn't answer at first. He wasn't ready to talk.

'I've been thinking, Bill,' she continued.

'Yeah, I know,' he mumbled. 'I reckon there's a bit to say.'

Nancy pushed a pillow behind her back and sat up to be next to him. 'I don't think it would do any harm to tell him.'

'I'm not so sure,' he answered, shaking his head slowly. 'I reckon it'd do his head in.'

There was a silence, a moment that marked the chasm between what they each wanted.

'I'm so sick and tired of hiding behind all the lies, Bill. All those years, grasping for a thread of hope.'

Bill grimaced, wishing that Sam was at home so he would have to leave. 'What hope?' he said, immediately regretting what he asked.

'Ah, c'mon Bill,' she snapped, 'all those years we were together, forced to be hiding in the closet.'

'What choice did we have? You were my sister!'

'Stepsister!'

'Not as far as everyone else was concerned, Nancy,' he said, 'Especially...'

'Who? Especially who?' she said, 'Just say it, Bill, or I will for you... Especially your father and my mother! You, we... could've stood up to them! What's it matter anyway... they're not here anymore!'

Bill hung his legs over the edge of the bed, facing away. 'It was more complicated than that. Do you know how much I was looking forward to seeing him after the war?'

'That's understandable. You were just a toddler when he went away... but he came back.'

'He did, but he was a broken man. Getting together with your mum was the only thing that kept him going; even when he found out that she had a kid, he didn't mind.'

'Yeah, I remember we got on alright, back then at least.'

'It would have been hard, but I know he wanted to make a go of it. After meeting your mum and then finding out about you, he did his best, really did. He tried to look after his own mum too until she died; that knocked him around too. So, it was more complicated than just standing up to him about us. Can't you see that?'

'And this isn't complicated?' she said. 'There's a difference with us, Bill. We still have a chance to make it right - tell Leon that he has a mother and a father who love him.'

'Are you serious?' he said looking over his shoulder. 'What about Sam? He couldn't possibly understand. Do you think he wouldn't hate me for it? Hate you? I was married to his mother for Christ's sake.'

He planted his feet on the carpet, stood and walked past the bed. Nancy watched the outline of his naked body move through the shadows cast by the streetlights. She listened to the running water from a bathroom tap and the splashes it made over his face.

'So that's it,' she called out, 'walk away as if we've finished what we were talking about.'

He grabbed a towel, patted his face dry and wrapped it around his waist. Slowly he ambled back into the room and sat on the bed next to her. 'Nah, that's not it,' he murmured. 'Just need a smoke.'

'Well, that might make you think more clearly,' she said, 'might help you see things from my point of view.'

'Hmph,' he grunted.

'You know Bill,' she continued, 'all those years together and then you met Anne; you dropped me cold - like I didn't exist anymore.'

'It wasn't like that.'

'It was exactly like that,' she said, 'and before we know it, the two of you were married, miserable pair you were... Why'd you do it, Bill? Was it to make sure that you and I were finished?'

He walked to the window and opened it as far as it could go, cold air rushing onto his face with the hum of the inner suburbs sucked in with it. He grabbed for his tobacco and pinched a wad. 'You hated her, eh?'

Nancy stood up, reached for a dressing gown, and did her best to stay calm. 'I never hated her,' she said. 'There were times when I hated you. I almost resigned myself to the fact that you were gone, well and truly out of my life and then...'

'I know,' he said, resting his brow in his hand. 'I couldn't stay away.'

There were two chairs, one either side of the window. He sat on one and waited for her to sit on the other.

'Roll me one of those, Bill.'

In the quiet and amongst the flickering shadows, the red tips of cigarettes glowed while, from a distance, a siren reminded them of the world outside. She allowed herself to remember being young, a time when she was firm and inviting. She thought back to when they were thrown together as a family, that first time at Sapphire Point, when a bare-chested sixteen-year-old was showing off in front of her, diving under the breaking waves and emerging the other side of the white foam.

She thought of that same day, so long ago, when Bill's father, Tom, drove for hours to show her and her mother the sea. She drew on her cigarette, snapping herself out of the past.

'When Leon was born... well before that actually,' she said gazing into the black night, 'all that time, so many years, I waited for you and then...'

'Go on,' said Bill. 'Let's get it all out.'

She puffed on her smoke again, more words building. 'All the years, and then we had a beautiful baby. We could have been a real family, Bill.'

The words hung in the air until he could say something. 'You make it sound so easy,' he said. 'Just like that and everything would have been alright, and we'd be playing happy families.'

'It would have been hard at first,' she said, 'but not as hard as it's been for me ever since. I never got over it, Bill, giving him up to Thelma like that and hating myself ever since. Then you go off with Anne like everything was fine.'

'It was hard for me too, Nancy. It just seemed like it was the best thing for everyone. Thelma really wanted him...'

'So did I! I wanted him... and I wanted you too.'

'We just couldn't have made it work, Nancy.'

'You want to believe that. A year later, Sam comes along, just to make sure of it.'

'That's not fair, Nancy. We talked it through, remember? You were a part of what we did too.'

'Ah Bill,' she said. 'What choice did I have? You made it sound so sensible, like it was the best thing for Leon. My mind wasn't in a good place; I didn't know what I was agreeing to.'

'It was the best thing to do at the time.'

'Best thing for you maybe... you go off with Anne and Leon goes to Thelma. Me? Be a good girl Nancy and just get on with your life.'

'Nancy...'

'You don't know how much my whole body aches every time he calls me Aunty Nancy.'

'I know it's been tough,' said Bill. 'He's my kid too.'

She looked at him, her eyes pleading. 'Maybe it's not too late, Bill, we can still make it right.' She spoke softly, her words breaking up. She placed a hand on his bare knee. 'We could still do it, be a family... the four of us.'

'I'm listening to you, Nancy. I really am.' He waited, reaching for the right words, impossible words that could placate her. 'Don't you want Leon to be happy? Thelma takes good care of him, treats him like her own. And we're still important people in his life; we're that right now... but if they knew, it would destroy them both. They couldn't understand.'

'You underestimate them. Sam would love to have a mother too.'

He looked through the window, to the black sky above the rooftops. He sucked his cigarette and breathed the stream of smoke into the cold air, clouding his view. She had said what she needed to; he'd heard it before but never with such conviction. He wondered how long it would be before she told Leon the truth. The guilt settled on his shoulders like a heavy blanket. He closed his eyes and tried to escape, to when he was sixteen and amongst waves at Sapphire Point, swimming out further and further, waving back at her then diving deep into the green and disappearing.

~

The last morning of the camp started earlier, yellow fog lights on top of the tall poles glowing in the semi-dark. There was a lot to be done after breakfast, the feature event being a team obstacle course around the back part of the grounds where climbing walls, cement tunnels and tree-rope obstacles were to be conquered by the competitors. The camp organisers and the teachers had planned it well - kids exhausted from a lack of sleep followed by a flogging through the physical contest, making for a very peaceful bus ride back to the city that afternoon.

Sam was determined to suck the most out of the last day before it was all over. He made sure he was one of the first in line at breakfast, urging Mark to hurry up, but not waiting for him when he dawdled. With a full belly, he had almost an hour of absolute freedom before he would have to get together with his teammates at the obstacle course.

With a bit of luck, Kim, the pretty girl from the school in the western suburbs might be on his team. Her pretty face, long dark hair and big almond-shaped eyes had caught his attention a few times over the past days.

For now, though, he'd created some valuable time, maybe the last opportunity to go and sit on his secret rock. It was barely light, and the sun was rising behind him casting the first shadows of the day and glistening on the branches of leaves around him. His bottom felt icy on the rock but that didn't matter; the view of the vast valley in front of his misty breath filled his senses. He looked to the horizon where the green of the mountains was starting to show with first light. The tallest peaks were capped in a white that touched the sky, the same endless sky into eternity that he gazed into last summer at Sapphire Point.

It was easy to think of the sea and catching mullet with Leon; they'd done that since they were little kids. He thought of the beach and the first time they walked past Archie's place to get there.

He remembered back as far as he could. On that cold rock, he felt the warmth of the rising sun soak through and massage his shoulders and he fell deeper into his memories. Soft hands slowly pushed him on the tricycle, around and around. He turned his head to look into the yellow glow that made him squint, black hair and a pearly white face with red lipstick that hugged her smile.

'Mum?'

20. Wounded

Bill slowed as he drove past the warehouse, looking from the corner of his eye to make sure no lights were on. It was one o'clock in the morning, and the signal was to be a garbage bin at the back in the laneway, with two wooden stakes protruding from the top.

There was no one to be seen, so he rolled to a stop and reversed back up into the lane, a thin divide with the backs of dilapidated warehouses and small factories on one side and high fences of inner-city backyards on the other. It all looked straightforward; break the lock and feign an altercation with Steve, the extra security hired by the business since there had been a recent run of break-ins in the area.

That was the part of these jobs that he hated the most; planting a full-blooded punch on the willing collaborator who could then show how he put up a good fight, albeit not enough to stop the burglary. After that, load up the car with the boxes of cigarettes, make the delivery and hold his hand out for the cash.

Bill's heart was thumping, and his breathing was rapid, like it always was when he did one of these jobs. He looked at his watch and stepped silently past the bin that was to let him know everything was good to go. *Hang on a minute, where are they? Fuck! Are those old brooms supposed to be wooden stakes? Fuck Hoc, you stupid prick, gotta make it clearer than that!*

He saw a light flick on and off in a small back window on the back of the second floor. That must be Steve, right on cue, letting him know. He breathed deeply and tried to remain calm as he stepped up to the back door. With two swift movements he used the iron rod in his hand to lever under the door handle and break it, pulling it back and taking a section of plaster with it. He was inside and pointing his flashlight ahead; he saw the way to the storeroom when he heard heavy steps pounding down a wooden stairway. A strong light came towards him, obliterating anything else from his vision. 'Fuck, Steve! Point that thing somewhere else!'

'What the fuck!' shouted the man as he bounded towards him.

'Jesus! What the...'

The man spoke into a crackly walky-talky as he rushed a surprised Bill. 'Break-in at...'

Whack! With one hand over his eyes to shield them from the glaring light, Bill brought the metal rod up and across the guard's hand that was holding the device, smashing it from his grip. Instinctively, the next blow followed, a brute of an upper cut into his jaw, knocking him backwards and onto the ground. Bill stood over him, not sure what his next move would be until the dazed guard attempted to get to his feet.

Whack! This time the blow came from Bill's work boot, smashing into his head and dropping him again. This time, he stayed down. Fleetingly, Bill thought of the hundreds of cartons of smokes just one room away. The guard moved again, trying to sit up and speak. 'I don't give a fuck,' he mumbled from a broken mouth. Take what you want.'

This is too hot... gotta get out of here. Fuck you, Hoc! He turned and stepped over the man who was almost sitting up and fled. Hurried steps back into the lane and into his car, dropping the rod on the floor of the passenger side and quickly turning the motor over. The tyres spun in the gravel. He looked over his shoulder to see the dark outline of the guard outside the back door of the warehouse, the shrill of a continuous bell piercing the night sky.

Not until he turned onto the empty street did he turn on his headlights and accelerate away. He navigated his way through the narrow streets and lanes, putting distance between himself and the botched break-in. Soon he would be home where he would turn in for the night without anyone being any the wiser. He knew that Sam would be sound asleep inside, totally unaware that he had been left alone while all of this was unfolding. He told himself that everything would be okay, yet the more he tried to believe that, the stronger was the niggling of doubt in his head.

He dimmed his headlights and rolled to a stop outside the small frontage of his house. He checked that he had everything important, the metal rod and the flashlight. *Shit! Where's the flashlight?*

He flipped over everything in the car that he could get his hands on, looking for it. At some stage in the struggle, he'd dropped it. He'd left some potentially damning evidence at the warehouse or somewhere near it, but there was nothing he could do about that now. He got out of the car as he and softly pushed the door closed, stepping towards his front door. He produced a key and almost jumped out of his skin when he heard his name called.

'Bill... over here, near the telegraph pole.'

He saw the shadow at the pole a few car spaces away and immediately hurried over, knowing who it was. 'What the fuck happened, Hoc?'

'I came here as soon as I knew the job was off,' he answered, 'but you'd gone, must have just missed you.'

'So, you let me go on with it?'

'No mate. No wooden stakes in the bin out the back.'

'There were fucking broom handles in it, you prick...'

'Don't tell me you went ahead with it,' said Hoc. 'Broom handles aren't wooden stakes!'

'Let's walk; I can't talk about it here. What a fuck-up!'

'Only found out that Steve got switched at the last moment. By the time he called me it was too late. What happened?'

Bill relayed the story as they walked, Hoc shaking his head as he heard the details.

'That was going to be a big one, Bill, for both of us,' he said. 'We can kiss that haul goodbye. Did the guard see you?'

'Of course he did! But it was so rushed with his flashlight all over the place, no way would he ever recognise me. One problem

232

though, I dropped my light somewhere, inside the warehouse I reckon.'

'Ah shit!' said Hoc. 'Wait a minute, Bill... You've got no form as far as the cops know, eh? Not unless you've lied to me, and I hope not because that's one of the reasons I hire you.'

'Nah, nothing.'

'No record of your prints.'

'S'pose not.'

'Okay, should be right then,' said Hoc.' Let's get some sleep. Tell your kid you'll be late home tomorrow; we need to talk it through. Zetland Hotel.'

'Wednesday tomorrow... he won't be home till after dinner anyway.'

They walked off in different directions, Bill checking his wristwatch to see that it was just after two. So much had happened in little more than an hour and his heart was still racing. He cursed Hoc, bitter about the night on many levels, not the least that this bloke, ten years his junior, was already a notable player in Sydney's seedy underbelly. He was the one with the contacts, the one who told Bill what to do and it didn't sit well.

He tried to think of other things. With a bit of luck, he could still get a few hours' sleep before having to wake up Sam for school and carry on as though it was just another ordinary day.

~

On the final Wednesday evening of October, after the first proper hot day of the season and after leaving Leon's place, Sam didn't walk around the corner and go straight home. Instead, he took the long way, giving himself some time on his own to mull things over in his mind. Since the last morning of the school camp, when he sat on his special rock and looked into the sun, the same ghost-like image had flickered through his mind.

He sat on the bench at Thompson's Park and tried to feel like he did that morning on the rock. The dark of night softened the hard bricks and mortar of the streets, and the hum of the city hung in the breeze, almost as hypnotic as the sound of the wind through the trees at his rock. When he closed his eyes, the urban buzz could even be the sound of the waves at Sapphire Point. Black hair covered her white face, and so desperately he wanted to brush it out of the way.

He wanted more time, the night settling over him and freeing his thoughts, but he knew that he had to go. His Dad had been acting strange lately. Sometimes Sam would have to ask the same question two or three times before his father would answer, and when he did, it was short and sharp. His father had always been gruff, but lately he had been worse than ever. He'd better get home before it was too late.

That night, half an hour later than usual, Sam came through the front door surprised to see Aunty Nancy and his dad, sitting around the table. It didn't look right; for one thing, it wasn't Friday with fish and chips, laughter and long-neck beer bottles. It was smoky and quiet, and they wore straight, expressionless faces as though they'd been fighting and Sam had just interrupted.

'It's about time,' said his father. 'I was just about to go and see Mrs Green.'

'Sorry.' He could smell that his father had been drinking. 'Hi Aunty Nancy; it's not Friday.'

'Hello Sam. Your Dad is going to drive me home; he won't be long tonight...'

'We'll have a talk when I get back,' said Bill.

Nancy got up and kissed the boy's forehead on her way to the door.

'Like she said, Sam, I'll be back soon,' said his father just before closing the front door on his way out. 'Keep the door locked.'

The bewildered boy turned the television on and flopped onto the lounge. He stared at the screen without even noticing what the program was. He had been baffled about his father for weeks but now everything was even more confusing. There was something wrong and Aunty Nancy was in on it. Unaware of what was being played out as his father drove Aunty Nancy home, he lay still, sure of one thing - he was about to find out stuff that he may not want to know.

'You're driving too fast.'

'I'm driving exactly the same as I always do,' Bill mumbled through his clenched jaw.

'There's nothing the same about this,' she snapped. 'You call me from the pub and tell me to meet you at your place, just to tell me you've done another job... after promising me you were done with all of that.'

He wound down the side window, feeling the rush of air give him some distraction, some respite. He knew she was right. A job gone wrong and now he was paying for it. Worst of all, he had no choice but to drag her into it. 'I can handle it,' he managed. 'Just might need you to take Sam for a while. Can you do that or not?'

He drove erratically, the uncomfortable silence needling an anger and tightening what felt like a vice on his head. Nancy's hands gripped each side of the seat as the tyres screeched when he cornered sharply. 'For Christ's sake, slow down!'

He took a deep breath and eased off on the accelerator. 'Look Nancy, I said I'm sorry.'

'Just drive.'

Nancy let out a deep breath when they arrived at her place. Bill cut the motor and pulled up the hand brake. 'So will you help?'

Nancy breathed slowly, wanting to make sure that she was in control of whatever she was about to say. 'What else haven't you told me?' she said. 'If I am going to help you, I want to know everything.'

Bill sat, both hands gripping the steering wheel.

'Bill,' she pressed, 'everything.'

'Okay,' he said, preparing to tell her what happened. He owed her that much. 'The job was a fuck up, didn't get a cent out of it.'

'That much I know.'

'For some reason, they changed Steve's shift and put on some prick called Marco. Maybe they got wind of something. I don't know. Maybe they don't trust Steve after the last run of break-ins. Like I said, I don't know. By the time Hoc found out, it was too late.'

'Go on.'

'Anyway, Marco gave me a bit of a surprise and well...'

'What?'

'Well, what I've found out from Hoc is that Marco's good looks have been... well... he's not so pretty anymore.'

'He didn't deserve that, Bill.'

'Look, do you want to know what happened or what?'

'Yeah.'

'Okay. A few things about those guards,' he went on. 'Steve is dumb as a nail, and he talks too much. So, he gets talking to Marco, went to see him in hospital after he had his jaw wired up. They talk about it and Steve, the dumb prick, well he mentions my name.'

'So... police?'

'Nah, that's not going to happen. Hoc has shit on all those blokes. The thing is that Marco fancies himself as a bit of a hero; the word is that I can expect a midnight house call from him later this week when he gets out of hospital... and he won't be bringing me flowers.'

'Bill! You left your son there tonight by himself!'

'I checked. Marco is still in St Peters Private... There's a couple of other things about him.'

'Shit, what else?'

'Marco is the sort of bloke who holds a grudge... likes to get square, if you know what I mean...'

'So?'

'Well, I have it on very good authority that he can be spooked... scared off.'

'And how the hell are you going to scare him off?'

'Let's just say that I'll be ready for him when he pays me a visit.'

'No, Bill!'

'Just hear me out. If he's on the back foot, a bit worried about his future well-being, I shouldn't have much to worry about.'

'Don't make this worse than it already is.'

'All I'm asking is that you take Sam for a week or so, just 'till it's sorted out.'

'Don't have much choice, do I?'

'Thanks, Nancy.'

They sat in silence and the longer it lasted, Bill became worried that she would have more to say. He wanted to lock in the agreement. 'After I have a talk to Sam tonight, I'll call you... make the arrangements?'

'There's more to say first, Bill, more to talk about.'

'I guess you're right...'

'What are you going to tell him? We have to get our stories straight.'

'Maybe I've got to get something medical done, nothing serious enough to make him worry, just some straightforward thing, and I'll be in hospital for a few nights.'

'He'll want to visit.'

'Aw, we can get around that somehow; let me think about it.'

'There's more.'

There it was, that jolt that made him realise that she wanted more out of it. 'Like what?'

'I want Leon to be with us too.'

'What? How is that going to help anything?'

'It will help me, Bill!' she said. 'If I'm going to look after Sam, I want to be able to look after my own son as well. It's probably the closest I'll ever get to being a mother to him.'

'But...'

'But nothing!' she said. 'Take it or leave it.'

'What will I tell them? What will I tell Thelma?'

'You'll work it out,' she said, 'and then you'll tell me. You'll have to work things out with their schools too. Just keep it consistent, Bill.'

'Jesus, Nancy,' he said. 'Orright.'

He leant over to kiss her goodbye, falling short as she moved away.

'You'd better go. I'll expect a call in about an hour.'

He drove off as details began to settle in his head. Through the back streets, he went, assembling the story along the way, keeping it as simple as possible. It started to fall into place, though there was something else that troubled him. He knew what Nancy wanted more than anything in the world. With the boys in her house for a week or more, what would she tell them?

21. Losing Control

'I'm old enough to stay here on my own,' he pleaded. 'I don't want to stay at Aunty Nancy's for a week! What about school and everything else?'

'No, Sam,' said his father, 'you're not old enough. Don't make this any harder, I've already got enough to worry about with hospital.'

'Is that why you've been so shitty?'

'What?... I haven't been shitty, just a bit worried.'

'But you said it was nothing to worry about, just a straightforward thing and some time to rest afterwards.' For Sam, the temporary move to Nancy's house and some story about cutting out a postate, or prostrate, or something, didn't ring true.

'Look Sam, it's just how it is, and I need you to do this, okay?'

He sat on the side of his bed looking down. He'd been told what was going to happen and he knew there was no way out of it.

'I'll tell your teacher, just so she knows.'

There was no reply.

'And it won't be so bad. You'll have some company. Leon will be there too.'

'No way!' he snapped as he looked at his father. 'I spend plenty of time with him already. Look, I'm happy to go there every Wednesday and he even comes with us to Sapphire Point instead of any of my other friends. Why does he have to come to Aunty Nancy's too?' He vented, although he knew it was pointless to argue.

He was angry, knowing Leon would at least have a choice, something his father wasn't about to give to him.

'I'll take the two of you over tomorrow,' said Bill. 'Aunty Nancy's looking forward to it so don't get shitty with her, okay?'

~

Bill spent the next couple of nights pretty much on tenterhooks. He quickly settled on a routine of sleeping for a few hours straight after work and then waiting anxiously for something to happen. Hoc had told him that it would happen on Friday night, but he'd come to learn the hard way that Hoc's information could be loose. What he did bank on, as far as Hoc was concerned, was that Marco's address was the real thing; that was important, for if his plan to sort out this whole mess was going to work, he had to know exactly where Marco lived.

In the meantime, his routine included setting up the house for the night, a system of amateurish strings attached to cups that would rattle out a warning hanging off every door and window that could be opened from the outside.

In both his bed and Sam's, he'd arranged a bunch of pillows under the blankets, and in the dark of night they did the job of appearing as sleeping targets. He turned the wireless on that sat on a small table next to his bed. From it came the soothing sound of late-night radio that men such as he would fall asleep to.

Bill had pushed the old wardrobe in Sam's room away from the wall to make a space behind it where he put a single mattress. It was there he made a camp of sorts, and when everything was set up, he'd have one last smoke and lay there. From time to time he'd doze, responding instantly to any creak or other noise of the night by grabbing the metal rod next to the pillow.

The hyper-vigilance was exhausting, and on the second night of living like this, about an hour before dawn, he fell into a deep sleep. It wasn't until the sound of rattling cups from a window at the back of the house disturbed him, and with that his heart pounded as he grabbed a piece of rope and the iron bar. He stood and waited in the dark for the next sound.

Cold sweat dripped from his forehead, his hands shaking as they gripped the piece of hard iron. Nothing. He waited in the tense quiet, hearing himself breathe, but still nothing. He swapped hands to hold the rod and wiped the sweat from his clammy hands on his singlet. Still nothing but a faint squeak and sound of a scuttle across the laundry floor. *Fucking rats.*

Still, he took no chances and crept through the rest of the house, holding the iron bar up and ready to fight. When he was certain that the visitor was just the rodent, he relaxed a little, and even though the sun was yet to rise, the adrenalin in his system had him already thinking about the new day ahead.

By the time he got to work, the morning sun was glaring at him. His head was bleary from a lack of sleep, and the day was too bright, making him squint as his foggy mind tried to focus. He thought of the two boys and wondered how they were going at Nancy's. He hoped she wasn't fussing over them too much, and more importantly, he hoped she wasn't telling them anything they didn't need to know.

He thought of the words he had with Thelma Green and how hard he had to work to convince her that the week with Nancy would be good for Leon, an opportunity for him to do something different.

For the moment, however, he needed to focus and move the forklift accurately about the warehouse. Twice that week already he had almost dislodged a pallet, coming dangerously close to causing serious harm to the others there. The morning dragged on painfully slow, and by morning smoko, he was on the verge of going home early. Coffee, nicotine and ten minutes of resting his head and closing his eyes in the lunchroom, however, gave him a second wind, and thankfully the afternoon passed less arduously.

It was Friday afternoon again, though a very different one than usual. There'd be no Nancy with a bottle of soft drink for Sam and Leon when he got home with the fish and chips. Instead, he went through the same procedure as the night before; by now, his fatigue and the state of his nerves brewing anger and the need to sort this thing out. He drank just one long neck beer to take the edge off and smoked to stop his hands fidgeting while, outside, the light of day faded once more and the streetlights began to flicker.

By the time he bedded down behind Sam's wardrobe, he felt as though he could sleep for a week, and despite his best efforts to stay awake, he quickly fell into a deep slumber. Hours later, he opened his eyes, unsure what it was that disturbed him. It took a few moments for him to gather his thoughts and realise where he was.

A surge of adrenalin shot through his body like electricity as the sound of cups rattling came from the back of the house. He was standing before he knew it, shoving the rope inside his pants and grabbing the iron bar, peering through the gap he had left between the side of the wardrobe and the wall. His heart thumped when he saw a narrow beam of light move up the hallway, changing directions to shine into the kitchen and then into the very room he was waiting in. Soft and slow footsteps trailed the light as it returned to the hall and then flickered towards the lounge room.

Bill fought his instincts to charge at the shadowy figure as it passed the open door of Sam's room. He made himself breathe slowly channelling his concentration, knowing that the soft radio playing in his bedroom would muffle only so much of any noise he would inadvertently make. The tranquil tunes and the smooth tones of radio's late-night love-God drew the intruder towards the false target.

Soft steps as he surreptitiously followed. His eyes were now accustomed to the dark and he watched the figure move inside the main bedroom and closer to the mound under the blankets. He watched the attacker silently raise a baseball bat high and then bring it down hard on the pillow imitation of Bill.

THWACK!

In that split second of confusion, Bill moved from behind and swung the piece of iron across the side of Marco's head. Stunned, he turned around, using every bit of energy he could muster not to stumble and fall, and raised the bat to retaliate. The next blow, however, was Bill's vicious straight right fist through the partly mended jaw. The intruder stumbled to the floor dropping the bat and landing on his knees, trying desperately to stay upright. Bill swooped on the bat, and after a swift backswing, followed it through the line of Marco's testicles. With the sickening groan of someone who has just had the life belted out of him, he fell onto his back until Bill rolled him over pulling his arms backwards and almost out of their sockets so he could tie the hands tightly behind his back.

'Thanks for dropping by, Marco,' he snarled. 'How about I give you a ride home.'

Marco mumbled something indistinguishable through his pain.

'Nah, don't thank me,' hissed Bill. 'Now get up!'

From the small concrete yard, they made their way through the rusty gate that had been left open, into the narrow lane and onto the street where a corner light post cast a smoky glow over the pavement.

'Take the lead, Marco... your car.'

Bill's eyes moved up and down, side to side, making sure there was no one around. When Marco faltered and staggered, he snapped his arms up high, extracting a sharp gasp of pain and moving him along until he stopped around the corner at a souped-up Datsun.

'You're fucking joking,' he said as he raided Marco's trouser pockets for the keys. 'Should've guessed.'

Bill unlocked the passenger door and pushed down on his shoulder, forcing him into the vehicle. 'Get in.'

'Where... you... tak... ing... me?' Muffled words from a broken mouth.

'Home,' said Bill as he got into the driver's seat, '78 Apex Street, Randwick. The thing is Marco, I know where to find you, wherever you go... just so you know.' He turned over the motor and they drove off. 'Better see someone about that jaw... looks nasty.'

~

The weekend brought a hint of respite for Sam. The abnormality of not going to school for a few days had finished, and now the streets were full of kids riding bikes and skateboards instead of wearing grey and blue uniforms. Through the week, Nancy had done her best to keep the two boys occupied, taking them on the bus to movie theatres and to the shops. Sam, despite his reluctance to be away from school and his mates, had begun to warm to the attention. He thought of his father from time to time, thinking that whatever he was having done in hospital couldn't have been too serious; otherwise, Nancy would have told him about it.

Nancy had managed to take some time off work, albeit to the annoyance of her supervisor at the government office block. She knew this was above any commitment she had to Bill, yet she could not deny that since she had agreed to it, having the boys with her gave her a warm contentment.

When talk came up about going to the park after Sunday lunch, she was thrilled to be included in that part of the boys' lives, although what they wanted from her was a far cry from how she saw herself being involved. Sam simply wanted information, how to find a decent park in the neighbourhood with trees to climb and enough space to kick a football around. Once Leon was used to the idea of their special holiday, he was happy enough to be there, and what he wanted was to go to a park and catch insects, just like the ones Sam had collected.

For Nancy, the motherly instincts she had been forced to suppress for so long had been stirred, and in her mind's eye she pictured herself when Leon was just a toddler, pushing him on a swing and then waiting patiently on a blanket spread in the shade of a wide oak tree. In her fantasy, she'd have a picnic ready to be rolled out as soon as he had exhausted himself playing. She longed to go back in time and take him home after such a busy day, feed and bathe him before tucking him into bed with a story about pirates and monsters.

In reality, she had to be content with sharing the twenty-minute walk with them to Newfield Park, an urban green space that boasted metal slippery dips, rusty swings, a merry-go-round that wobbled as it went around and a row of fig trees to climb and claim as their own territory. Reluctantly, she walked home by herself, leaving them there to their own devices and trusting them to be back before it got dark.

As she walked, her imagination picked up where it had left off with thoughts of Leon falling from the swings and running to her for a cuddle to make it all better. She knew her fantasies were futile, though, for the moment, she allowed herself to savour the serenity they evoked.

A calmness that is, until she had dwelled on them for too long, and as one thought cascaded into another, a bitter envy began to grow inside - resentfulness towards Thelma Green for being the one who had lived those moments with her son and a malignity to Sam's mother for not knowing how blessed she was, before walking away from a child.

She walked through the front door again to see the tell-tale signs of sharing life with the boys. She went to the sink and washed a collection of cups and plates. Then, she picked up a shirt that Leon had thrown on the lounge and saw a rip in it that needed to be fixed. Small tasks, but ones that kept her connected to her son. Her time with the boys was fleeting; she had only a few days left of being the mother.

She went into her room and reached under her bed for an old wooden sewing box with 'Nancy, 1947' carved into the top. She carried it to her son's torn shirt and sized up the length of cotton needed to repair it. She knew too that, when she was finished with Leon's shirt and while she was still alone, she needed to talk to Bill.

~

With the weekend all but over, things were not sitting well in Bill's head. *God knows what Marco's next move will be. For the whole thing to work, he has to be more scared of me than he is desperate to get even.*

Nancy's call had made him more edgy, hearing for himself how content she sounded, a joy in her voice that took him back in time to when they were punching their way through their restless, teenage years when everything seemed possible. He had asked her for a few more days, wanting to make sure that it would be safe when the boys came back, and now he was even more perturbed at how willing she was to keep them with her for longer.

He sat at the kitchen table, noise from voices on the television filling the room as he smoked and flipped the top off another longneck of beer. Outside, shadows crept over the narrow brick houses to the west as the late afternoon sun began to dip behind the factory rooftops that towered over them.

He thought about his two worrying predicaments. Firstly, if Marco's desire for revenge was stronger than the fear he had for him, there might be a revenge hit. Secondly, what was Nancy saying to the boys? He smoked and drank and became more restless. He had to do something, or he'd splinter. If nothing else, he had to find out what Hoc knew by now.

He'd been told to sit tight until there was any news, but he'd had enough of waiting. He took a long swill from the bottle followed by a deep drag of his smoke before stubbing it out. He stood and reached for the telephone handset that sat on the kitchen bench.

For the second and third time it rang out, frustration building and driving him to make another decision. He'd try once more, and if he didn't pick up, he'd go there in person. He dialled again - three rings then four and five and then finally a voice.

'Ngyuen residence.'

'What the fuck is going on, Hoc?'

'Jesus Bill,' said Hoc, 'I said that I'd call you; I don't want my missus picking up the phone with you on the other end.'

'I've had a gutful of waiting. You should have called by now.'

'And if you waited another five minutes I would have. I haven't been sitting on my arse doing nothing!' he said, trying to stifle his voice. 'Listen, can you get to the Zetland in twenty minutes? I've just finished talking to Steve and there's a bit to say.'

Bill always felt on edge when he was at the Zetland Hotel. He pushed open the door to the bar and saw Hoc. Inside, the long bar extended between two distinct camps. On one side of the smoky bar were moustached men in suits mingling with off-duty coppers wearing track suit tops over their uniform shirts. They'd stand, most of them with one hand in a trouser pocket and the other holding a large beer.

On the wall at the opposite end of the bar were two enormous prints of footballers decked out in red and green with rabbits on their chest. There was another gathering near the pictures, shifty in demeanour, smoking and drinking, and talking to one another in hushed tones. Occasionally, one of them would slip a piece of paper into another's pocket and walk out the door. Bill and Hoc gravitated towards the football pictures, nodding to a few of the men who were standing there.

'I've seen Steve, just about an hour ago,' said Hoc.

'Ok, what's he told you?'

'He went to see Marco in hospital after he found out about his accident,' said Hoc. 'Jesus! What did you do to the poor bastard?'

'Keep your voice down, Hoc.' He took a sip from his glass. 'I let him know that I don't like unexpected visitors. Then I drove him home.'

'Steve saw him yesterday and he was a mess, not sure if his face can be fixed this time, not to mention his ruptured nuts.'

'Is that it?'

'There's more. Steve went back to see him today, only a couple of hours ago.'

'And?'

'He'd pissed off, discharged himself and he's gone. There's something else too... So, Steve goes around to his place and he's not there either, him or that fucken Alsatian mongrel he has. Steve has a snoop around the place and it's clear... he's shot through... vanished.'

Bill was quiet for the moment.

'Did you hear what I said?'

'Yeah, I heard you,' Bill said. 'You've got plenty on him, eh?'

'Plenty on both of them,' said Hoc. 'Plenty on you too, Bill.'

'Could say the same thing,' said Bill. 'That's why we can trust each other, eh?'

'S'pose you're right.'

'Well maybe it'll all be okay after all. It's nice when a plan comes together.' He held up his beer, inviting Hoc to clink their glasses together. 'Cheers.'

'You're a cruel bastard.'

'You're no Saint either, Hoc. The difference is that you don't like getting your hands dirty. One more thing...'

'Who taught you how to talk like us?'

'Say what you mean, Bill - like an Australian?'

'Well, er, yeah I suppose, like an Australian.'

'Been here twenty years,' he snapped. 'I reckon I am Australian, just like you. We look different but we're just the same... same as Marco - we all bleed red.'

'Hmph, okay, so I'm a cruel bastard... but like you said, we're just the same, Hoc.'

'Maybe you're right,' he said. 'Now listen... Could be a good job coming up next week.'

'For fuck's sake, Hoc, let me get over this one first!'

~

It was after ten o'clock at night when the phone rang in the lounge room at Nancy's house. Although both boys had gone to bed in the adjacent spare room, they were still wide awake with any sleep pattern gone along with regular school hours. Sam was happy to be on the blow-up mattress next to the spare bed that Leon occupied. They lay there with Leon doing most of the talking, mostly about animals and Sapphire Point and his wildlife club.

Sam said what he needed to keep Leon happy, though his mind was mainly elsewhere. Nancy's night-time hugs and motherly fussing had rekindled the images of black hair, the white face and ruby red lips, and he tried to imagine them once more. His thoughts were broken by the sound of the telephone ringing.

'Hello,' said Nancy. 'So, what's going on?'

At first the phone conversation was of no interest to the boys, just a couple of grown-ups talking about boring stuff. That changed when her voice grew terse. The boys' ears pricked up as she was interrupted mid-sentence, only to raise her voice to speak again. With the mention of his father's name, Sam sat up in bed and tried to listen.

'That's rubbish, Bill... You said a few more days, not tomorrow.' More silence, save the sound of frustrated deep breaths. 'No, I haven't said anything to them... but I'm not ready to send them back... Bill, this might be my only chance to ever do this, don't take it away from me yet!'

It was too much for Leon to take on; Nancy's terse words were overwhelming him.

'Two more days like you promised!' she snapped. 'They are in good hands, Bill... I know you want what's best for them, of course I know... you are their father, but don't forget that I am Leon's mother too and I want that time with him!'

More silence as the words hit Sam hard. *Their father? What does she mean? He's my father! She can't be Leon's mother because that's Mrs Green! How can Dad be his father? What about my mother; he was with her, not Aunty Nancy!*

Tumultuous thoughts cascaded through his head, one realisation and then another hitting him in a barrage. He felt sick in his belly, hot and sweaty and then cold and clammy. He thought of all the Wednesdays, how it was always Leon at Sapphire Point with them and why it was always Leon who got what he wanted from his father. He felt confused; the only thing for certain was that he was angry with his father and Nancy for lying to him for all this time.

'Okay then,' she continued, 'two more days. I'll tell them that you're nearly better; the operation fixed everything, just need a bit more rest.' Nancy hung up the phone, breathing heavily after having to bargain for what she wanted, for what was rightfully hers, unaware that the two boys were standing in the hallway looking at her. She gasped at the sight of Leon who was confused and upset, while Sam stood there, straight faced and with a spiteful glare in his eyes.

'You heard all of that?'

22. Fragile

Nancy couldn't bring herself to forewarn Bill of what the boys had heard, and when he walked into her house that Tuesday afternoon after work, he knew things were not right.

She danced around the issue at hand, lots of small talk and being way too pleasant as far as Bill was concerned, especially since he was here to take the boys away. He saw it in their faces too, bewilderment in Leon's eyes and defiance in Sam's.

'What's going on, Nancy?' he said as they moved to the kitchen.

She avoided the question, instead looking at the boys and telling them to go and grab their bags.

'You told them something, didn't you?'

'I didn't Bill,' she spluttered, 'but they know a bit now...'

'Know what?' he said, putting both hands on the table and leaning forward.

'The phone call on Sunday night.'

'What about it?' he said. 'Wait a minute... Were they listening?'

'I didn't know.'

'It was late, Nancy. Why weren't they in bed?'

'They were in bed, Bill! But they must have been awake because they heard us talking.'

'Jesus Christ!'

'They heard, just like they're probably hearing this too, so calm down! I've had to explain a lot to them since. There was no way around it. But anything else from now on must come from both of us.'

Anger, then silence. Panic pulsated through Bill's veins as the first cracks around his secrets began to appear. He looked at Nancy, his eyes fixed on the bump in her nose, the same bump that he had, before his was rearranged in a fight. Her dimples, the same as his, only his were perpetually hidden under a three-day growth. Barely a minute passed while they waited for the boys, enough time, though, for a myriad of consequences to rush through Bill's mind.

He had to think of other things or he'd snap. He remembered the breaking waves at Sapphire Point all those years ago before there was any of this mess. He saw himself diving under them while she waited for him on the beach. He wanted to stay under but couldn't hold his breath anymore, bursting up through the blue ocean again to see her waving him in. Again, he saw himself dive under, deeper this time and holding the secret in the depths of the ocean, where it had to stay.

'Bill,' said Nancy, 'we have to talk about this.'

He was in damage control, desperate to contain the remainder of the awful truth that only he knew.

'I'm not up to it yet.'

'We have to talk to the boys.' She'd practised the spiel all day. 'It has to happen here tonight, before you all leave.'

'I... I can't.'

'Well, let me. There's no other choice.'

In his mind's eye he was diving under another frothy wave, holding his breath down where the green water touched the sand, vowing to never come up again.

'Go on then.'

The car ride home that night was surreal, each of them with a different interpretation of what had been said. Leon was scared, afraid that he would have to leave Ma and live with Aunty Nancy; only he wouldn't be able to call her that anymore because she would now be called Ma and that wasn't right.

Sam felt that he didn't know who the people in the car really were anymore; the mate he had always had to look after was now his brother because of what the man driving the car had done. He gritted his teeth, glaring across at the man who also made his mother go away.

Bill went quiet; enough had been said that night already. He knew he couldn't take Leon back to Thelma that night, not while he was like this.

Wednesday came and went with Bill having a day off work to talk things through with the boys, a fruitless effort as far as Sam was concerned. His father may as well have saved his breath.

By lunchtime, Bill had had enough of being on tenterhooks and attempted to create a small amount of normality by making some sandwiches and calling the boys to have something to eat.

'I'm not hungry,' said Sam when he came out of his room.

'Not hungry too,' said Leon in a grab for solidarity.

The stand-off was hitting the mark, the silence getting into Bill's head. 'Jesus Sam,' he snapped, 'I've just about had enough of this!'

'Dunno why you're the angry one,' said Sam. 'Seems like our lives have all been bullshit!'

Leon stood behind Sam, his hands shaking. He hated confrontation and although he didn't understand much of what was happening, he knew he was in the middle of it. 'Stop, stop.'

Bill saw the panic on Leon's face and did his best to calm down. 'It's not all bullshit. Nancy and I were always going to tell you when you were old enough to handle it.'

'Don't reckon,' said Sam, 'if we didn't hear Aunty Nancy talking to you on the phone, don't reckon you'd ever tell us. At least I know now why you like him more than me.'

'Who? Leon?' said Bill. 'I don't... but I don't like him any less either. It's just that... I'm... I'm his dad too.'

Leon stood holding his hands over his ears and shaking his head. 'No! You're Uncle Bill not Dad.'

'It's okay Leon,' said Bill. 'Things can be just the same as they've always been... I can still be your Uncle Bill.'

'I want to be with my Ma,' he added. 'I don't want to live with Aunty Nancy and call her Ma. I want to go home and go to the

Wildlife Club coz it's Wednesday and I want Sam with me coz he has tea with me and Ma on Wednesdays.'

Sam turned around and saw the despair in Leon. He put his arm around him. If nothing else had grown out of what was revealed on Sunday night, this had, a deeper connection, that of blood. 'It's okay Leon,' he said. 'I know its Wednesday and we can go to the Wildlife Club and have tea with Ma and...'

'And you can stay with her and still call her Ma,' said Bill, 'and you can still call Nancy Aunty Nancy like you did before.'

'And can I still call you Uncle Bill?'

'Yes mate, I'm Uncle Bill.'

'Can Sam and I go soon?'

'After we have some lunch,' said Bill, shifting his attention to Sam. 'You two can go to your Wildlife Club, but I'm coming over a bit later. I'll take the envelope over this week because I need to talk to Mrs Green.'

'Does she know? Does she know that I'm his brother?'

'Yeah, she knows.'

Sam picked up a sandwich and took a bite. He picked up another and gave it to Leon before looking downwards and slowly shaking his head.

'What? I've told you all there is to know,' lied his father. 'What's done is done and we have to get on with it.'

'It's still all shit, Dad.'

'Look, I don't know what else -'

'It's shit Dad,' said Sam, cutting him off. 'Leon has his Ma, and he even has Aunty Nancy too.'

'It's best that way.'

'I'm happy he has that, I really am... but...'

Bill knew where the conversation was going, and he wanted to close it down. 'That's good then that you're happy for him.'

'I'm your son too,' Sam said, cutting him off once more, 'Don't you get it? Where's my mum? I don't know what you did to her.'

'Nothing! I did nothing to her. She shot through when you were just a baby. You knew that!'

253

'And now Leon knows his mum,' he pushed on. 'What about if I want to find mine too!'

The discussion was left exposed like a gaping wound.

'Can we go soon, Sam?' said Leon. 'I want to see Ma.'

'Yeah, mate.'

For Sam though, nothing was normal anymore. The following day and the day after that, he left early for school as normal, being the first to get to Thompson's Park where he waited for Stephen and Mark. He'd never wagged school before but didn't need any persuading when Stephen suggested they head off to the tree park and maybe get a bus into the city instead. Mark wasn't interested, taken aback by Sam's unusual compliance with Stephen's mischief, and trudged off to school, promising not to tell anyone what they were doing.

Things had changed forever, and no one it seemed, was really who Sam thought they were. While the distance between him and his father had widened, he wasn't sure how long he could stay angry at Nancy.

From Bill's point of view, enough information had been disclosed. If he wanted to stop any more coming out, he knew he'd have to make sure that both Sam and Nancy felt as though they were getting something out of it. Then, hopefully, they'd be satisfied with that. That's why, when he received a phone call on Friday afternoon, asking when Sam was likely to return to school, he knew that he had to broach the issue more carefully than his instincts would have it.

Friday night rolled around again, with fish and chips on the table and Nancy there once more with her bottle of orange soft drink for the boys. On the surface, things looked normal, Bill swilling from his long neck of beer; though, beneath the thin veneer of small talk, there had been a shift in their world.

'Sam, there's something I have to ask you,' said his father. 'Don't worry; I won't go off my nut.'

'Yeah, what?'

'You been wagging school?'

'Maybe.'

'It's not a maybe,' he said. 'It's yes or no.'

Sam grabbed a couple of chips and shoved them in his mouth. He wasn't about to squirm, for in comparison, skipping a couple of days school didn't amount to much at all. 'Well, it's a yes then.'

'Okay,' said Bill, 'so on Monday, you'll be right to go back to school?'

'Er... Well, yeah.'

'Good,' said Bill. 'Now leave some of them chips for us too, eh.'

Nancy saw a softer side to Bill, something she hadn't seen since their time together, thirteen years earlier, before things went sour. She wondered if they could ever be like that again.

With full stomachs, Sam and Leon went out into the small back yard for a while. There wasn't much there to do, but Leon always enjoyed that part of the evening, trying to catch moths that would hover about the back light. With little success that night, Sam soon grew weary of the pursuit, leaving Leon to carry on by himself. He wandered back inside to where Bill and Nancy were talking.

'I was thinking,' said Nancy.

'About what?' asked Bill.

'We all know things are a little bit different than they were before.'

Bill reached for the tobacco on the table and braced himself for what was to follow. 'Not that different.'

'I was thinking... What would be the harm in me picking up Leon a little bit earlier on Fridays, so I could spend some more time here with him before you got home?'

'I'm not sure he'd want to,' interrupted Bill. 'He's only just getting over what we've told him already, I reckon it'd upset him even more.'

Nancy breathed in deeply and drank from her glass. 'He'd be fine, and I could get to know him a bit more. I don't see what the problem is.'

Sam could see the desperation in her face, a sadness he recognised. He looked at his father knowing how he could twist words around to get what he wanted. 'Why can't he? Why can't my brother come over earlier?' said Sam, more lippy than usual. 'Leon can still call you Aunty Nancy if he wants, but we know that you're his real mum. He can have two mums,' he continued. 'I wish I could call someone mum one day.'

It was unrehearsed, but it felt like an ambush. Nancy watched Bill lick the cigarette paper and finish making his smoke, the only distraction he could find from Sam's stinging words. He felt the walls closing in on him.

He was anxious to contain the wreckage, and he knew that he had to give them something. 'Looks like I'm outnumbered,' he mumbled, striking a match and breathing in the smoke deeply. 'Only if he wants to.'

'I'll go and ask him,' said Sam, turning around and making for the back door again.

~

The final days of primary school came and went. Afternoons were spent at the tree park, their oasis in the concrete, bricks and steel of the inner city. It was there, with Stephen and Mark that the days melded into evenings, when the birds and bats on flight from the Botanic Gardens made use of the fig trees, squawking and screeching as the golden sun began to dip behind the rooflines in the west.

Sam was clinging onto his boyhood while he still could, making secret hideaways with his blood-brothers in the upper forks of the fig trees, almost as high as the bats. His life was changing though, being wrenched into the problems that grown-ups had made.

He stayed at the park later and later each day, pushing the limits, one night getting home just as the streetlights began to flicker, the next night twenty minutes after that and the following one not until it was fully dark outside. Yet Bill said nothing other than that there were some sausages and potatoes for him in the fridge.

Things had changed alright, but soon he'd be back at Sapphire Point, and for a week or more, he hoped that everything would be the same as it had always been.

23. Exposed

Nancy had made sure she was to come along to Sapphire Point that summer, and now she was there, it felt strange. Stirred in her mind was a familiarity about where she was, pricking the memories of her first time there long ago, as an excited teenager.

To Sam, the holiday house felt more crowded, not so much because of the space that the extra person occupied, but rather from the sound of Nancy's voice, emanating from where she was sharing a bedroom with Bill. Sam was torn in how he felt, for now he wondered if Nancy was the real reason his mum had left. He hated thinking like that because it made him feel bad, and Nancy had also been the closest thing to a mother in his life.

Her insistence that she go with them to Sapphire Point was difficult for Bill to argue against, knowing in his heart that she had a right to be there. Not that he was happy about it. In his mind, the more they were all together the more likely it would be that another part of their history would unfold.

For Nancy, she loved being with Leon, though it still hurt every time he called her Aunty Nancy. 'What if you just call me Nancy?' she said to him one morning before the boys escaped to the rocks.

It was already hot, and Sam had scoffed down some cornflakes. Now he was waiting for Leon to finish his breakfast so they could go.

'But you're Aunty Nancy, not Nancy.'

'I mean, both of you,' she continued, desperate to remove the title that always kept her a step further away. 'Because you're getting older now, no need to call me Aunty anymore.'

'If Sam does too, I guess it would be okay.'

'I don't care,' said Sam, eager to get to the ocean. 'I'll call you Nancy if you want, doesn't matter.'

'Okay, I will too,' said Leon, 'but I might forget.'

'Then I'll remind you,' she said smiling. She wanted to gather her son in and hug him and tell him all sorts of things, but she knew that would push him away and she couldn't risk it. 'Now you both be careful out there today. Have you had enough to eat? What time will you be back? I'll have some lunch ready.'

Bill looked at the boys and shook his head slowly, knowing they were on the wrong end of a bunch of questions that ate into their Sapphire Point freedom. 'Go on, you fellas,' he said. 'We'll see you when you're hungry.'

The screen door slammed shut and they were gone.

'But Bill,' said Nancy, 'what time...'

'Relax, would you,' he said. 'There's only two times that matter while we're here.'

'And what are those?'

'Lunchtime and teatime,' he said, sitting down and reaching for the teapot to top up his cup.

'And when do they happen?'

'When we're hungry,' he said, 'the rules are pretty loose.'

She let out a sigh, sat down next to him and slid a cup towards him to fill. 'This might take a bit of getting used to.'

'You'll be right if I duck over the road for an hour or so later?'

'But I was thinking we might...'

'Might what?'

'Might go...'

She stopped herself mid-sentence, feeling for the first time since they got there like an intruder. *It wasn't meant to be like this; I thought we'd be like a family.*

'Doesn't matter,' she said looking into her cup.

Bill reached for his tobacco and grabbed a pinch. He looked at her, picking up on a familiar aura that he knew, if left unattended, would come back to bite him. 'I won't be there long,' he said, 'and what's say after we finish our cuppa, we go for a walk, maybe have a look at the water.'

She put her hand on his. 'That would be lovely, Bill.'

In the tidal pools on the rocks next to where the river began its meandering journey towards the foothills, Sam and Leon did as they had always done at this time of year. They searched for creatures in the crevices until they got too hot and then jumped into a pool as a wave crashed further out, with the cold water from it rushing across the rocks and splashing over them.

For Leon, being there reassured him that all was well. For Sam too; the child in him remained excited with the catch of a decent sized crab, one that could rip into the flesh of his fingers if he didn't hold it in just the right spot behind its nippers. The roar of another wave crashed over the rocks, making him feel excited by the big seas.

While his brother scouted for another crevice chock full of starfish and anemones, Sam trailed him around to the safe side where the rocks were protected from the crashing waves. Leon looked every bit the year older than when they were last there. Facial hair now sprouted over his masculine jawline, but inside he was the same. A simple child. He squealed with delight as he slid into a pool through a grove of rubbery kelp that had been washed in overnight by heavy seas. Sam squatted and watched him, knowing that if he liked it, he'd stay there for ages. He looked for a comfortable rock to sit down and lean back onto.

His mind wandered, massaged by the sounds of the ocean. The sun etched into his shoulders, and he gazed over the blue seas to the horizon, trying to picture his mother. He could see her long black hair hiding the white face and there was a splash of red lipstick. The image dropped easily into his mind's eye, but he wanted more, to see her eyes, for if he could do that, he knew that he'd remember her. He gave in to his imagination, letting it take him on a fantasy. He watched her lift her hand, fingertips of red, and pull back her hair. 'I love you, Sam,' said his faceless mother.

~

On the beach towards the Ocean-Spray Hotel, Bill stood with Nancy at the water line. She grabbed his hand as another wave broke and rushed up and over their ankles. 'Think I'll go in,' she said, turning around and running away from the water. She stopped and pulled her floral dress up and over her head, dropping it on the sand.

Bill watched her walk back towards him in her swimsuit, the same fifteen-year-old girl that excited him so long ago. He looked at Nancy, his heart pounding as she grew nearer and his thoughts taking him back to when everything was alright and when he wasn't ashamed, wishing that he'd never learned the truth.

~

That night, long after their bellies were full and the effects of the sun and sea had them weary and content to be in bed, strange noises woke Leon. Soon he was up and standing next to Sam, shaking him awake. 'Is Uncle Bill hurting her?'

The slice of moon shone through the gaps in the blinds that were moving back and forth from the sea breeze, flickering light about the dim room. Now awake and hearing the moans and groans through the wall, Sam felt nauseous. 'Ah shit,' he said. 'Don't worry Leon, he's not hurting her; it's just something that grown-ups do. It'll stop soon and Dad will start snoring. It's okay - go back to bed.'

'Sam,' he said, 'Uncle Bill is your dad and mine too...'

'We've been over this, Leon. He's your dad too, but you can still call him Uncle Bill if you want.'

Leon moved back to his bed and lay on top of the sheet. 'I tried to understand, Sam. But it doesn't make any sense. Why is he now my dad when he wasn't before?'

'Jeez Leon,' said Sam, yawning and trying not to hear the noise from the other room. There was a squeal, then an intense groan, then silence. 'To make you get born, they rooted, Aunty Nancy and my dad. So, he's always been your dad, but we just didn't know it.'

'What's rooted?'

'What they were doing when you woke me up. Rooting makes the baby grow inside the mother. Go back to sleep.'

The breathing from the room next door got slow and loud, then deeper and deeper until the first snorts sounded out.

'I can't sleep,' said Leon trying to make sense of it all.

'Okay, like I said, they rooted to make you and that's why Aunty Nancy is really your mum, but you can still call her Nancy.'

'But she's not your mum?'

'Nah, Dad rooted someone else to make me,' said Sam. 'He rooted my mum, but I can't remember her.'

'But we're brothers coz Uncle Bill rooted both of our mums.'

'Yeah,' said Sam yawning, 'we're brothers. Now go to sleep; sun'll be up soon.'

~

Birdsong said that dawn was breaking, soon followed by the drone of cicadas in the bush, a cacophony that woke the boys as usual. Behind the nest of green, fibro holiday houses was a vacant block of land with forest behind it. Eastern Grey Kangaroos would come out of the bush and graze there in the wet, grey dawn. The boys knew that if they were quick, they'd catch a glimpse of the kangaroos out the back before they'd bound away.

'C'mon Leon,' said Sam in his early morning raspy voice, 'let's get out early, before they wake up.'

'Okay,' he replied, 'but I'm hungry.'

'Put your boardies on,' said Sam while he pushed his legs through his shorts and grabbed yesterday's t-shirt from the floor. 'There's cold sausages in the fridge. I'll write Dad a note and grab some snags for us to eat on the way.'

Leon followed his brother, holding back the back screen door so it closed slowly and silently behind them. They walked to the back of the small yard and looked out through the gaps in the fence. It was invigorating to feel the fresh air on their faces, cool enough so that Leon's bottom lip shook as his voice quivered. 'Look Sam, f-f-five!'

'Let's see how close we can get before they jump away!'

They pushed open the rickety gate slowly, the creaking catching the attention of the large animals that looked up at them with startled eyes before taking off into the bush.

'Here you are,' said Sam, offering Leon a sausage. 'Have one of these. Let's go.'

The street was empty and wet. It had rained through the night, and for the boys, it was exciting to be the only people around. They walked past the empty beer kegs that were stacked on the footpath outside the Spray, towards Archie's place and the track that went down to the beach. Just as they got to the old man's fence, his front door opened, catching them by surprise, making them stand dead in their tracks.

'Look Sam, it's Archie!'

'Shh, Leon.'

'Good morning, young fellas.'

Was this the crazy old man, the mysterious and dangerous threat to any kid that got too close? He continued up the broken pathway, the sun now an orange ball glowing on the rocks at the end of the beach. He took full advantage of his walking stick, hobbling to the front fence, his morning ritual to grab anything that had been put in his letterbox from the previous day.

'Er... hello,' said Sam.

'I've seen you two boys plenty of times when you walk past... you're Bill's boys.' He looked at Leon. 'And you look a lot like he did when he was a kid. All these years and it's taken' till now to meet you.'

'You're Archie,' said Sam, taken aback by the old man's words, 'I know lots of kids who are mean to you, but...'

'Ah, don't worry about that,' he said, 'silly buggers, they don't know any better.'

'How do you know my dad?' Sam asked.

'I've lived here all my life. Bill came here with his folks... must have been near on thirty years back. Yeah, that's right, the war was over for a few years. I took 'em all fishing a few times, his sister too.'

'What?' said Sam with wide eyes, 'Aunty Nancy? She's not his sister.'

'Well, you could have fooled me... peas in a pod, those two. Nice kids,' he went on, enjoying a rare audience.

Sam's interest was tweaked; the old man must have been confused about a few things, like forgetting that Bill and Nancy were just stepbrother and sister, not real ones. 'Did you know my mum too - you know, when Dad came back as a grown-up?'

'Nah, only saw him and you kids. Thing is, haven't spoken to Bill for years... best that way.'

'How come?'

'Ah, you don't wanna know about that stuff.'

'Come on,' said Sam, 'you can't say that much and then stop.'

'Yeah,' added Leon in support. 'You're not scary anymore!'

'Ha,' chuckled the old man, 'don't s'pose it matters anymore... Thing is... I used to drink a bit... too much if the truth be known. Well, one night coming out of the Spray, 'bout eight or nine years back I reckon... you two were here back then, just littlies...'

'Was my mum with Dad then?' asked Sam. 'Was my mum here too?'

'Nah, I remember it was just your dad and you two youngsters. He'd get you fed and washed up and into bed... Then he'd come over for a drink or two... just leave you for a little while, and he could pretty much keep an eye on the place from the pub anyway.'

'Okay, so what happened?'

'Yeah, so what happened?' echoed Leon.

'Ah... Well, like I was saying... I was leaving the Spray, bit too full I'd say, and a couple of blokes from out of town, young blokes they were... well, they have a go at me, try to get my wallet.'

'Did they,' said Sam. 'Did they get it?'

'Probably would have, but your old man must have been watching; he'd have his drink on the veranda of the pub, like I said;

kept an eye on things... Well, they didn't know what hit 'em. He cleaned 'em both up.'

'Whoa,' said Sam, a touch proud of the man he was still angry with. 'But I don't get it...why haven't you two spoken for so long?'

'Ha. Well, not sure what happened to them two young blokes, but I do know that they went to the coppers about being bashed up.'

'But...'

'Yeah, I know; don't make any sense. Well anyway, your dad gets a visit from the cops, and they tell him he could be in big strife... on account of the head injuries. Anyway, the coppers know what's really going on and pretty much tell him to keep his head down if he knows what's good for him... stay away from the Spray and stay away from me and let them worry about everything else.'

'And that's it?' said Sam.

'Yeah, that's about it,' said Archie, shuffling around to begin heading back to the house. 'Just habit these days... he steers clear of me and that's fine. Tell me... does he tell you to stay away from me too?'

'Nah,' said Sam, 'he just says for us not to bother you like the other kids do.'

'Fair enough,' said Archie walking away.

'Hey Archie,' called Sam after him.

The old man stopped and moved his head slightly to the left to hear. 'Yeah?'

'Probably catch some mullet later,' said Sam. 'Want some for your tea tonight?'

~

The rising sun was still low in the sky when they got to the rocks, and although most people at Sapphire Point were still in bed, the day was already heating up and getting sticky. The solitude upon this pristine part of the coastline fed their imagination and the threads of boyhood created their escape. Over the expanses of ocean rocks, there was no trace of civilisation to be seen, and they could be explorers venturing into the great unknown.

By the time it was afternoon, the boys were once again fishing for mullet. Sam was intrigued by Archie, and having said that he would bring him some fish, he couldn't go back on his word. For all his faults, Bill had taught him well.

They stopped outside Archie's place where Sam opened the squeaky gate to take a step towards the front door. It felt like they were encroaching upon forbidden territory. Sam knocked and they listened to some movement inside and the sound of slow, shuffled steps before the front door partly opened.

Archie's eyes took time to focus. 'Ah, it's Bill's boys,' he said in a croaky voice that wasn't accustomed to much conversation, 'Wanna come in, I've got fresh milk.'

'Sure,' said Sam, and they followed the old man slowly inside the house, 'Gotcha those fish!'

'Thanks for that, 'said Archie. 'They'll make a nice meal tonight. Drop 'em in the sink.'

Archie had a good look at Leon. 'My word, you look like your father when he was a kid, same nose I reckon.'

Talk of his father still didn't sit well with Leon. 'Does he mean Uncle Bill, Sam?' he whispered.

'Yeah, mate. We've been through this; you know that's who he means.'

Archie went on with what he was saying. 'Yeah, dead spitting image, a lot like his sister too... those dimples, just like hers; only they looked a lot cuter on her,' he chuckled.

'We've gotta go now, Archie,' said Sam, once again convinced that the old man was totally muddled up. Nancy didn't look anything like his dad.

When the boys returned to the holiday house, they told Bill and Nancy about meeting Archie. Bill took a deep breath and glared at Sam.

'He said he loved us calling in, told us about how he used to know you and that you're a good man... remembers you too, Aunty Nancy.'

'Archie?' she said, 'from across the road, down past the Spray?'

'Yeah. He said he used to take you two fishing, years ago.'

'I remember him,' she said. 'He's a nice old bloke... didn't know he was still around.'

'Funny thing is,' said Sam, 'he reckons that you and Dad are real brother and sister, on account of how your noses are the same, dimples too... like Leon's.'

Bill felt a cold sweat form on his brow, and for a moment he couldn't draw a breath. 'Ah, silly old bugger,' he managed, 'probably a bit doddery, his age n'all.'

His words caught Nancy's attention; they sounded defensive, as though Bill was rushing in to quash what had been said. 'Er yeah,' she said. 'I remember when Hazel, my mum, introduced me to Tom and you, Bill. I was fifteen when I met you. Tom and Hazel brought us up here for a holiday.'

'Yeah, I was sixteen. I remember.'

'Well enough of that,' said Nancy, 'who's getting hungry? I was thinking that maybe for a special treat, we get some take-away Chinese for tea?'

'Whoa, yeah!' said Sam.

'Can I have some fried rice?' said Leon.

'What do you say, Bill?'

'Yeah, sounds like a good idea,' he said, eager to send the conversation in a different direction.

For the first time in a long time, the events of the day had Sam feeling pretty good about the world.

'Leon and I love Chinese,' he said. 'I love that you're here with us, Aunty Nancy... I mean Nancy.'

For Nancy, they were words that, for so long, she wanted to hear. It caught her unaware and she felt a touch light-headed. Turning her head away so that the others couldn't see the emotion in her eyes, she dabbed them dry with the sleeve of her blouse.

Leon followed Sam's lead, wanting to add to the moment. 'And soon we'll have another baby, maybe another brother or even a sister. I don't really want one, but it might be orright.'

'What?' snapped Bill. 'What are you talking about?'

'Where did you get that from, Leon?' added Nancy.

'It's okay,' said Leon, 'we heard you rooting, you and Uncle Bill. I know it's what grown-ups do, like when Uncle Bill rooted you to make me and when he rooted someone else to make Sam.'

'That's enough of that, Leon,' yelled Bill.

'It's okay, I know that rooting makes babies.'

Sam stood, gob-smacked at what was being said. He tried to say something, anything, but words wouldn't come.

'Well Leon,' said Nancy finally, 'it doesn't always make babies, only sometimes. There's not going to be another baby.'

'Promise?' asked Leon.

'Promise.'

'Okay. Can I have some spring rolls too?'

It had been the strangest day that Sam could ever remember. Despite the sleep he had during the day, events had caught up with him, and after dinner, with a full belly he was very sleepy as he sat in front of the small television.

'Why don't you wash up and get a good night's sleep?' said Nancy, when both boys started to yawn. They needed no encouragement and Leon followed his brother to the bathroom where they started brushing their teeth.

When they were alone, and the soft snoring could be heard from the boys' room, both Bill and Nancy could feel the tension from unfinished conversation. 'Leon does have your nose, Bill,' she said softly, 'and so do I.' There was a pause and Bill again felt the walls closing in on him. 'And I've seen your dimples when you've had a shave... I know you try to cover them up, but I've seen them, they are the same as mine.'

Bill sat staring blankly at the screen, shaking his head slowly.

'How long have you known, Bill?'

It was useless to deny it any longer. 'I knew after you got pregnant with Leon,' he said in a quivering voice. 'Tom told me then. He was so angry; said that you had to get rid of it. Then he goes and kills himself. I guess he couldn't handle it.'

'I always thought he just couldn't go on without Hazel.'

'More like he couldn't face what was happening without her.'

'Jesus,' she said, shaking her head, 'all that time and you never said a word; that's why you married Anne! Marry her and you could never be with me; it was a fresh start for you.'

'For you too!'

'So you said at the time... But you knew! You knew about Tom and Hazel! And you didn't tell me anything. I was a wreck, Bill! You didn't say a word. How could you have done what you did?'

'I was just trying to make it better for both of us.'

The room went quiet; the secret for all those years had escaped its enclosure.

Finally, Nancy spoke. 'And Anne leaves you and Sam, and you come knocking again. I was stupid to let you back in my life.'

'I was trying to protect you.'

'Ah Bill,' she said looking down and holding her brow in her hands, 'You were looking after yourself. All this time and you didn't tell me what you knew; all the time since, doing what we've been doing. I'll never forgive you.'

'I couldn't stay away,' he blithered, 'I knew it was wrong, but I just had to see you, be with you. I'm sorry...'

'Sorry that I've found out, you mean! It makes me feel so...'

'Tom and Hazel should have told us at the start.'

'And you kept the lie going all those years!'

'I couldn't say anything; didn't want anyone to know, not even you. After a while, I figured that if no-one knew, it might not matter anymore.'

'Of course it matters! Oh God, I feel sick! Bit by bit, it starts to come out. What about the boys?'

'They know enough, Nancy; they don't need to know anymore.'

In the next room the exhausted boys slept, while outside, the noise of cars and shutting doors told them that it was closing time at the Spray. A couple of plovers squawked and made swooping sounds when more people leaving the pub got too close. Bill lifted his head and looked at her, his legs feeling like jelly; there was nothing he could say.

She returned the stare. 'Bill... the boys can never know.'

Part Five: Sisters and Brothers

5th August 2000

24. Chasing

The main street at Sapphire Point had changed a lot. It was the year 2000 and Sam was now a family man in his thirties. He parked the car outside the same old holiday house he once spent a week of his childhood at each summer.

He was sad when he knew in his heart that it, along with the other dilapidated houses with it, would soon be bulldozed to make way for something much grander. Progress was sure to be on its way.

Kim got out of the car and opened the door for Leon while Sam went to the other side of the car and lifted their new baby boy, Anh, out of the safety capsule. They would walk from there.

It was late winter, with the Sydney Olympic Games only a couple of months away. Expectations of the event, and how the city would present itself to the world as the host, was the talk of the town. It had been a wonderful year for Sam and Kim so far, highlighted by the birth of their son just a week before Sam's thirty-second birthday. When Kim first told him that she was pregnant, he was so excited; after all the years wondering if they would ever be parents, it was going to happen at last.

For weeks after the announcement, in the quiet part of the evening they would watch television and chat about names for the baby. One night, about a month before Anh was born, Kim was lying on the lounge, her head on a pillow and her legs resting on Sam while he ran his hand over her glorious baby bump. They were watching a popular drama series called 'Sea Change' when one of the guest characters in the show caught their attention.

'He looks Vietnamese,' said Kim, 'reminds me of my brother.'

'Yeah, I think I've seen him on some other show. In fact, I'm pretty sure he's a refugee like you. I've heard something about him before, can't quite remember his name,' said Sam.

'Check when the credits come on, the show's nearly over.'

A few minutes later, Sam was doing as he was told, watching carefully as the names of cast and crew rolled up the screen. 'There it is,' he said, 'Anh Do. Yep, sounds Vietnamese alright.'

'Nice name, don't you think?' said Kim.

'Which one, Anh or Do?' joked Sam.

'Anh, silly!'

'Mm,' murmured Sam, nodding, 'yeah... what do you think... Anh Davis?'

'I like it,' said Kim.

'Me too.'

A few months later, in the main street of Sapphire Point with his wife, new son and brother, Sam breathed in the salty air. It was the first time in fifteen years they had come back to the seaside town of their childhood summers.

The last time they were there, in 1985, was when Sam was a teenager and had just gotten his driver's license. Bill and Sam, along with Nancy and Leon, set off in the new Ford Fairlane for the annual pilgrimage. It was a week of respite from the complications of life, before they'd once again return to their separate houses, coming together as they had done for so long, on Friday nights.

That summer holiday of 1985 was a test of patience for all. Leon, physically a young man but mentally still a child, grew increasingly frustrated because no one wanted to go to the rock pools with him. He continued to be out of sorts since Thelma had passed away from a massive heart attack one year before. After that, he had gone to live with Nancy, and although he knew that she was his real mother, he missed his 'Ma' terribly.

In that final week at Sapphire Point, Nancy had done her best to keep Leon calm, all the while feeling as though she was walking on eggshells, trying to smooth the persistent ruffles between the others. Each night they had each hoped that the next day would be better. Unfortunately, it wasn't, and so they finished the wretched holiday early and went home. With that, the yearly ritual of summer holidays at Sapphire Point had come to an end.

Since that final summer trip to Sapphire Point, Nancy had come to accept that her life would never bloom into what she wanted it to be. Even the short time each summer when they would be together as a family had ceased to exist. Sadness and disappointment were now her forever companions.

There had been a time when her instincts told her to cut ties with Bill, for when it came out that he was her brother, she felt that they existed on the wrong side of what was decent. Beneath the anger from being deceived, she constantly struggled with the shame of what she had done.

Yet out of the mess, her beautiful son, Leon, had emerged. With each day, he grew more important in her life, and she was constantly drawn closer to him. While the rest of the world remained oblivious to the circumstances between her and Bill, she lived as though she was trapped in a bad dream.

Her only moments of escape came from her interludes with Bill and the love she had for Leon. For years, she watched him grow physically to become a man, and cherished the child-like innocence that kept him from being corrupted by the adult world.

It was too difficult for Leon to think of her as his real mother, yet despite this, love grew between them as it was always bound to do. She had become a sad woman, but always pushed past that to care for him, unwavering in her maternal companionship.

Such was Nancy's life for the fourteen years after their final trip to Sapphire Point. Right up to when he was a man in his early thirties.

In the winter of 1999, Leon's life was to be upended once more when Nancy's sad life ended in a tragedy that took her and Bill together. It had been a long working week and finally Friday was upon them, and with that came the ritual that had helped carry them through the years, meeting for some take-away food and a few drinks before coming together in union, their taboo remaining hidden from the world.

As usual, Bill drove from work and called at Nancy's to collect her. Although Leon was developmentally delayed, he was a grown man, and Nancy felt that he could now be left on his own for a few hours. He too had a Friday night routine of watching some animated videos while he ate Chinese food.

After saying goodbye to Leon and going over the usual rules with him, she left with Bill. They were going through the motions, prepared to have as much alcohol as they needed to dull the torment of what their lives had become and be together for a wisp of respite from the world.

Three streets from home, Bill looked into the rear vision mirror, noticing something that jolted him out of the banal routine. Nancy picked up his reaction and asked him why suddenly he looked worried.

'Just sit tight,' he snapped, and put his foot down on the accelerator putting some distance between them and the black car behind.

'What's going on, Bill?' Nancy shrieked. 'Slow down!'

'We've got some company,' he mumbled, concentrating on getting further away. 'Bit of a misunderstanding, that's all...'

'Be careful!' she yelled as he swerved sharply to the left to speed through a laneway. 'What have you done?'

'Like I said, a misunderstanding... He thinks I've ripped him off, taken some stuff I wasn't supposed to...'

'And did you?'

'Kind of.' He reached the end of the lane, turning a sharp right and knocking over some bins in the process.

'Can't you just give it back?' she yelled. 'I'm scared, Bill.'

'This fella, he doesn't like talking. I don't know how he figured out it was me.'

Bill knew his way around the labyrinth of back alleys and laneways and wasted no time in weaving through them towards the suburbs in the south.

'Where are we going?' said Nancy in a panic.

'Not sure; just need to think.'

He joined a busier street, satisfied for the moment to slow down and join the flow of traffic. They were silent, Nancy petrified and Bill struggling to think of a way out of his latest mess. He checked the rear vision mirror every few seconds. They continued down King Street into Newtown, seemingly out of trouble for at least the present moment when as if out of nowhere, he saw the same menacing car speeding up on them from behind.

'Shit!' he said. 'Hold on!'

Again, the big Ford Motor took him away from the pursuer with Nancy feeling that her heart was in her mouth. He weaved through the traffic, risking all as he passed slower vehicles, swerving onto the other side of the road, only just missing oncoming traffic. He could still see the black car in the distance behind and was determined to get out of King Street and onto the highway as soon as he could.

There were traffic lights at the intersection he was fast approaching and they were green, allowing the cars in front to take the highway turn.

Stay green you bastard!

Closer he came, still green, closer.

Shit, yellow. We're not stopping!

Yellow lights changed to red. 'Hold on, Nancy,' he yelled, 'hold on!'

The tyres of his car screeched as he tried to beat the traffic that was beginning to move in front of him. Cars skidded to a halt, their horns blaring as he swerved through them and almost onto the highway south when a fully loaded truck sat motionless right in front of them. The collision was immense with a crash that could be heard back in Newtown.

~

For Sam, this trip in 2000 to Sapphire Point with his wife, child and brother was to say goodbye to his father and to the aunt whom he had grown close to since he was a boy. Leon knew about death and that he was farewelling his Uncle Bill and Aunty Nancy. For Leon, they were now in somewhere called heaven with his Ma.

The loss of his father took something else away from Sam, the link to his real mother. While Bill was alive, it was a subject that Sam had found too difficult to broach with him, and he had put it off for so long. After the crash a year earlier, it was now too late. The only shred of connection he had to her was the complicated timeline on art paper from 1969, a confusing yet cherished testimony of love from the first woman in his life.

His father was gone now, along with Nancy, and he wondered if this mysterious woman who somehow continued to make his heart pang had also passed away. They had a long walk ahead of them, but that's how he wanted it, breathing in the nostalgia as they passed by one part of their history and then another.

~

Sam breathed in the salty air, the smell taking him back to the summers at this scruffy town on the coast, where his father taught him how to fish and where Leon played in the sun for hours. The cold wind coming off the ocean felt strange to the brothers for they had only ever been there in the heat of summer. They were rugged up, each of them, with Anh tucked cosily into a baby carrier that fitted onto Kim's chest. Sam and Leon each carried a string bag holding an urn of ashes.

Sam wrapped his spare arm around Kim's shoulder as they walked. 'Thanks for doing this,' he said softly. 'I mean, my old man wasn't the nicest man in the world.'

They ambled along, with Leon by their side, dutifully carrying the string bag. It felt strange traipsing down the track from the main street to the beach on such a cold day. They continued to the rocks where they once played as children. Waves crashed further along, but they were protected where they stood, where the water came calmly to them and then receded in a hypnotic rhythm.

'This is the perfect spot,' said Sam.

'Do you want to say anything?' asked Kim.

'I don't think so,' he answered, as he spilled the urn's contents into the water. 'It's just about remembering them, I think.'

'Alright,' she said, holding his arm.

'Your turn, Leon.'

With that, the final remains of Bill and Nancy blew through the windy air to settle across the ocean.

25. Disclosure

Belinda-Anne made sure that every detail was complete so the beautiful seascape could rest against the wall in her studio and be totally dry by Friday. She had been on tenterhooks since phoning Sam to tell him that it was ready.

She had painted for him before, and on several occasions since he left school, she had helped him with his own artwork. This painting, though, was so much more than just an eye-pleasing image. She was desperate that it was perfect and had done her best to capture the mood of Sapphire Point from the photographs Sam had given her. She wanted to be sure that when he looked at the painting, he'd be taken back there.

The night before Sam and Kim were to collect the painting, Belinda-Anne kept herself busy, tidying up the living area of her studio and planning what she could cook for them. She had never been nervous about them visiting before.

Where she looked at the painting, through the glass door that separated the living area from her art studio, she was satisfied that it was good. It stood against a wall in prime position and that was where Sam was going to first lay his eyes on it.

There was something else that was making her feel uneasy, and she knew that it existed somewhere in that studio. Pulling open the partition, she made her way past the painting of Sapphire Point, to a large cupboard that she rarely opened. More than a dozen of her works were inside, stacked up against each other, paintings that for some reason had not seen the light of day for a long time.

She lifted the closest one out and rested it on the side of the cupboard, then another and another. Finally, she took one more painting out, exposing what she had been looking for. After all this time, the lines and arrows, the deep purple and black hues and most of all, the desperation in the woman's face called out to her. It was the first time she saw the jewel that could have been a famous showpiece, her work, 'Luna Flight', since she locked it away years before. With trembling hands, she extracted it from the cupboard and carefully carried it to where she placed it next to the Sapphire Point seascape.

Giving herself a moment to gather her thoughts and to make sure she knew what she was doing, she packed the other paintings back into the cupboard. They were coming for the seascape, but she now knew that there was a further dimension to their visit. Would 'Luna Flight' be a magnificent and mystical addition to Sam's gift or was she exposing it to the world to finally come to terms with her past?

~

Friday morning was busy at Sam and Kim's house. By seven in the morning, Kim was nursing Anh after he had woken from a solid sleep, having farewelled Sam for the day. She had been looking forward to the day off work so she could spend it entirely with Anh before the planned visit to Belinda-Anne's that evening.

Sam was already driving Leon to his sheltered workshop on his way to work, using it as a chance to explain how he was going to be on his own that night until they got home very late. 'There's plenty of food in the fridge, Leon,' he said, 'and you know the list of things to do.'

'I know Sam,' he answered, 'and make sure I lock the door tonight before I go to bed.'

'You've got this,' he said with a smile that boosted Leon's confidence.

'Yeah, I've got this!'

Sam pulled up the car, watching his brother get out and walk to the gates of the workshop. He noticed how much older Leon was looking, more stooped and with a bit of a limp.

Friday afternoons were always welcomed, but on this day, there was a sense of urgency when Sam collected Leon on his way home. 'You look worn out, Leon,' he said as they drove. 'Are you feeling okay?'

'I'm okay.'

'You know what to do when Kim and I aren't there tonight?'

'I follow everything that's on the list and there's plenty of food in the fridge and lock the doors at night.'

By the time they got home, Kim was ready and had Anh fed, hopefully so he was content to sleep on the way into the city. Sam was also eager to get going and had a quick shower to freshen up before they said goodbye to Leon.

When it was time to go, they backed out of the driveway, arms out of the window waving as they went. Sam stuck his head out of the side window and called out to his brother, 'You've got this?'

'I've got this!' he yelled back, holding up an arm and waving them off.

They drove away, tooting the horn as they went, watching in the rear-view mirror, at Leon limping back inside. 'He doesn't look very good,' said Kim. 'Is he alright?'

'He doesn't look well; we need to get him seen to.'

~

Belinda-Anne was cutting and slicing vegetables. They would be there within the hour, and if anything, the nervousness that had given her a disrupted sleep the night before was more intense now. She finished preparing the bowl of salad, as colourful and creative as one of her paintings, and carried it towards the dining table.

In her peripheral vision, she saw through the glass partition to where the lights in the studio were shining on the fervid mood of the Sapphire Point seascape and on the haunting image of 'Lunar Flight'. Placing the dish on the table, she turned and looked more fully at the paintings, and when she did this, it made her heart skip a beat. Was she ready to do this?

She had decided to wait until they arrived before having a glass of wine, but changed her mind and poured a small glass, just to take the edge off. The vegetarian lasagne was cooking beautifully in the oven, the first aromas starting to waft into the room, telling her that everything was going to be alright.

She did her best to remain calm and sat down to take a sip of wine. The sudden sound of the phone made her spill a bit on the table.

'Hello, Belinda-Anne here.'

The connection was crackly with interference. 'Hello Belinda-Anne, its Kim.'

'You're still coming, aren't you?' she said. 'I mean, is everything alright?'

'Yes, of course... I can't hear you very well - I'm on a mobile phone. Can you hear me okay?'

'Kind of.'

'I only rang to say that the traffic has been awful and not to worry if we are a little late.'

Belinda-Anne let out a sigh of relief. She had worked herself into a state and wanted to see this thing through. 'Ah, that's fine,' she said. 'See you when you get here.'

She picked up a magazine from the bench near the phone and sat at the table to flick through its pages to kill a bit of time, topping up her glass on the way. The distraction worked for a while until she gulped what was left in her glass and looked again into the studio. The display lights weren't quite right, and so she opened the glass partition and went to address the situation, shifting the beams so one now focussed on the white water crashing over the rocks of the seascape and the other on the woman's face of 'Lunar flight'. Walking back into the living area, she decided to leave the glass doors open.

She wondered what time it was, the hands on the out-dated clock on the wall having stopped moving. She figured that it must be getting towards six o'clock, although at this time of year the bright daylight made it hard to tell. She decided against pouring more wine, choosing to check that the lasagne was not getting overcooked.

Turning the oven temperature down, she tensed suddenly when there were four knocks on the door at the bottom of the stairwell.

Breathing in deeply she slowly took a step forward. Trying to muster some confidence, she took a series of more determined steps down the stairwell until she saw the silhouettes of Sam and Kim, holding the precious child, through the small stained-glass piece at the top of the door. With that, she held her breath and stood motionless, unable to take another step down. Again, there were four loud knocks on the door, and she turned around, scurrying back up the stairwell and into her apartment.

Running through the living area and into the studio, she lifted 'Lunar flight' and carried it back to the cupboard from which it had briefly escaped. She closed the door on it and turned the key to lock it back into its imposed hibernation. A wave of relief fell over her and she felt as though she could breathe again. She walked through the apartment and to the stairwell once more. 'Coming!' she called out as she traipsed down the steps.

26. Tides

'It makes me feel like we're actually there,' said Sam looking at the seascape on the wall in their home a few days later. He stood gazing into it, immersed, and for a moment he thought he could hear the waves crashing on the rocks.

Kim stood next to him while Anh played on the floor. 'She's done a beautiful job; it's an amazing gift.'

Anh let out a cry, bringing them both back to the present moment. 'Are you taking the whole day off?' she asked.

'Yeah, I think I'll have to,' he answered. 'The doctor's appointment is at 9:30, that's if he's on time. Then if it's anything like last time there'll be some running around to do. Not sure how long it will take, and I want to get as much sorted as we can today.'

'He seems worried, Sam. I don't like seeing him so sad.'

'That's the other thing. I want to spend some time with him, hopefully doing something he likes.'

Leon appeared from the bathroom. 'I'm ready to go to the doctor.'

'Alright, let's go.'

Sam kissed Anh's forehead and then Kim on the lips. 'See you later this afternoon.'

It was a long morning for the two brothers, beginning by waiting until well after ten before the doctor could see them. Sitting in a waiting room was difficult for Leon because it was Thursday and that should be a workday at the nursery.

Finally, inside the consultation room, the doctor asked Leon a lot of questions to which he responded with simple answers and monosyllabic groans. Sam did his best to fill in the gaps of his brother's replies and to add whatever information he thought was relevant. After recording some observations and taking a few notes, he asked Sam for a private discussion without Leon.

'What do you think, Leon?' said Sam to his brother. 'The doctor and I need to have a long talk. It might be confusing and boring. Do you want to listen, or do you want to wait outside? There's a shop next door, you can have a treat and a drink if you want.'

Leon didn't need to be asked a second time. 'Can I have some money, Sam?'

'Sure,' said Sam reaching into his pocket and extracting a bunch of dollar coins. 'There you go. Make sure you save some room for lunch though,' he said passing over the money and putting a brighter light on his brother's mood.

As Leon closed the door behind him, Sam felt that he was about to hear a lot more than had been disclosed so far. The doctor began with a few more questions about what Sam had noticed recently and if there had been any notable changes in his brother, either physically or in his demeanour. At first, Sam struggled to add anything to what had already been said but as the doctor probed with specific queries, it prompted him to say a bit more.

Over the next ten minutes or so, Sam had elaborated on several points about Leon, his worsening fatigue and how he had aged so dramatically in recent months, not only in his physical capabilities but also in how he was getting confused about things.

As the consultation ended, the doctor printed out a series of request forms for blood tests, several scans and a referral to a specialist that shocked Sam. It was for Leon to see a geriatrician, a specialist who oversees the care of the elderly.

'But he hasn't even turned thirty-four yet,' queried Sam.

The doctor nodded and drew a deep breath. 'In terms of calendar years, he is a young man,' he said. 'However, in terms of his physical state, the same cannot be said. We can investigate causes, especially genetic, but I must be as honest and frank with you as I can be...'

'Please, be honest.'

'Science and medicine have never been able to reverse the aging process; if we could, do you think the world would cope?'

'But Leon is still a young man. It's not fair.'

'It is absolutely not fair,' said the doctor. 'We can't say how quickly he will continue to age, and there are things that people can do to keep them feeling as young as they can...'

'Good diet, a bit of exercise and fresh air?' said Sam shaking his head. 'He needs more than that.'

'You can certainly help him with those things, but more importantly help him be happy... We will run more tests to investigate likely scenarios and syndromes.'

'I'm sorry,' said Sam. 'It's all a bit much to take in.'

'There's nothing to be sorry about. You came here for solutions, to know what to do to make him better. What we are having is a difficult conversation - I understand that. Remember, for now the most important thing is to help him to be happy. What does he like to do? Does he have a favourite place?'

Sam absorbed the doctor's words and nodded slowly. 'Sapphire Point.'

~

It was obvious to Kim that the day had delivered information that was disturbing for Sam. During the late afternoon, he was quieter than usual, spending most of the time in Leon's company. He put on a facade however, that all was well, and over dinner he was too chatty, a thin disguise over his preoccupation, one that Kim easily saw right through. She knew that when they were alone there would be much more to talk about.

As the evening meal finished, Leon began to clear the dishes as usual, happy that things seemed to be back to normal, with Sam and Kim staying at the table for a while, just like they always did.

'So, are you going to tell me what the doctor said?' asked Kim while Leon made kitchen noise in the background.

'Sure,' he answered, 'when he goes to bed.'

'Okay,' she said. 'Meanwhile, I'll tell you about our day.'

'Please.'

'The big news is that your beautiful boy said his first word today!'

'What was it?' he asked, immediately feeling uplifted.

'Dada, of course,' she said smiling. 'Maybe you'll hear it for yourself later when he wakes up.'

'Hope so,' he said. 'Any other news from today?'

'Belinda-Anne rang.'

'Did she want to know if we've hung the painting and how it looks in the house?'

'Well, yes, she did ask about that,' said Kim, 'but she was more interested in how Anh was.'

'She was certainly taken by him, wasn't she? Couldn't take her eyes off him.'

'Yeah, I noticed,' she giggled. 'I didn't realise just how close she was to you though.'

'Why? What did she say?'

'When she asked things about Anh, she made a few comments about what you must have been like as a baby... and what you were like as a kid.'

'I guess we do go back a long time now... She had a pretty big impact on me when I was learning to draw and paint at school. She's one of the reasons I became an art teacher.'

From the adjacent kitchen, Leon finished his nightly chore and walked back to the dining room to remind Sam that the dishes were ready to be dried and put away. 'I'm tired tonight,' he continued, yawning, 'I'm going to get ready for bed.'

'Thanks, Leon,' said Kim. 'Come and say goodnight before you do.'

'Okay,' he replied, walking away towards the bathroom.

Kim looked at Sam. 'He doesn't seem himself lately.'

'They're doing a heap of tests,' said Sam, beginning to open up. 'Thing is, he's not going to get any better. He's an old man, Kim; can't you see that?'

She placed her hand on his arm. 'Are you okay?'

'We have to make an appointment to see a geriatrician... for a man in his early thirties.'

She could see the distress in his eyes. 'Oh Sam,' she said, 'there must be something the doctors can do.'

'Not really.'

'So, what now?' she asked. 'What can we do?'

Sam breathed in deeply and let it out with a sigh. 'The doctor did say something. It doesn't sound like much in the grand scheme of things, but when you think about life, it's often the little things that mean something.'

'Sam, it's nearly always the little things that count,' she said. 'What did the doctor say?'

'He said that we need to make him happy,' he said with glassy eyes, 'so I'm thinking to myself, what would make him the happiest he could be?'

Kim nodded slowly, knowing what he meant.

'I'm thinking just him and me,' he said looking for approval, 'maybe a few days, like we were kids again. Remember when we went there to spread the ashes?'

'I do, Sam,' she said, squeezing his arm gently. 'He would have loved to have gone over to the rock pool to sit in it, it didn't even matter that it was winter and the water was freezing cold.'

'I can take him back so he can sit in those pools, like when we were kids,' said Sam. 'We could catch mullet, explore down the river... eat Devon sandwiches...'

'While he still can.'

'Yeah, while he still can,' said Sam as the moisture in his eyes formed a drop that trickled down his cheek. 'Will that be alright with you?'

'Of course,' she said, leaning over and kissing his forehead. 'Maybe you can find your own inner child too while you're there.'

He smiled and looked over his shoulder at Belinda-Anne's seascape. 'You know, the weird thing is that I feel like a boy again when I look at the painting, like I could step into it and be a child again.'

'That must be a beautiful feeling.'

'But when we were there in winter, the ashes day, it wasn't like that... We had things to do, and it didn't feel like that at all. Why didn't it, Kim?'

'Ah Sam. Reality, I suppose,' she whispered. 'You're not a little boy anymore.'

He nodded in sad reflection. 'But Leon is.'

~

While Sam and Leon spent time at Sapphire Point, Kim had her sister, Mai, come and stay with her. They spent time cooking their favourite Vietnamese dishes and sharing stories on the couch. It was fun to be together and on Mai's first night, time passed very quickly.

The night was getting on and Mai began to yawn. 'I'm getting tired,' she said. 'I think I'll get ready for bed.'

At that moment, Anh began to cry, and Kim got up to feed him. 'Me too. I'll be going to bed as soon as Anh is fed and settled again. You sure you don't mind sleeping in Leon's room? All clean sheets and everything has been tidied up.'

'Of course not,' she answered. 'I'll try not to disturb all those papers on the desk.'

'Oh, sorry,' said Kim. 'I forgot about that, I'll get them out of your way in the morning if that's alright. They're all our birth certificates and special documents, ours and the ones that came with Leon when he moved in. Sam asked me to try and find them and have a look through them; he wants to see if he can find anything about the family history... I think he's trying to find out if there was anyone else like Leon, you know some relative hidden away somewhere in the past with the same affliction.'

'It all sounds intriguing,' said Mai. 'I'll make sure not to touch them at all.'

'Okay,' said Kim. 'I better get to Anh, he sounds like he's got a wet nappy.'

'Goodnight.'

~

It was easy to book a few days at the same holiday house at Sapphire Point. There were many other more salubrious dwellings in high demand, but Sam was sure that the dilapidated place they had stayed in so many times was where Leon would want to be. Now with green paint flaking from its exterior, the old place was simply in waiting, the land beneath being the real value of the property. Any holidays had in the old places were a bonus for the owners, just some extra cash in their hands as they waited for the right time to sell to developers.

Inside, it had hardly changed from the last time they stayed there fifteen years ago. There was a new television with an outside aerial, and the cumbersome refrigerator that had always been too noisy had been replaced with a smaller one that made the kitchen look bigger. The same kitchen table and chairs were there, and the two bedrooms made Sam feel as though no one had been in them since they were last there.

It was dark now but with the limited amount of moonlight when they looked outside, they could tell that someone had done a few makeshift repairs on the backyard fence.

'What room do you want, Leon?' asked Sam, sitting a bag full of groceries on the bench, and still holding his overnight bag.

'I always sleep in this one, the bed near the window, remember?'

Sam laughed, loving his brother's recollections and how such a small detail was so important to him. He figured it meant that Leon was truly making the intended journey back through time to when they were kids. He wished that he could too. 'You get the whole room to yourself, not like it used to be.'

'Why?'

'There's just the two of us, so I can put my things in the room Uncle Bill used to sleep in.'

Leon went quiet, taking a few steps into the old bedroom and dumping his bag on the floor.

'You hungry?' Sam called out.

'No thanks... I thought...'

'What, Leon?'

'You said that it'll be like when we were kids.'

'Kind of. I mean it's just you and me, but we have to do the grown-up stuff too.'

'But the other room...'

'What about it?'

'We used to both sleep in here, me on this side of the room and you over there.'

Sam nodded and smiled. 'Okay, so if we do that, you in that bed and me in this one, then everything will be fine?'

'Yeah,' he answered, 'and then we can get up early and see if there's kangaroos on the grass behind the fence, near the bush.'

'Then go down to the rocks?' added Sam.

'Yeah, the rock pools!'

'Hungry now?'

'Yeah, we can make Devon sandwiches.'

'Happy?'

'Happier than ever!'

'Well, that makes me happy too,' said Sam, smiling and remembering when they were kids.

~

'It smells different, Sam.'

'What does?' he answered with bleary eyes, still coming to terms with the new day after such a disturbed sleep on the narrow bed with a worn-out mattress.

'Here,' said Leon, 'the house.'

Sam tipped some cornflakes into a bowl and more into another. 'Want a banana chopped up on yours?'

'Yes please,' he answered. 'I'll get the milk. I saw some kangaroos before, you were still sleeping, but I had a look outside.'

'Ha-ha, how many?'

'I counted five, but when they knew I was there looking through the fence, they all jumped away.'

They ate some of their cereal and Sam began to liven up. 'I think I know what you mean,' he said, 'it does smell different.'

'Yeah, it doesn't smell like Uncle Bill.'

'Ha-ha. It's the cigarette smoke... There's none here, that's the difference.'

They finished eating their breakfast, and with no need for conversation, they fell into a routine that had been entrenched in their childhood. Sam went out to the car, returning with some fishing gear while Leon pulled a few pieces of bread from the loaf on the table and threw it in a bucket. 'Mullet for tea, tonight... We can cook up some spuds with 'em, eh Sam?'

'Yeah mate,' he answered. 'Rock pools first? It's still a couple of hours before the tide turns.'

Their conversation had been lifted straight out of 1980. Out through the back screen door they went, hearing it snap shut behind them on their way out to the main street. The early morning dew was still sitting on the ground where the sun hadn't yet burnt it off. Looking down the road, they could see small family groups in the distance and a few teenagers with surf boards under their arms, walking down the track to the ocean. Sam and Leon crossed the road and followed their familiar route towards the rocky headland, walking past the Seaspray Hotel and then Archie's house. 'He's not really scary, is he Sam?'

'Archie?'

'Yeah, he's nice and he likes the fish we bring him.'

They walked on, passing right by the old man's front gate. 'You do know that he's not here anymore, don't you Leon?'

'Yeah, I know,' he answered. 'He's with Ma and Uncle Bill and Aunty Nancy.'

'That's right. And you're right, he wasn't scary.'

'But that means he is somewhere; they are all somewhere. So, he is still nice.'

Sam looked at Leon, knowing that it wouldn't be that many more years before he would be with them too. 'Yeah, you're right, they're somewhere; it's just that we don't really know where that is.'

'Are you sad, Sam?'

'No, mate. I'm here with you. How could I be sad?'

'Sam,' said Leon, 'I know we can't bring Archie fish anymore, if that's what is worrying you... I'm not silly.'

A smile spread across Sam's face. He swapped the hand he was carrying the rods with, freeing up his other arm as they walked, to put around his brother. 'I know you're not silly, Leon.'

~

The next day, Kim asked if Mai would like to help her sort through the folder of birth certificates and documents that Sam had asked her to find.

'Are you sure you want me involved in that?' asked Mai, 'it sounds very personal.'

'I'm sure I can share things with you... especially after some of the things you told me last night!' said Kim giggling.

'Ha-ha,' laughed Mai, 'I suppose you're right.'

Kim fetched the thick folder of papers and brought it to the dinner table where they sat down to begin work. 'I really should get all of Nancy's certificates and things sorted; they should be put in with our stuff, Sam's special documents and things... keep them all together.'

'What exactly are we looking for?' asked Mai.

'I'm not sure really,' pondered Kim. 'I think that first we put them in order, oldest to youngest; we're looking for unfamiliar names, maybe a long lost relative of some kind. For some reason, Sam's Aunty Nancy built up a collection over the years, and we've put all our stuff with it - it's all mixed up.'

'Mm, I wonder,' said Mai.

'What?' said Kim.

'What Nancy was looking for.'

'Well, you do know that she was actually Leon's mother.'

'I remember something about that, but I was always confused about that - who was Thelma Green?'

'She raised Leon from a baby,' said Kim shaking her head. 'Don't ask me why - it was all pretty messed up. Maybe Nancy was looking for some answers of her own. Anyway, there are quite a few documents here.'

'Sounds like Sam's Dad had an interesting life,' said Mai with a smirk.

'Shady character, let's just leave it at that.'

For the next hour, they shuffled pieces of paper around on the table until they decided to break for a cup of tea. With that, Anh began to stir, a murmur first and then a more pronounced cry.

'Good timing,' said Kim. 'How about you make the tea and I check on Anh?'

'Sure,' said Mai, 'and then when he's settled, we can get back to it. It's looking interesting so far.'

Drinking her tea, Kim was happy for Mai to nurse Anh back to sleep, especially since it was her last night there.

'Hey, there's something else I'd like to show you... Sam hasn't tried to hide it or anything, because it was with the document folders in the cupboard, but he's never actually showed it to me. I had a look when I was getting all these papers together.'

With Anh in Mai's arms, Kim went and fetched the subject of her conversation from her room. Returning, she unfolded a large piece of paper, holding it up so they could both see.

'What is that?' said Mai.

'I have no idea. Look, there's a long line with arrows and words going all over the place, and it all leads to this symbol of a rocket with Apollo 11 written on it... lots of written descriptions. Ooh, what's this bit?... Something about Soviet space travel, and on this bit it says something about America... How strange!'

'What's written across the bottom, Kim? It looks like a message.'

'It says, *"My darling Sam, this is how the world was just before your first birthday. I will always love you, Mum."*'

'Whoa,' said Mai, 'and you've never seen it before?'

'I have, but I've never really taken any notice of it. I'm starting to think that Sam wants me to find it and ask him about it. It must be special to him... probably the only thing he has from his mother... Maybe he finds it hard to talk about and he wants me to ask him about it. What do you think?'

'You could be right. What are you going to do with it?'

'I think I'll fold it back up for now and put it back when we finish. Then when the time is right, I'll tell Sam I found it, and then if he wants to say anything, he will. I'll let him get over this trip away first.'

The discovery added a new sense of purpose to their work. Kim resumed sorting things into chronological order, occasionally picking up a document for closer inspection. She was happy for Mai to return the sleeping Anh to his cot while she continued. 'There are a few names I've never heard of,' she said as Mai came back. 'They may help Sam with what he is looking for, who knows?'

'There's a familiar one,' said Mai pointing, 'William Thomas Davis... Sam's and Leon's father.'

'Ah good,' said Kim, lifting the birth certificate from the few remaining papers underneath. 'Ooh, and look at the one underneath; it's Nancy's I think... Nancy Jane O'Brien...'

'Not Davis?'

'They were never married; I know that for sure,' said Kim. 'Bill was married to Sam's mother, who ever she was.'

Kim looked closely at the birth certificate of William Davis, absorbing each detail. She put it down and replaced it with that of Nancy O'Brien. A strange look gripped her face as she flitted from one to the other, checking and re-checking what she was reading.

'What is it?' asked Mai, seeing the bewilderment in Kim's face.

'I'm not sure I'm seeing this correctly... Someone has written on Nancy O'Brien's certificate.... It says the child is Nancy Jane O'Brien. Father - Thomas Charles Davis. Mother - Hazel Mary O'Brien.'

'Okay,' said Mai. 'I'm not sure...'

Kim picked up William Davis's birth certificate again. 'It doesn't make sense... If you look at this one,' she continued, 'it says that the child is William Thomas Davis. Father -Thomas Charles Davis; Mother- Hazel Mary O'Brien.

She looked gobsmacked at Mai, shaking her head. 'That can't be right... Can it? Was Bill Nancy's brother?'

~

The light through the window and the chattering birdsong woke Sam early on their last day at Sapphire Point. Leon continued to sleep soundly, worn out by their activity at the rocks and river catching fish. When he did finally stir, it took him a long time to get out of bed and start his day. Slowly, he walked to the kitchen. 'Today is the last day,' he said in a croaky voice.

'That's right, Leon. But you know what?'

'What?'

'We can come back another time. Would you like that?'

He nodded, starting to feel good about the day.

'Banana on your cornflakes?'

'Yes please,' he answered. 'Fishing today?'

'Sure,' said Sam, 'but we might need to go soon; it'll be high tide in a few hours, and we need to get down there to catch some mullet on the run in.'

Back at the river, Sam was content simply to be with Leon. 'Remember when we were kids,' he said, 'and you didn't want to catch the fish?'

'Yeah, I remember.'

'You just wanted to watch them in the bucket.'

'But Sam, I'm not a kid anymore, am I?'

The comment caught Sam by surprise. 'No mate,' he said, 'you're a grown up, just like me.'

~

That evening after eating, they sat in front of the television in the house that smelt of cooked fish, satisfied and sleepy. Sam thought of the few days they had just shared, knowing that tomorrow it would be over, and he'd be driving home to his family and Kim's news of the past few days. He looked at Leon who was happy to watch the television.

'You feeling good tonight?' asked Sam.

'Yes. This is the best holiday I've ever had.'

'Ever?'

'Ever! Thanks for taking me here again. I love you, Sam.'

It was the first time that either of them had ever said that to each other and it shook Sam to his core. His life alongside his older brother had all been worth it, from the days at the Wildlife Club in the shed of Thelma Green's backyard, sticking up for him when he couldn't do it for himself and now having him as an uncle to his baby boy. He had given Leon so much of himself, but only there and then, in the shabby living room of the old holiday house, did he finally know that Leon had given him so much more in return.

They were at Sapphire Point together, and that moment in time was all there was.

Epilogue

12th June 2021

Sam sat next to Kim at the extra table they brought into the living room. She was holding one of the nine hundred remaining pieces of the jigsaw that was spread in front of them. The other hundred or so formed the edge to the picture. It was just the fourth day of a government-imposed lockdown in the winter of 2021. Sydney's population had been confined to their homes to be kept safe from the latest outbreak of the COVID-19 pandemic.

Anh was stretched out on the lounge chair, earphones linking him to the music on his phone. He was frustrated because, months earlier, that night had been planned as a dual celebration. It was to mark the end of semester examination results with his friends and to get together for his twenty-first birthday.

Anh's lanky body filled the length of the lounge, his head on a pillow at one end and his sock-covered feet hanging over the arm at the other. The chatter of his parents was incessant as they searched for pieces, and their laughter was annoying whenever they found a piece that fitted into the picture. He loved them dearly but there was only so much of their company he could stand. He had the volume of his music turned up high.

He craved the faces and voices of his peers, for at his age there was always something going on and each day that passed was another day lost. Lately, one of his friends had introduced a couple of new girls to their group and Anh was pretty sure that one of them,

Casey, liked him. Instead, he was stuck at home with his parents whose quirky habits were driving him crazy.

'Anh!' his father called out, 'we can hear that from here. Turn it down or it will damage your ears!'

'He can't hear you,' said Kim. 'I'll go over and tell him.'

She stood up and walked to the other side of the room and shook her son's shoulder.

'What?'

She motioned for him to take out his earphones.

'Please turn down the music,' she said. 'If we can hear it from over there, it must be too loud.'

Sam used the interruption to go to the kitchen and make a pot of tea. It was nearly four-thirty. 'We're having tea, Anh, want some?'

'No thanks,' he yelled back, looking up from the lounge, firstly at his mother, who, at fifty-three, remained slender in the blue jeans she was wearing, and then at the thinning grey hair on the back of his father's head as he walked to the next room. 'I've got to get out of here, Mum.'

'There's still plenty of light, why don't you go for a run? You are allowed to get out and exercise, even if it is a lockdown.'

'Maybe... Well, yeah, it might make me feel better.' He nodded towards the kitchen. 'Doesn't he get on your nerves sometimes?'

'Ha! Of course, we're married,' she said with a smile. 'Now sit up for a moment and give me a bit of room.'

Anh put his feet on the floor and his mother sat next to him. He had her looks, the high cheekbones and almond shaped eyes beneath his head of jet-black hair. 'But he has a heart of gold, and he loves you to bits.'

'Yeah, I know,' he conceded. 'I'm just a bit bored at the moment.'

'It's hard for us too,' she said. 'Your father misses his job; working from home on computer screens doesn't come naturally to him.'

'He's a dinosaur; he needs to catch up with the rest of the world.'

'It's not that, Anh,' she was quick to say. 'The thing your father has always loved about teaching, is being with the kids through thick and thin, good times and bad. I mean quite literally, being there with them... He's struggling with this lockdown. He's worried that it will go on as long as the last one.'

'Yeah, I suppose you're right,' said Anh with a smile. 'Come to think about it, I wish more of my teachers were like him and had his patience.'

'He learnt that a long time ago, looking after his brother.'

'I wish I knew him,' said Anh. 'I've heard bits and pieces about Leon and what he was like, but I can't remember much about him.'

Sam returned with a pot of tea and two cups on a tray and carefully put it down on the jigsaw table.

Anh took another look at his father. 'Actually, Dad,' he called out, 'I'll grab another cup.'

'Ah, good,' said Sam, his face lighting up with a smile, 'come and join us.'

~

Belinda-Anne was cocooned in her studio apartment at Darlinghurst. She had been out to grab a few supplies, mainly vegetables and some grains, but the restrictions of being allowed out just once each day for essentials made her feel trapped. She had struggled up the stairs to her studio's front door, having to pause halfway to give her aching knees a break. It would be another day before she could briefly venture outside again.

Now in her late seventies, and spending far less time painting, she had to plan out her day thoughtfully, spreading out the tasks so that she wasn't ready for bed at a ridiculously early hour. Earlier that day, she had worked for an hour on a portrait she was doing from pictures in a book, but she'd had enough of that for now. It was nearly time to begin preparing something for her dinner. Not that she was hungry or that she would eat very much, but it would occupy that empty stretch of time between late afternoon and dark.

This lockdown was particularly cruel because it was coming up to Anh's birthday, and she had planned to put in a huge effort to get to the other side of Sydney and take him a gift. In all her years of knowing Sam and then his family, her company with them was always guarded, always insisting that their get-togethers would be at her place. Consequently, she had never once visited their home. Now that Anh was older and had his own life to get on with, he had stopped accompanying his parents when they went to see her. What saddened her now was that she could feel in her waters that this one and only planned trip to their house would be her last chance.

Over the years, her work with people across the local art scene had kept her busy. However, following a health scare a few years earlier, she'd dropped out of many functions and few of the people she knew remained in touch. It was Sam and Kim who took the time to make sure that she wasn't alone and that she truly had friends. Her fondness for Anh, as well, never waned, and whenever they visited in the past, she loved to have something special for them to take home for him.

That night, after managing to eat a small meal, she considered reading her book for a while, another Bryce Courtney story she was halfway through. She had always liked his descriptions of people and places, some of them providing inspiration for her to paint. Usually while she read, the sounds of life in hectic Darlinghurst would penetrate her walls and give her a comforting backdrop which kept her feeling connected to the world. Now though, as it had been for days, it was eerily quiet, and it unnerved her.

She sat in the silent room, with her book unopened on the table, feeling old and lonely. In that frame of mind, she pondered her mortality and what she had done with her life. She tried to think of what she was leaving as her legacy. There were paintings of hers hanging on walls all over the country and that gave her solace, especially the seascape that occupied a prize position in Sam's home. But would anyone else remember her and know her story?

The one piece of work that told the world who Belinda-Anne was remained locked away in a cupboard on the other side of the glass partition in her studio, and if she happened to die that night, that's where it would stay. In that reticent apartment, one of many in a comatose city, she yearned for the connection that her work once provided. She pondered her pieces of art, especially 'Luna Flight', lamenting that it had only seen the eyes of appreciative onlookers for the briefest of moments before she was bombarded with questions about it that she did not want to answer.

The world, her life, were different now. As if being given notice from some form of oracle, she knew that there was something she now had to do. Rising slowly from her chair she opened the partition into the working space and walked to the cupboard of old paintings. Lifting the key from its dusty top, she unlocked it and leaned the first paintings in the stack forward. She pulled a couple more towards her and then another one until she saw what she was looking for. She lifted out her greatest ever work of art and returned the other paintings.

Carefully, she carried it back to the living room section of the studio apartment, where she stood it up against the table. She removed her Bryce Courtney book and put it back on the shelf, leaving the table clear. Back through the partition she hurried, returning with a roll of brown paper, bubble wrap, tape, scissors and a thick felt pen. For the next twenty minutes, she spread out the paper on the table and put layer upon layer of bubble wrap on top, onto which she placed the framed masterpiece face down. On the back of the frame, she began writing. When she was finished, she thoroughly wrapped it, and with the thick felt pen, began writing an address. She grabbed the phonebook and searched for a courier.

~

It was still morning, though to Sam it felt much later. He had started the day's work early in the cluttered room that served as a study. By nine o'clock he already had the instructions for his students uploaded and ready for them to work on remotely through the day. With that done, he had time to read what his older students had sent him to mark and critique, before updating himself with photographs of progress his senior students had made on their major works. How he missed doing all this face to face, the screen in front of him hurting his eyes and giving him a headache. He decided to listen to some music for a while and flopped into the lounge chair to do just that.

His concentration was interrupted by the sound of Anh finally stirring after a late night of study. The beats of hip hop sounded through the walls, and rather than make an issue of it, Sam got up from the lounge and lifted the needle from his vinyl. It was time to get back to work anyway. Before he got back to the study however, the doorbell rang. No visitors were allowed during the lockdown and so, with excitement he rushed to the front door knowing that it could only be one thing, that moment of joy during isolation when a postal delivery is made.

'Expecting a delivery, Anh?' he yelled on his way to the door.

'No,' was the answer from behind the shut door, 'probably something Mum ordered.'

Sam opened the door to find a large rectangular package resting against the front of the house. 'Thanks!' he shouted to the delivery man who was already at his van.

He lifted it up and carried it inside, resting it against the jigsaw table in the living room. In large letters it was marked 'Fragile' and was addressed to the Davis Family. He was eager to rip the brown paper off and look inside but forced himself to be patient and wait until Kim got home before doing that.

The break had been good; he was refreshed, and he knew there was not going to be a better time than right then, to get back to work. Back at the computer desk, he worked through to the afternoon when the sound of Anh in the kitchen and the aroma of the onion and garlic in the stir fry being cooked made him hungry. He pressed 'save' on the file he was working on and joined his son.

'Smells good,' he said. 'Looks like you're making a lot.'

'Yeah,' said Anh, 'I knew you would be wanting some lunch and I figured that Mum would be home soon. She had an early shift, right? At least being a nurse, she gets out to work.'

'She'll be back soon, but we need to look after her; she'll be exhausted.'

'Well, there's plenty of food, lots of rice in the cooker too. Help yourself.'

'Thanks Anh, that's great. Going to join me?'

'I'll take mine to my room, eat it while I work.'

Sam looked at his watch and realised that Kim would be home within the hour. He decided that he would wait and eat with her, and then they could open the big brown package together. He grabbed a spoon and took a large mouthful to try on his way back to the study. If he worked hard and fast before Kim got home, he might be able to have the afternoon off. He sat back down and reopened a file.

Just before three o'clock, he heard keys opening the front door. He saved what he was working on and shut the computer down, happy that he wouldn't be using it again that day. He could see by the look on her face that Kim had put in a huge day. 'Come and relax,' he said. 'When you're ready, I'll get you a drink.'

'Thanks Sam,' she said, 'just let me get these shoes off. Cup of tea would be great.'

She went to her room to change out of her work clothes. 'Something smells good,' she called out from the room. 'Which one of you has been cooking?'

'Anh,' he answered. 'I waited to eat with you. It'll be a late lunch, that's if you're hungry.'

'I am,' she said, returning to the kitchen. 'And what's that over there, in the living room?'

'We got a delivery,' said Sam. 'Did you order anything?'

'No,' she said, 'aren't you going to open it?'

'Do you want to eat and then open it?'

'Let's open it first; could be something exciting!'

'It's addressed to the Davis Family, so we should call Anh too.'

Anh heard the conversation and emerged from his room to greet his mother.

'Thanks for cooking lunch,' said Kim, 'but let's see what we've got here first.'

In the living room Kim and Anh sat on the lounge while Sam peeled off the outer layers of paper.

'Be careful, 'said Kim looking on. 'It could be breakable.'

He pulled off the numerous protective coverings. 'It's a painting,' he said with a look of intrigue as he pulled off the remaining wrapping and rested it against the wall.

'Whose it from?' asked Kim.

'It doesn't say... but what an interesting piece! It's absolutely striking... See the look on the woman's face in the sky, the pain in her eyes...'

'It's pretty weird, Dad.'

'Certainly different, kind of... cosmic. I don't know how else to describe it... Look there's initials in the corner... B-A.D. That's...'

'Same as the seascape of Sapphire Point,' said Kim. 'That's one of Belinda-Anne's.'

Sam lifted it up, taking a closer look at the detail. 'There are the familiar swirls that she does so well. He held it out in front of him so the others could see what he meant. From that angle he saw the back of the frame, noticing the handwritten message. 'There's a note on the back. It's to me.'

He started reading it silently to himself.

'What does it say, Dad?' said Anh, to which there was no reply.

As Sam continued to read, his face changed shape and his lips began to quiver. He turned ashen white, and he put the painting back down against the wall.

'Are you okay?' asked Kim.

'Dad,' said Anh, 'what's the matter?'

'I'll be alright,' he answered. His hands were shaking. 'I just need to be by myself for a minute.'

He went to his bedroom.

'Sam,' called Kim, 'what is it?'

'Just leave me, please.'

The mother and son looked at each other, confused and perplexed.

'What was written on the back?' said Kim.

'I'll bring it over and we can read it together,' said Anh.

'Shouldn't we wait until your father is with us?'

'We need to know what's upset him,' said Anh, getting up and retrieving the large painting. 'Come on, Mum.'

Anh lifted the painting, turned it around and rested it back against the wall. Together they crouched down, and Kim began to read it out loud...

My darling Sam,

A long time ago I left you a note about the amazing world you were born into. It was such a complicated yet wonderful place, and when I made that timeline of what was happening on our planet, the first men were about to fly to the moon; what an incredible thing that was. It was then that I also took flight because, my beautiful son, I honestly felt that I had no choice. I don't expect you to understand, and I can only ask that one day you will be able to forgive me. I have always kept you close, to my eyes and ears, but mostly to my heart, intoxicated with the life you have made and the love you pour on your beautiful family, Kim and Anh. I see you too, when I look into the face of my cherished grandson. Perhaps this wretched lockdown has forced my hand in opening up to you at last, not knowing when it will ever end and making me feel at times as though I may never see you in person again. I'm not getting any younger. This painting has spent its days locked away in a closet, a dark cupboard, just as my secret has also been locked away. In freeing the painting, I am freeing myself, and it is the biggest risk I have ever taken. I have and will always love you,

Belinda-Anne Dawes (Anne Davis, your mother)

Kim left Anh stunned and squatting in front of the painting and went to Sam. She found him sitting on the bed, looking numb and distant. 'Sam,' she whispered, kneeling on the floor and wrapping her arms around him.

'All this time...'

'Oh Sam, what are you going to do?'

He stared blankly ahead, trying to come to terms with what had just happened. 'I've wanted to have a mother for so long.'

'And now?'

'Kim, can you do something for me?'

'Yes, of course.'

'Wrap it back up and hide it away somewhere. I'm not ready for this.'

~

In the silent studio apartment that was now her world, Belinda-Anne lay on her bed, regretting. The loneliness and perception of her own twilight years made her free 'Lunar Flight' along with her secret from their dark chambers. She was now wondering if, on the other side of Sydney, what she had done was causing pain to the people she loved the most. *Hadn't I already hurt Sam enough, so long ago when I walked out of that house in Surry Hills? What right do I have to seek his understanding and forgiveness?*

She reached down to the wall at the back of her bed side table where her only phone line was plugged into the wall and yanked it out, descending deeper into the exile she believed she deserved.

~

At the end of another day, across the suburbs, Sam remained preoccupied with Belinda-Anne's disclosure. He tried to be communicative, though it was easy for Kim to see how troubled he had become.

'Are you alright?' she asked one night while they sat on the lounge chair.

'It's like Belinda-Anne has fallen off the face of the Earth.'

'Try ringing again,' said Kim, passing over her phone to him. 'Here, use mine.'

He took the phone and pressed Belinda-Anne's name on the contacts, only to hear once more that the person he was trying to reach was unavailable. 'I know she is still there, so why won't she answer? I don't understand why she would send us the painting and tell me everything, only to close up like that.'

'I suppose she was ashamed of what she had done... to you,' said Kim. 'It can't have been easy for her.'

'All those years, even way back at school,' said Sam, 'she was right there with me, my mother, and I had no idea. I can't believe she let me go through my life longing for something that she could have given me. It's so cruel.'

After dwelling on it for days, there was much more he wanted to know. Had it not been a lockdown, he would have gone to see her to ask things to her face, but that was out of the question right now.

'There was always something between the two of you though, something strong,' said Kim. 'She was right in what she said... She has always kept you close.'

Sam thought about the woman who had held his heart in her hands the whole time, yet never wanted to have the relationship with him of a mother. He just didn't understand her.

'Sam, in a couple of weeks, things might be different,' said Kim, trying to console her husband. 'You could go and sit with her and talk it through.'

He sat there without responding, staring ahead.

'Sam?' said Kim, 'did you hear what I said?'

He turned to look at her and nodded. 'Yeah, I heard you... There's something I need to do.'

He stood and walked towards the study.

~

Merely existing in her isolated studio, Belinda-Anne was surviving yet another day. It felt much later than it really was when she was shaken by a knock at her door. It was the first hint of company for months, and she was reluctant to answer it. Traipsing down the steps and walking slowly to the door, she turned the handle and pulled it open to see a delivery man already walking away.

'I left the parcel there once I heard you were inside,' he called.

She bent over to pick it up, recognising the familiar touch of a framed painting, and carried it back inside, instantly coming to morbid conclusions. *What a fool I was in believing he would have behaved any differently.*

For a while she let the package rest against the table in the kitchen, simply looking at it and wondering if there was any correspondence enclosed. Was he disappointed, or worse, did he hate her for what she had done? Lifting it up onto the table, she started to carefully peel off the protective wrapping, removing one layer and then several more until the back of the painting was face up and exposed.

She recognised the words she had written months before, most of them covered by a large envelope that had been taped over them. She was sure that Sam's words of rejection were inside the envelope, and as she opened it, she braced herself for what she was about to read.

She extracted a large piece of art paper and unfolded it. It was the timeline she constructed of events leading up to the moon landing in 1969. It shocked her to see it, hitting her as though she had been stabbed in the heart. A total rejection of everything she had given him. She sat heartbroken on a chair next to the table and lifted out the other piece of paper from the envelope and began to read.

Dear Belinda-Anne,

I must say that when I received the painting I have now sent back to you, I fell into shock and disbelief, a state that it has taken me some time to climb out of. Part of getting over my initial response was to remember as much as I could about the times we shared each other's company. Doing that has taken me on a journey of its own. The more recent times have been easy to recall. Somewhat more challenging was to remember before that, when you were the special artist at my school. I remember that so clearly, though I had no idea who you really were. Remembering further back than that has been incredibly confusing, and perhaps it was you, whose soft hands held me safely and pushed me on a red tricycle. I think of all those things, and I feel loved.

I don't know why you left, leaving me only a sketch of a strange timeline about what was happening in the world up to 1969, when I was probably just taking my first steps. I've held that thread of connection to you closely ever since; it was all that I had. When I look at the painting I've returned to you, it adds to your story, and I can hear it trying to make me understand what has happened.
I've tried to call you but without success. Soon this awful lockdown will be over, along with the enforced social distancing it has entailed, and when that happens, I want to ask something of you. When you are ready, will you please see me? If you are willing, I want you to explain each and every part of that crazy timeline to me, so I know what your world was like way back then. There's more: I want you to tell me everything you can about 'Lunar Flight' and why you painted it, and then will you give me both things again, only this time in person and with the loving embrace of my mother.
And finally, should you be willing, I would like you to accompany Kim, Anh and myself on a small trip. It would mean so much to me if we all slept soundly one night in a cabin on the coast, so that we can wake up in the morning to gaze across a sparkling blue ocean at Sapphire Point. Like a family.

With love,
Sam (your son)

Belinda-Anne made no attempt to stem the flow of tears as she read the letter once more. She held it to her chest before carefully folding up both the letter and the piece of art paper and sliding them back into the envelope. Standing slowly, she felt a strange euphoria, like nothing she had ever experienced, and walked to her bedroom, placing the envelope under her pillow.

She put her hand behind her bedside table and reached down to pick up the plug of her home phone line that had been collecting dust on the floor for more than a month. She inserted it back into the wall. She lifted the receiver, listened for the purr of a dial tone, and pressed some numbers.

At first her words would not come and then when they finally did, they broke up between her gasps. 'Sam... is... that... you?'

Authors Note.

I remember visiting the Museum of Sydney, a year or so after the Global Financial Crisis of 2007 - 2008. There was an exhibit called 'Skint – Making do in the Great Depression', and I was drawn to the faces of people in some of the photographs, particularly those from shanty towns such as Happy Valley, which had sprung up around Sydney.

My interest had been sparked in this part of our history, and for years after my visit to the museum, I observed the increasing incidence of destitution in some parts of the wider community. The faces in make-shift squats of city and suburban parks, or in camps near riverbeds, and in the bush further out from town, wore similar expressions to those in the photographs from Happy Valley.

When I spoke to people in these marginalised communities, I began to think that for some, life is not so different from how it was at Happy Valley in the 1930's. Over a period of many months, I spoke to some that through terrible circumstances, hadn't been able to work for years. Others departed their makeshift dwellings each morning, to wash in a public amenity before taking their place in the workforce.

They each had a story worth listening to. In my mind's eye, I imagined some of the people I spoke to, living in the shanty towns of 1932. The inspiration for writing this book had been born. One person who gave me his time for a chat, was Bill, and when I began writing Rabbit Town, his disposition became embedded in one of the central characters of the same name.

Many who endured the years in improvised dwellings of shanty towns like Happy Valley, went on to play a significant role in subsequent phases of history, including times of war and social upheaval.

I wish to acknowledge my father, Tim Radley, for his posthumous help in Part 2 of Rabbit Town. Whilst the characters and their personal stories are not based on him, I was able to use my father's war records, notably his attestation papers, to trace his life as a soldier through World War Two. The movements of two central characters, Charlie and Tom, follow the real movements of my father, through Northern Australia, the Middle East, New Guinea and Borneo.

There are others I wish to acknowledge. I am grateful to my beta readers for their time and honest feedback. They include Robert Radley, Brett Worsley and Julianne Radley.

To Robert, thank you for your encouragement during the early stages when I asked for your opinion of my first draft. To Brett, thank you for your advice and the sensitivity you demonstrated when critiquing. To Julianne, thank you for your honest and sometimes brutal feedback when it was needed. Many pages of rewriting followed our robust conversations, and as well as improving the manuscript, you helped me grow a much-needed thicker skin.

Thank you to my editor, Fiona Smith, from Beyond Words Literary Agency. Her advice in the first structural edit was invaluable and made for a deeper and richer narrative. Thanks also to Phoenix Raig for the exceptional attention to detail in his proofreading, along with thanks to the entire team at Contempo Publishing.

Finally, to those who have read Rabbit Town - my wish is that you somehow connected with the characters of the five generations of the Davis family. I hope you enjoyed the ride. For taking the time to read about them, I sincerely thank you.

www.ingramcontent.com/pod-product-compliance
Lightning Source LLC
Chambersburg PA
CBHW011149290426

44109CB00025B/2543